W9-CSX-253

Literary Criticism and Cultural Theory

Edited by

William E. Cain
Professor of English
Wellesley College

A Routledge Series

Literary Criticism and Cultural Theory

William E. Cain, *General Editor*

"Foreign Bodies"
Trauma, Corporeality, and Textuality in Contemporary American Culture
Laura Di Prete

Overheard Voices
Address and Subjectivity in Postmodern American Poetry
Ann Keniston

Museum Mediations
Reframing Ekphrasis in Contemporary American Poetry
Barbara K. Fischer

The Politics of Melancholy from Spenser to Milton
Adam H. Kitzes

Urban Revelations
Images of Ruin in the American City, 1790–1860
Donald J. McNutt

Postmodernism and Its Others
The Fiction of Ishmael Reed, Kathy Acker, and Don DeLillo
Jeffrey Ebbesen

Different Dispatches
Journalism in American Modernist Prose
David T. Humphries

Divergent Visions, Contested Spaces
The Early United States through the Lens of Travel
Jeffrey Hotz

"Like Parchment in the Fire"
Literature and Radicalism in the English Civil War
Prasanta Chakravarty

Between the Angle and the Curve
Mapping Gender, Race, Space, and Identity in Willa Cather and Toni Morrison
Danielle Russell

Rhizosphere
Gilles Deleuze and the "Minor" American Writings of William James, W.E.B. Du Bois, Gertrude Stein, Jean Toomer, and William Faulkner
Mary F. Zamberlin

The Spell Cast by Remains
The Myth of Wilderness in Modern American Literature
Patricia A. Ross

Strange Cases
The Medical Case History and the British Novel
Jason Daniel Tougaw

Revisiting Vietnam
Memoirs, Memorials, Museums
Julia Bleakney

Equity in English Renaissance Literature
Thomas More and Edmund Spenser
Andrew J. Majeske

Equity in English Renaissance Literature

Thomas More and Edmund Spenser

Andrew J. Majeske

Routledge
New York & London

Routledge
Taylor & Francis Group
270 Madison Avenue
New York, NY 10016

Routledge
Taylor & Francis Group
2 Park Square
Milton Park, Abingdon
Oxon OX14 4RN

Routledge is an imprint of Taylor & Francis Group, an Informa business

Printed in the United States of America on acid-free paper
10 9 8 7 6 5 4 3 2 1

International Standard Book Number-10: 0-415-97705-3 (Hardcover)
International Standard Book Number-13: 978-0-415-97705-0 (Hardcover)

Library of Congress Cataloging-in-Publication Data

Majeske, Andrew J.
Equity in English Renaissance literature : Thomas More and Edmund Spenser / by Andrew J. Majeske.
p. cm. -- (Literary criticism and cultural theory)
Includes bibliographical references and index.
ISBN 0-415-97705-3 (alk. paper)
1. English literature--Early modern, 1500-1700--History and criticism. 2. Law and literature--History--16th century. 3. Law and literature--History--17th century. 4. Spenser, Edmund, 1552?-1599 Faerie queene. 5. More, Thomas, Sir, Saint, 1478-1535 Utopia. 6. Spenser, Edmund, 1552?-1599--Knowledge--Law. 7. More, Thomas, Sir, Saint, 1478-1535--Knowledge--Law. 8. Equity--England--History--16th century. 9. Equity--England--History--17th century. 10. Equity in literature. I. Title. II. Series.

PR428.L37M35 2006
820.9'3554--dc22 2006007109

Visit the Taylor & Francis Web site at
http://www.taylorandfrancis.com

and the Routledge Web site at
http://www.routledge-ny.com

For Andrea and Owen

Contents

Acknowledgments

I want to thank my wife Andrea for her support and limitless patience. I wish to thank Professor George Anastaplo and Professor Emily Albu, without whose help I would have floundered in the deep waters of classical thought and languages. I also must mention the support of Professor Margie Ferguson, without whose encouragement and flexibility this book would not be possible. Thanks also to Professor Winfried Schleiner, under whose direction this project started. Finally, I want to acknowledge Professor Larry Peterman, a kindred spirit, and to thank him for his input.

This book was made possible in part thanks to various University of California Fellowships, a Francis Bacon Fellowship at the Huntington Library, and a Woodrow Wilson Foundation, Charlotte Newcombe Fellowship.

Figure 1. The "Garden of Equity" from Del Bene's *Civitas Veri*, 1609, reproduced by permission of The Huntington Library, San Marino, California.

Figure 2. The blindfolding of lady justice from William Brandt's *Das Narrenschiff* ("Ship of Fools"), 1494, reproduced by permission of The Huntington Library, San Marino, California.

Introduction

This book focuses in considerable part on works now classified as literary to trace the shift in meaning of the concept of equity that began to be evident in the early and late sixteenth-century especially in England, but also on the Continent. To describe Thomas More's *Utopia* and Edmund Spenser's *The Faerie Queene* as purely literary is, however, misleading. These "literary" works are part of larger philosophic discourse involving, among other things, political theory and what is now termed the history of ideas—works which span millennia and easily include dialogic works such as Plato's *Laws*, and I suggest, can even include more "treatise" like works such as Aristotle's *Rhetoric*, *Ethics*, and *Politics*.[1]

Certainly, authors such as More and Spenser were profoundly concerned with the changing meaning of justice, and explored its relation to equity and other concepts. A close examination and comparison of their literary treatments of justice and equity, one from 1515–16, the other from the mid-1590's, reveal the beginnings of a dramatic shift in equity's meaning over that period—a shift that is hard to discern in more conventional works of the era addressing issues of legal and political theory. At the outset of this period, More, drawing upon a comprehensive understanding of equity, presented equity as perhaps the core element of justice—a common association during the Middle Ages and early Renaissance. More also highlighted that in one of its conceptions equity concerned the ideal political order. At the same time, More senses that the meaning of equity is in flux and he even predicts some of the wide-reaching practical consequences of these changes. In Book V of *The Faerie Queene*—a book entirely devoted to the virtue of justice—Spenser's treatment of equity merely nods at the expansive conceptions of equity highlighted by More, while centrally focusing on the shift in equity's meaning to a more narrowly limited concept, with a severely curtailed jurisprudential function.

This book will establish a broad historical context for the English Renaissance understanding of the concept of equity, particularly the idea's derivation from the classical Greek concept of επιείκεια,[2] in order to explain equity's various significations in More's *Utopia* and Spenser's *The Faerie Queene*. The several meanings associated with equity in England at the beginning of the sixteenth century derived from a Christian melding of the respective classical Greek and Roman concepts of επιείκεια and *aequitas* modified as necessary to serve the purposes of Christian doctrine. The Christian scholastics combined the meanings of these two terms under the rubric of *aequitas*. Many of the meanings were modified to varying degrees to fit within the Christian hierarchical system by tethering them to an overarching framework of natural and divine law. The classical (pre-Christian) conceptions of επιείκεια and *aequitas* had very different associations to the transcendent—or, none at all. At the beginning of the Sixteenth century, with the dissemination of the newly available classical texts, particularly those of Aristotle, Plato, and Cicero, direct access was again available to the full range of the pre-Christian meanings of επιείκεια and *aequitas*. These texts made clear that the awkward conglomeration that was Christian *aequitas* could not comfortably accommodate the meanings of επιείκεια, since επιείκεια*'s* meanings and functions were clearly of human origin and involved human political problems—there were no natural or divine law implications. English equity, derived from the post-classical (Christian) *aequitas* by way of the Old French *equité*, reflected this tension. An alternative English term, "epiky," deriving directly from the classical Greek επιείκεια, attempted unsuccessfully to enter the English language in the first half of the sixteenth century to make up for the term equity's inability, especially, to reflect Aristotelian επιείκεια. Towards the end of the sixteenth century, two treatises addressing English equity simply retained the Greek word "επιείκεια" in their titles—a reflection that the term equity alone was insufficient to accommodate classical επιείκεια*'s* meanings.

The meaning most frequently and famously associated with επιείκεια was a device that intervened between the laws and the specific cases to which they were applied. Since, as Aristotle observed, the laws were necessarily general in statement, and the cases to which they were applied specific and unique, the strict application of the laws was frequently unable to fit the penalty to the offense. Επιείκεια resolved this difficulty by quietly intervening between the laws and the specific cases, and producing outcomes that were fitting by taking into account the unique circumstances of each case and ignoring where necessary the strict letter of the laws—a very human and practical solution to a profound political problem. Επιείκεια invisibly created the impression that the laws were in fact capable of consistently producing fitting outcomes. This meaning involving as it does a solution to a political problem carries through in somewhat changed form and emphasis in the English term equity. A more esoteric meaning for επιείκεια, discussed at length below because of its role in More's *Utopia* and to a lesser extent in Spenser's *The Faerie Queene*, involved its role in the relation of the theoretically best possible commonwealth (utopia) to the best possible commonwealth actually achievable in practice.

Classical *aequitas*' core meaning aimed at equal application of the laws. It sought to create equalness—to diminish the relevant differences between cases in order that the application of the same law to different cases would be considered fair. Classical Roman *aequitas*' objective was conflicted with επιείκεια's, since επιείκεια sought to highlight the distinguishing characteristics of specific cases in order to achieve a result fitting to the circumstances particular to each case. These two concepts, later forcibly and uncomfortably combined in the English word equity, promoted radically different visions of what should be considered "fair;" *aequitas* achieved fairness by artificially eliminating difference, επιείκεια achieved fairness by in effect celebrating difference. The word equity attempted to encompass these two contrasting visions of fairness—of justice, a combination rife with both productive and destructive tension. This tension is, with good reason, much more apparent in the ambiguous and nuanced literary treatments of the concept than in its specifically jurisprudential treatments. This difference is a major factor behind the present study's approach to the concept from the discipline of literature while continuing to be sensitive to and informed by the disciplines of history and law.

In the area of English jurisprudence, how equity operated and was regarded underwent a tremendous shift during the course of the sixteenth century. A number of factors shaped the change. Most prominently, the basic understanding of the nature of laws was itself changing. At the outset of the sixteenth century, human laws were perceived as inherently defective on two counts. From a Christian perspective, people, who were by nature fallible, devised human laws and these laws shared the people's fallible nature. From a classical Aristotelian perspective, laws were defective in nature since they needed to be formulated in general terms to apply to a category or categories of situations, but each case to which they were applied was specific, with unique facts and circumstances. As a consequence, laws applied to specific cases resulted in outcomes for which the penalty tended to be disproportionate to the offense.

In both of these situations equity's role was to assist—to work with the laws, not to be considered in tension with or adversarially related to them. In the Christian context, equity was modified to the extent that it was considered to flow from the "infallible" sources of natural and divine law, and consequently could potentially correct fallible human laws in any given case. In the classical Aristotelian context, equity helped the laws by quietly intervening between the laws and their application to specific cases. Equity took into consideration the facts and circumstances of the particular cases and fashioned appropriate outcomes—apparently with the overriding objective of satisfying the expectations of fairness of the people who were subject to the laws. Equity thereby preserved the authority of the laws. The consequence for the laws losing their authority was tremendous—the rule of law itself would be in danger.

English jurisprudence of the early sixteenth century was unique as compared to the jurisprudence of other European nations in that under the Common Law system, equity had essentially been severed from laws. An equity jurisdiction separate from the Common Law had developed in the Chancery. As a consequence, the Chancery itself became in part a court. Persons aggrieved by the unfairness of rigorous Common Law court decisions complained to the king, who delegated responsibility for such matters to his Chancellor. Thus developed the Chancery court's so called equity jurisdiction. Rather than quietly intervening between the laws and particular cases to help the laws achieve fitting results, English equity had become adversarial to laws, even directly overruling the decisions of Common Law courts in specific cases. The Chancery's actions tended to undermine the authority of the laws, which consisted principally of the Common Law and Parlimentary statutes. One result of this undermining was to highlight rather than disguise the problems with laws identified by Aristotle. In effect, the authority of both the Common Law and Parliament's statutory laws were being openly challenged for all to see.

The perception of the nature of laws itself began to change, perhaps in part as a consequence of this confrontation with equity. Laws began to be viewed not as defective, but as sufficient. If sufficient, the laws no longer needed equity—at least equity based on επιείκεια—because they were considered adequate to address the facts and circumstances of specific cases to the extent necessary to preserve and maintain the authority of the laws, and thus also the rule of law. Some factors influencing this change in the perception of the nature of laws included the beginning of the rise of legal positivism, and the decline of theory-based systems in favor of practice-based ones in the wake of Machiavelli. Spenser appears to prefer practice-based systems as reflected in portions of his Letter to Raleigh.[3] Another factor was the more scientific approach to laws and legislation advocated by persons such as Francis Bacon. This new "equality" based conception of what would be considered "fair" continues to hold sway in Anglo-American jurisprudence.[4]

But, of course, the nature of laws had not really changed—what changed was the view that the laws' inability to deal adequately with individual cases made the laws defective. If the facts and circumstances of individual cases were to be considered irrelevant to the appropriate outcomes of those cases, then the laws could be considered sufficient and adequate rather than defective. Provided the focus shifted from the facts and circumstances of particular offenders and their offenses to the equal punishment of those committing a particular offense, then the laws no longer needed equity to quietly intervene on their behalf. The laws themselves could be authoritative, and the rule of law maintained. The drawback to this line of thinking is that a corresponding change needed to occur in people's expectations as to what was fair. Their expectations of what was fair needed to shift away from a concept of fairness that looked to appropriate outcomes based on the specific circumstances of individual cases, as classical Aristotelian επιείκεια did, and towards the sort of equity deriving from the classical Roman conception of *aequitas*.

Under *aequitas*, or equity based on equality, what mattered was not the ability of laws to address the facts and circumstances of specific cases, but the ability to disregard the facts and circumstances that made specific cases unique. If the people could be persuaded that what was fair was equal treatment under the laws of a multitude of artificially "uniform" cases rather than tailored outcomes in specific cases, then the laws certainly could be reconceived as sufficient. Once the laws were accepted as sufficient, by whatever reasoning, equity based on επιείκεια would be no longer necessary.

One way to approach equity's shift in significance is to observe both how it became a tool of political power in sixteenth century England and how equity as a political tool causes a transformation of its jurisprudential role.[5] At virtually the same time that the Chancery court's jurisdiction became explicitly associated with the term equity in the late 1520's, this jurisdiction's political potential began to be realized and tapped. Perhaps the long tradition of warnings about the potential for the abuse of equity based on επιείκεια, highlighted especially in the works of Aristotle and Aquinas, helped to identify for persons such as Thomas More, Oliver Cromwell, and Christopher St. German the political potential of the Chancery's equity jurisdiction. Certainly, equity's unique separation from the laws in the English legal system played a role since the Chancery court, under Royal control, could effectively overrule decisions of the Common Law courts, which were under Parliamentary control.[6] English equity, rather than working with the laws to achieve just outcomes, could now be viewed from a political perspective simply as a means of overpowering laws in order to achieve politically advantageous outcomes.[7]

This book explores the significations associated with the English concept of equity in Thomas More's *Utopia* and Edmund Spenser's *Faerie Queene* in light of classical, medieval and renaissance treatments of equity and its predecessor concepts of *epieíkeia* and *aequitas*. The book intervenes in at least two critical conversations. Principally it engages recent developments in the criticism of literature and rhetoric undertaken by scholars such as Victoria Kahn and Lorna Hutson in their collection *Rhetoric & Law in Early Modern Europe* (2001). Secondarily, it enters into the critical arena variously termed the history of ideas or intellectual history. While the book's emphasis on "great texts" is at odds with the stated theoretical position of two leading scholars in this second area, John Pocock and Quentin Skinner, it appears consistent with their practice, which uses such texts as touchstones. Certainly the transformation of the meaning of the English concept of equity over the course of the sixteenth century traced by my project fits well within the linguistic paradigms these scholars use to uncover the "beliefs and attitudes" of the age (Sharpe 4).

The early modern historian Mark Fortier observes that "various attempts have been made to restore ideas as a basis for understanding early modern history" (1257). Historian Kevin Sharpe further suggests that "a better understanding of [the early modern period] requires a fuller study of the relationship of ideas . . . to politics and the exercise of power" (*Politics* xi). However, as Fortier notes, because "self-contained ideas" rarely "have a direct impact on historical events," it is difficult to assess the extent of their influence (1257). One way of assessing their influence, Sharpe suggests, is to examine the way "ideas [are] woven through the textual and linguistic life of the culture broadly conceived" (*Politics* xi). This book undertakes the exploration of the idea of equity in the "linguistic life of the culture" of early modern England. Specifically, it examines the complex significations associated with the idea of equity in Thomas More's *Utopia* and Spenser's *The Faerie Queene*, focusing especially on their uses of equity in a now lost classical sense deriving largely from Aristotle and Plato that makes it a kind of nexus between the ideal political order—the *best* theoretical state of a commonwealth—and the best *practically achievable* commonwealth.[8]

This book complements the ongoing exploration of the rhetorical significations of equity in both the early modern literary and legal discourses. The essays contained in *Rhetoric & Law* suggest an early modern rationale for associating ideas of equity and commonwealth; this rationale grows out of an early seventeenth century worldview based increasingly upon the scientific method and progressively more divorced from divine will and religious doctrine. The essays in the Kahn and Hutson volume view equity and commonwealth as practical concerns—theoretical concerns formerly critical to these concepts, namely, its relation to the theoretical "ideal," are disregarded to the extent they cannot be directly and substantially related to practice.

Equity from this early seventeenth century perspective is simply a device to circumvent laws by reinterpreting them to suit one's purpose, and commonwealth's meaning is limited to a generalized notion of the common good. The observations about equity and commonwealth made in *Rhetoric & Law* have permitted textured and nuanced readings of various early modern literary texts resulting in novel interpretive insights, several examples of which are contained in the collection. But the typical approach to these concepts in works such as *Rhetoric and Law*, especially to the concept of equity, is nearly entirely forward-looking, and is consequently limited in a critical sense. This forward looking approach effectively treats equity as though a break or rupture with the past has occurred. It does not address the history and context that makes equity such a "slippery and "most ambiguous term." (Austin 61). Important to the forward looking approach is a perception of the early modern period as having a special connection to later periods; somehow the dynamic changes occurring in the areas of politics, society, and religion during this period help us better understand subsequent historical periods, even perhaps contemporary times. In turn, so the argument goes, this relationship reciprocally permits special insight into the early modern period by contemporary scholars.

I do not object that a kind of special relationship between the early modern and later periods exists. Rather, I suggest that this special relationship derives in the final analysis from the early modern era's complicated relationship with the past. The key to this relationship is the momentous impact caused by the direct access to classical thought arising from the dissemination of the newly available classical texts. The profound ways in which this classical thought became integrated into early modern thought helped set the stage for the dramatic changes of the early modern period that some scholars tend to associate with rupture from the past. Even though a return to the newly available worldview of classical political and social philosophy was considered unviable, we should not diminish the significance of the impact of this worldview in deconstructing the edifice of Christian scholastic thought. The classical worldview certainly played an important role in the early Renaissance in helping to transform all aspects of society for a new age, both by undermining the foundations of Christian scholasticism, and also by serving as a "nursery of refined and useful institutions" and ideas to draw upon to address the problems of the new age.

As already noted, a key distinguishing feature of this new age is the turn away from theory and towards practice. Machiavelli rejected both Christian and classical thought as overly theoretical. He advocated that theories in the area of political thought should be developed based on the way people actually act, not the way they theoretically "should" act. Francis Bacon greatly extended this shift away from idealistic and towards practical concerns with the scientific method he advocated. In this context equity began to be viewed as problematic since it derived from concepts which during the Christian era had been tethered to divine law—which both Machiavelli and even Grotius considered an ideal conception. However, this sixteenth century shift towards the practical focused principally on Christian era developments and ignored επιείκεια's older, extremely practical side. First and foremost επιείκεια's practical side allowed a pragmatic solution to one of the most fundamental problems of practical politics. Επιείκεια concealed the astounding fact that all laws were deeply flawed—they could not reliably achieve fair (just) results in any given case. Επιείκεια, closely identified with the infinitely malleable "Lesbian rule", permitted the laws to appear flexible—an appearance that is indispensable to the long-term maintenance of a healthy rule of law.[9]

There is another side to επιείκεια though—a very esoteric one. This side addressed another practical problem, one of the utmost delicacy: how to translate into practice the theory of the ideal commonwealth—the best conceivable though practically unachievable political order. This esoteric sort of επιείκεια is concerned intimately with an economic understanding of justice, as is clear from Aristotle's distinction in his *Ethics* among just, unjust, and equitable persons.[10] Unjust persons take more than their share—more than what they in theory deserve, just persons take their share—precisely what they in theory deserve, and equitable persons take less than their share—less than what they theoretically deserve (1129b; 1134a; 1138a). The seemingly altruistic equitable persons are assigned a very special, secretive role in moderate regimes.

Επιείκεια is the word associated with the people whose role Plato and Aristotle described as working to change a regime over the course of generations until it approached as closely as practice permitted the ideal of what I will term "absolute communism"—the form of government that in theory eliminated the "money loving" that inevitably accompanied "justice" in existing regimes (Plato, *Laws* 737a). Unsurprisingly, given human nature, this practically achievable level fell far short of absolute communism. According to Plato and Aristotle, the best that could be achieved was a ratio of four or five to one between a society's wealthiest and poorest segments. In this way επιείκεια became associated with the notion of commonwealth, but only an achievable—a practical one. The unachievable "ideal" commonwealth of absolute communism described in Plato's *Republic* and in much of book two of Thomas More's *Utopia* was not an objective at which επιείκεια aimed, though it was the touchstone from which what was achievable was determined. To reiterate, equity, by its derivation from επιείκεια, addresses both the supreme practical problem of how to make possible government based on the rule of law, when laws are inherently defective, as well as the vexed problem of how to improve existing regimes in the direction of a theoretically ideal regime, when such imrovment is antagonistic to the self-interests of the rulers of the regime, and would inevitably be forcefully resisted by the rulers and those who support them if the attempts were recognized.

In books such as Kahn and Hutson's *Rhetoric & Law*, English equity's early seventeenth century flexibility is celebrated because it permitted English common lawyers to present legal resistance to the regime without disturbing the "commonwealth." Equity permitted the lawyers to hypothesize legislative intent as they imposed competing, often contradictory, and usually self-serving interpretations upon the burgeoning numbers of statutes being enacted by Parliament. Equity could be drawn upon for such purposes precisely because of the flexibility so long associated with it. This book explores the classical sources for the protean nature of English equity, a character which owes much to its dual derivation from the classical Greek επιείκεια and the classical Roman *aequitas*, with their very different meanings, and the changes that occurred to these classical ideas under the influence of Christian thought.

This book provides a broader historical context than early modern equity typically receives by establishing how the meanings associated with the root words from which equity is derived underlie and even anticipate in critical respects equity's new seventeenth century role. Certainly the "flexible" version of early seventeenth century English equity is not new. It is in some degree an outgrowth of the meanings associated for two millennia with επιείκεια and nearly one millennium with the Roman Latin and Christian Latin versions of *aequitas*.

As Kahn and Hutson note, the "linguistic turn in history" has led to, among other things, new historicism and the burgeoning field of critical theory—especially in literary studies. This trend, they note, also encourages—in fact demands—a much more extensive interdisciplinary approach to literary studies. Many scholars who venture on an interdisciplinary excursion into the early modern period, rely for points of legal history upon the work of J. H. Baker. Baker's work represents perhaps the dominant voice in the contemporary legal history discourse in Anglo-American jurisprudence, at least insofar as the early modern period is concerned. Baker's critique of

Maitland addresses extensively the English legal establishment's treatment of the concepts of equity and commonwealth at the outset of the Renaissance. This book builds upon but also pointedly reacts to Baker's findings—particularly his summary dismissal of any practical relevance associated with the idea of commonwealth, and his presentation of equity as purely practical, completely dissociated from theoretical concerns—including the notion of commonwealth.

Baker approaches sixteenth century English equity and the practical influence of the idea of commonwealth with what appears to be a distinct agenda. This agenda advances the notion of laws as being perfectible rather than inherently defective—this approach is a direct descendant of the turn towards the practical at the expense of the ideal in terms of political matters associated with Machiavelli. One obvious consequence of viewing laws as perfectible is to eliminate the need for equity to correct or conceal laws understood as inherently defective. In effect, Aristotle's political thought is rejected. Baker also downplays any practical effect the concept of commonwealth may have had in sixteenth century England by utilizing an unduly demanding test to measure its influence. Baker's effort in this regard appears to be due to a well-meaning, and perhaps unconscious desire to promote the cause of capitalism over communism in the cold war climate in which his critique was written. Baker's analysis certainly makes it more difficult, for instance, to recover the critical message that Thomas More is conveying in his *Utopia* about how equity draws upon the best possible commonwealth in order to help fashion the best commonwealth achievable in practice—a message that directly draws upon the ways Aristotle and Plato dealt with επιείκεια.

I critique Baker's interpretation of the significance of the ideas of equity and commonwealth in sixteenth century England in more detail in Chapter One. There I also trace the long history of the idea of equity from its roots in the classical Greek concept of επιείκεια through the sixteenth century transformation that radically altered the course of its long history. I show how Christianity combined the meanings associated with επιείκεια with the very different meanings of the classical Roman *aequitas*, all under the rubric of what I refer to as Christian Latin *aequitas*. I further show that by choosing *aequitas* as the catch-all term, the Christian scholastics inadvertently distorted the meanings deriving from επιείκεια by associating *them* with the concept of equalness—of equality; the Christian scholastics also added to subsequent confusion by changing some of the derivative meanings of Christian Latin *aequitas* to fit within the Christian hierarchical scheme—it was deemed to flow from natural and divine law, associations with the transcendent absent from the classical Greek επιείκεια and classical

Roman *aequitas*, at least as formulated by Cicero. Later in Chapter One I concentrate on the various forces at work in Renaissance Europe, and England in particular, reshaping equity both in its abstract formulation and as a practical jurisprudential concept.

In Chapter Two I examine the more conventional meaning of επιείκεια conveyed in the significantly distinct treatments of the term in Aristotle's *Rhetoric* and *Ethics*, a meaning which involves its working closely and quietly with the laws to veil their defective nature in order to add to their authority with the overriding objective of helping to preserve and maintain the rule of law. I also explore the now obscure origins of the more esoteric meaning of επιείκεια drawn upon by More in *Utopia*. Beginning with a mere hint in Aristotle's *Ethics*, I trace this meaning into his *Politics*, which in turn points back to Plato's *Laws*, where this meaning finally is revealed explicitly. I show how this more obscure meaning for επιείκεια involves it operating to create the best commonwealth achievable in practice using as a touchstone or guide the best commonwealth in theory (utopia).

In Chapter Three I explore the two principal uses of equity by Thomas More in his *Utopia*. The first of these occurs in book one, a book concerned generally with practical political problems and specifically with the issue of whether wise persons, such as Renaissance humanists, are obligated in some fashion to enter politics to make practical use of their learning and experience for the common good. More's first use of equity is conventional in meaning but paradoxical in narrative context. It occurs as part of Raphael Hythlodaeus' "proof" that he would be ineffective as a king's political counselor. However, Raphael's "proof" in fact establishes him to be a highly effective counselor. Raphael succeeds in persuading Lord Chancellor Morton to address the very practical problem of equity Raphael has posed along the lines of the proposed solution Raphael himself has suggested—a solution that draws upon the practices of a fictional ideal society. In effect, Raphael is drawing on equity to utilize the theory of an ideal society for the practical improvement of an existing regime.

The second important use of equity in *Utopia* occurs in book two after the end of Raphael's uninterrupted exposition about the ideal place called Utopia—an exposition that occupies most of book two. It begins at the point Raphael resumes the very practical dialogue with the More persona and Peter Giles, which occupied the entire book one. This second usage associates equity with the political ideal of absolute communism—an ideal which in Plato's view eliminates the "money loving" that inevitably accompanies "justice" in existing regime—but it does so from the context of the debate about practical politics carried forward from book one (*Laws* 737a). Equity here represents the bridge between the ideal and the practical; its touchstone is the ideal of absolute communism, but equity itself remains based in the "real" world where this absolute cannot be achieved. In line with the esoteric meaning of επιείκεια in Plato's *Laws*, equity here points to the practical compromise that constitutes the best commonwealth that can actually be achieved—one which aims to create a limited gap between the wealthiest and poorest segments of society on the order of four or five to one.

Finally, in Chapter Four I address Spenser's equivocal use of equity in Book V of *The Faerie Queene*. I argue that Spenser, like More, is aware of and draws upon the esoteric Greek meaning of επιείκεια when he deals with equity. However, Spenser's treatment of equity differs radically from More's, as one might expect from their differing positions on the role of the monarch, on religion, and on whether and how theory relates to practice. Spenser's treatment advances a partisan political agenda aimed at replacing rule by women in England with rule by men. While the objective of Spenser's treatment of equity, like More's, is regime change, Spenser's treatment does not obviously seek change in the direction of the political ideal identified by Plato and Aristotle.

At a more superficial level, Spenser's treatment of equity also addresses its jurisprudential application. His treatment appears to draw upon the sixteenth century trend away from equity's traditional use as an infinitely flexible tool that assists the laws by concealing their defective nature. Spenser's treatment is consistent with severely limiting equity's jurisprudential role in order to promote the strict application of laws. Above all, Spenser's treatment advocates a certain idea of social order by emphasizing the achievement of quick, certain, and predictable results in legal disputes at the expense of flexibility and, consequently, perhaps also at the expense of justice.

Chapter One

Renaissance Equity in Classical Perspective

CONTEMPORARY EQUITY, THE EQUALITY PRINCIPLE, AND THE RULE OF LAW

This chapter surveys the long history of the idea of equity from its Greek roots in the concept of επιείκεια, through its alternative source in the Roman Latin *aequitas*. It then examines the uneasy merger and modification of these two concepts in the Christian Latin *aequitas*. Finally, it addresses the complex and rapidly changing idea of English equity as it transforms over the course of the sixteenth century. An overriding objective of this chapter is to highlight what I consider to be the core concern of English equity at the outset of the sixteenth century, a concern that derives from Aristotle's treatment of επιείκεια in his *Rhetoric* and *Ethics*. Sixteenth century changes to the meanings of justice, law, and the sort of equity present on the Continent, particularly in places with a Roman Law tradition, has tended to obscure this original core concern of English equity.

Initially, in order to overcome common preconceptions about what equity means, and to make clear its former meanings—meanings many readers may at first resist as being counter intuitive—I must briefly address contemporary perceptions, issues, and interpretations relating to equity.

Equity's jurisprudential meaning today is negligible. If it is mentioned at all in contemporary philosophy of law texts, is relegated to an historical footnote. The situation in political philosophy texts is similar—equity receives little or no attention. To the extent it is addressed at all, the concept is associated with a series of legal "maxims" or "principles" such as "equality is equity." This particular maxim is, of course, especially revealing—if "equality" is "equity," what independent significance or value does equity possess?

If there is still a general notion of the sort of equity once associated intimately with justice, separate from equality, it is when it means a kind of fairness involving even-handedness. But even this meaning, it is clear, partakes of equality. Consequently, equity, in the sense of fairness, is typically used today in situations such as those describing "gender equity" and "pay equity." The critical issue in these cases is whether a certain person or group is being treated equally as compared to another person or group. The question being addressed is whether disparate treatment or pay violates the equality principle; that is, what is considered fair is "equal" treatment or pay. Equity's almost universal identification with equality is a relatively new development in the long history of the concept, especially when we begin to consider its root principles stretch back to classical Greek επιείκεια and classical Roman *aequitas*.

We should especially notice that the contemporary conception bears little or no resemblance to the Aristotelian conception of επιείκεια, which is not equality-based. In fact, from a certain perspective, Aristotelian επιείκεια is directly opposed to contemporary equity based on equality. As already mentioned and as will be detailed in Chapter Two, Aristotelian επιείκεια emphasizes and deals with the unique aspects of each case—it highlights and concentrates on what distinguishes one case from another—what makes each case unique. In Anglo-American jurisprudence, equity has an opposing emphasis. It has been reduced into several objective categories (the "maxims"), and cases are aggregated into one or another category so that they can be compared (equated) with other cases, and dealt with in a similar fashion. The objective of this is to deal with (artificially) "similar" cases in "similar" ways. The problem with this approach is that square pegs are being forced into round holes. The distinguishing features of each case—what makes it unique according to Aristotle—are treated as irrelevant, or only taken into account in a limited way—for instance, as aggravating or mitigating factors in the sentencing phase of a criminal proceeding. By treating "similar" cases in "similar" ways, a kind of equality is manufactured, and the results can be viewed as "fair." Needless to say, the contemporary meaning of equity is in tension with its older meanings, and it leaves much to be desired in terms of its relation to "fairness," as commonly understood.

Equity based on equality, in short, enhances the predictability of the outcome in any given case because distinguishing circumstances are irrelevant. In this way numerous cases can be equated and decided based on the same principle. The supposed virtues of this approach are predictability, convenience, reduced expense, and the limitations placed upon the use of discretion. In contrast, the meaning of equity associated with Aristotelian επιείκεια (which I will refer to as "Aristotelian equity"), considers and weighs all of the distinguishing features of individual cases and is, consequently much more unpredictable as to outcome due to the unique features of each case, inconvenient, rather expensive since individual attention must be devoted to each case, and subject to more expansive judicial discretion.[1] Be all this as it may, I argue that most people would agree, upon sober reflection, that a truly equitable, that is, a *fair* result requires examining and taking into consideration the surrounding circumstances of a case before rendering judgment on it.

While much can and has been said about the virtues of the equality principle, which De Tocqueville described as that "well nigh irresistible principle of authority in the modern world," its shortcomings tend to be overlooked or obscured, except to the extent they interfere with other sacrosanct modern principles, like (individual) liberty and freedom (Jaffa 1975, 149). As I have already implied, the fundamental shortcoming that I would like to highlight here is the simple equation of equality with what is fair. This equation causes severe tension, because in the name of equality the unique circumstances of individual cases are ignored—and this results in outcomes that frequently defy common sense—the punishment assessed does not "fit" the offense. We intuit that these disproportional results are somehow unfair. But the long-standing identification of equity with equality, and the esteem with which equality is viewed, hinders a thoroughgoing critique of the premises of the equality principle from the perspective of an older understanding of equity.

The profound danger of not performing such a critique, and making adjustments warranted thereby, is that frequent disproportional results can cause people to question the justice of the legal system—to question the merits, viability, and desirability of the rule of law. In other words, such results present a danger to the regime itself. A solution to this problem, if there is one, might be to restore a full understanding and appreciation of Aristotelian equity. While a full return to this older meaning of equity may be neither possible nor desirable, at least being aware of it as an option might help to address problems stemming from what I consider to be an over-reliance on the equality principle. Perhaps we could view our contemporary "equality as equity" position as one extreme point on a continuum, and Aristotelian equity—treating each case as unique—as close to the other extreme. Viewed in this way, a new balance could be struck which takes individual circumstances more into account, yet still maintains an acceptable level of predictability, convenience, and expense.

Given the grave nature of the problem—one that could endanger the regime itself—some such effort at reevaluation seems especially worthwhile. A brief overview of a contemporary issue highlighting some of the problems with the contemporary identification of equity with equality will be instructive. This overview is intended to illustrate the nature of the contemporary inability to identify a way out of the predicament of the very constrained way in which equity and justice are conceived, and to suggest that once there was an alternative conception of equity, namely Aristotelian equity, that was not based on equality and that seems to point to a solution to this predicament.

The prime example of a contemporary issue that cries out for something closer to Aristotelian equity is that of "zero tolerance" policies, rules, regulations and laws (which I will refer to as "zero tolerance laws") adopted throughout the United States, and following our example, increasingly throughout the world. These zero tolerance laws are successfully defended against accusations that they are unfair by pointing out that everyone receives and can expect to receive "equal" treatment with everyone else. But this way of defending zero tolerance laws should only prevail if equity—what is considered fair—were truly identical to equality. That is, if equity still is identified with what is fair, doesn't it continue to resemble in some now veiled sense, Aristotelian equity? I contend that when the issue is pressed, there is no general agreement that equality is the only, or even the principal way, to determine what is fair. Common sense insists that at some level fundamental fairness requires taking individual circumstances into account, these must play some role or factor. Consider the irrationality of the following outcomes resulting under zero tolerance laws adopted by many school districts respecting drugs and weapons. Pursuant to these policies, a ten year-old Colorado honors student was punished for weapon possession because her mother's lunch sack, mistakenly switched with her own by the girl's mother, contained a paring knife for an apple. Does punishing the little girl for her mother's innocent mistake really seem to be a proportional outcome—does the punishment at all fit the offense? Does common sense allow us to disregard completely the apparent fact that there was no intent present to bring a "weapon" to school?[2]

Or consider the case in which a thirteen year-old Texas girl was punished for possessing Advil, or another where teenage Ohio girls were punished for taking Midol. In their cases, at least, they perhaps intended to bring a "drug" onto campus. But does this really justify their being treated in the same way as students who intentionally bring illegal drugs to school? The equality principle requires that all of these youths be punished in similar ways regardless of circumstances—this lack of "tolerance" overrides obviously relevant circumstances like mistake, lack of intent, capacity, or magnitude. Authorities justify the punishment as being "fair" because everyone can expect the same treatment regardless of circumstances, even obviously relevant ones. We sense that something has gone terribly wrong in some of these cases.[3] Ignoring relevant circumstances defies common sense and hints of extremism. But today there exists a profound difficulty identifying what the problem is precisely with the equality principle, and unless it can readily be identified, it cannot be adequately addressed. The problem cannot be identified because it is difficult to conceive of an idea of fairness, of a meaning for equity, which is not based on the equality principle. As long as the authorities can defend zero tolerance laws on the basis that people are being dealt with "equally," the fact that some outcomes are obviously unfair when surrounding circumstances are considered, will continue to create tension within the meaning of what constitutes justice. If this continues it will eventually become more and more obvious that many or all laws are unjust in some significant sense. As this fact becomes public knowledge, it will work to undermine the rule of law.[4]

Our elevation of the equality principle to near sacred status may prevent us from seeing other ways of perceiving fairness—most particularly of seeing or appreciating Aristotelian equity. Let me dwell for a moment on the nature of this blinder. Equality tends to mean that form of justice "that is seen as treating all" people alike. It culminates in the "rule of law," in which "the emphasis is placed less upon what the law should be than upon the assurance that all should have applied to them alike the laws of the community" (Anastaplo 1975, 63). The critical problem with the equality principle, so understood, is that the "rulers are left . . . free . . . to do what they choose—so long as the government is compelled to apply the same rules to all" (63).

The focus on equal application of the laws as being the cornerstone of fairness—of a broad sense of justice—draws attention away from the defects inherent in the laws.[5] The defective nature of laws, as identified by Aristotle, involves their necessarily general statement. This defect is hidden. This concealment is especially the case in western jurisprudential systems which claim that laws rule, not people—in these systems the "rule of law" is viewed with almost sacred reverence.[6] Another factor that tends to obscure the defective nature of laws includes the rise of legal positivism, the initial roots of which can be traced to Machiavelli, with a fuller expression in the works of Thomas Hobbes. This doctrine suggests that the laws enacted by the rulers are just per-se. Additionally, the rise of relativism has raised doubt that broadly accepted notions of fairness—of justice—exist, or can exist. Finally, the trend towards an undue emphasis on liberty raises deep suspicion of permitting anyone to wield the sort of broad discretionary power associated with Aristotelian equity.

There are of course objections to an undertaking like this book that seeks to resurrect an older notion of equity. Even those who would concede that there are some problems with the equality principle, might well defend it from encroachment by Aristotelian equity, contending that it rests on a surer foundation; after all in the sixteenth century equity ultimately drew upon natural law for its moral authority. People who object to Aristotelian equity tend to agree with Oliver Wendell Holmes Jr. and others who asserted that natural law based theories such as the common law are simply fictions: of the common law Holmes forthrightly stated that "there is no such body of law" (Anastaplo 1989, 320n.97; Jaffa, 1994, 88–91).[7] One response to Holmes' view is that while his interpretation has had the upper hand for at most several hundred years, various views based on natural law theories, some associated with Christianity and some not, held sway for nearly two prior millennia prior to that, and may well hold sway again. The wisdom of the past should not be disregarded simply because it is not currently fashionable—especially if we are encountering problems that this older wisdom can help us address far more readily than any contemporary alternative.

A more pointed response to these natural law critics, as I will show in Chapter Two, is that Aristotelian equity did not directly rely on natural law principles—the association of equity with natural law was a later development. Instead, Aristotelian equity relied in the final analysis simply on the intellectual virtue of prudence possessed by the person rendering it.[8]

CLASSICAL ROMAN (CICERONIAN) *AEQUITAS*

Although Aristotelian επιείκεια and the classical Roman concept of *aequitas* have often been considered to be synonymous, originally they were very different in meaning, as we have already glimpsed. Aristotle's επιείκεια, in its non-esoteric sense, means "a correction of the law where the law [is defective] by reason of its universality" (Riley 1948, 9). Etymologically *aequitas* derives from the same root as *aequor*, *aequalis*, and *aequare*, all of which evoke "the image of a level field that does not slant to any side." It "alludes and cannot but allude, to the idea of 'equality,' of 'equal treatment in equal cases'" . . . (Biscardi 1997, 7). Perhaps the clearest presentation of this principal meaning of classical Roman *aequitas* is by Cicero, who, in his *Topica*, states that "what is valid in one of two equal cases should be valid in the other . . . equity should prevail, which requires equal laws in equal cases" (IV.23). The identification of equity with equality, as previously discussed, has become so complete that equity has little other meaning today.

Cicero, in fact, according to some accounts, coined the term *aequitas*. He changed the traditional Roman formulation respecting justice, *bonum et aequum*, by reversing the factors, so that it reads *aequum et bonum*, moving to the forefront the "equalness" component.[9] He then used the term *aequitas* to capture this new dynamic (Van Zyl 1986, 68). In addition, Cicero gave *aequitas* a second major signification—one that appears to be drawn from the Aristotelian επιείκεια tradition. This secondary signification encompasses "fairness . . . moderation [and] even liberality" (Riley 1948, 10). This meaning represents a reaction to what Cicero identifies as the rigid or strict nature of law. *Aequitas* provides the counterbalance to this rigidity—a softening effect. Perhaps Cicero's most famous formulation related to this meaning is *summum ius summa inuria* (Van Zyl 1986, 67; Cicero *De Officiis*, 1.10.33). As *aequitas* evolved under Christianity, this second signification became more important as it came to mean the benign interpretation of law by the authorities. From this meaning arose what is perhaps the most characteristic Christian formulation—justice tempered by the sweetness of mercy, a formulation traditionally assigned to St. Cyprian (third century ce) (Riley 11).

What is most striking about the secondary Ciceronian signification is that while it incorporates elements of Aristotelian επιείκεια, it obscures the reason επιείκεια is necessary at all—the defective nature of law. Cicero, for some reason, prefers not to mention this at all. Instead, he characterizes law as strict and rigid by nature rather than defective in any way. Implicitly, Cicero suggests that there is nothing inherently wrong or defective about its strictness or rigidity, as Aristotle does.

The significance of this shift in emphasis cannot be overstated. Aristotle pointed out the essential problem of building upon a foundation of laws—you could and should appear to do so provided your regime was ruled by *statesmen*—persons possessing sufficient intellectual virtue to bypass the defective law and render judgment pursuant to επιείκεια in individual cases, taking into consideration all of the circumstances, and being governed ultimately by their own prudence rather than the laws. Cicero appears to silently reject the premise that law is inherently defective.[10] For him laws are the proper foundation upon which to build the regime—provided a certain moderating element is present to make the laws at times somewhat more flexible. Cicero does not allow the laws to be bypassed entirely by select officials, as does Aristotle. Cicero's *aequitas* is clearly subordinate to the laws. Laws may be characteristically harsh—but this does not make them inherently defective.

The meanings of Ciceronian *aequitas* and Aristotelian επιείκεια both become identified with the English word equity. Additional permutations developed under the influence of Christianity. As will be discussed below, at the outset of the early modern period in England, equity was a quite dynamic term, which is only appropriate given its diverse pedigree. Because of its sources in various traditions, its several meanings could be in tension with, or even contradict each other. Not surprisingly, accounts of equity in England written in the early modern period as well as historical accounts attempting to describe equity at this time are complicated and confusing (Riley 1–4).[11]

AEQUITAS—LATE ROMAN & CHRISTIAN

Between Cicero's time and the beginning of the early modern period the defining development respecting *aequitas* was its growing connection to natural law and, derivatively, to Christian divine law. This connection causes *aequitas* to depart radically from Aristotelian επιείκεια. Most important for present purposes is how Aristotelian επιείκεια is distinguished from the Christian Latin *aequitas* associated with natural law. As has become clear, επιείκεια, in its primary meaning, ultimately is more political in nature than theoretical—one of the most profound manifestations of the political, surely, but nonetheless political. To be precise, επιείκεια is of human origin and concerned first and foremost with humans and human affairs. However, it is not concerned with humans and human affairs generally, as natural law is sometimes considered to be, rather to those affairs relating to a particular regime—thus, a judgment in accord with επιείκεια by a statesman in one regime in a certain case may be not resemble the judgment of a statesman in another regime, though the facts of the cases be identical, since the statesman takes into account the expectations of the regime's people respecting what they consider fair—and people's expectations differ from time to time and place to place.

By becoming connected to natural law, *aequitas*' former close association with the supremely political επιείκεια became more attenuated. Even in its pre-Christian Stoic form, natural law is above the merely political—it applies to all persons, and is unchangeable and eternal. In the words that Cicero puts into the mouth of his Stoic interlocutor Laelius,

> [natural] law is right reason in agreement with nature; it is of universal application, unchanging and everlasting; it summons to duty by its commands, and averts from wrongdoing by its prohibitions. And it does not lay its commands or prohibitions upon good men in vain, though neither have any effect on the wicked. It is a sin to try to alter

> this law, nor is it allowable to attempt to repeal any part of it, and it is impossible to abolish it entirely. We cannot be freed from its obligations by senate or people, and we need not look outside ourselves for an expounder or interpreter of it. And there will not be different laws at Rome, and at Athens, or different laws now and in the future, but one eternal and unchangeable law will be valid for all nations and all times, and there will be one master and ruler, that is, God, over us all, for he is the author of the this law, its promulgator, and its enforcing judge.[12] (*De Re Publica* III, xxii)

This Stoic conception of natural law is in most essentials identical to the Christian idea of natural law in the late Medieval period. Consider the formulation attributed to Jean Gerson by Christopher St. German in his book *Doctor and Student*:

> The lawe of nature . . . which is also called the lawe of [reason] pertayneth oonly to creatures reasonable that is man/which is created to the Ymage of god. And this law ought to be kept as well among Iewes & gentyles/ as mong crysten men. And this is the law which among the learned in English law is called the law of reason, which natural reason has established among all men so that there is a natural instinct present in all men to observe it. And according to John Gerson it is a sign possessed naturally, which is indicative of the right reason of God which wills that the human rational creature shall be held or bound to do (or refrain from doing) something, in order to pursue its natural end which is human felicity—be it monastic, domestic, or political. Moreover, we may also regard as a sign naturally possessed that which is inscribed in every man who is not bereft of the due use of reason. Hence the law of reason is nothing else than the participation or knowledge of eternal law in a rational creature, revealed to him by the natural light of reason, whereby he has a natural inclination to act duly, and to a due end. (13)

Once *aequitas* becomes inextricably associated with natural law, its ultimate emphasis becomes elevated above the political realm. In its "highest" formulation *aequitas* can constitute the essence of divine justice; it can even be defined as nothing other than God,[13] since God is the fountain and origin of all justice (Landau 1993, 130). Once *aequitas* becomes associated with divine law, it becomes considerably less flexible than Aristotelian επιείκεια, which is not dependant on absolutes. Moreover, since the Christian God is above all a *merciful* god, the *merciful* element associated with Aristotelian επιείκεια comes to the forefront in the meaning of Christian Latin *aequitas*. As one might expect from the Roman temperment, this *merciful* element is not highlighted in pre-Christian Roman Latin *aequitas*.[14]

The best-known Christian formulation of *aequitas* that highlights the element of mercy is attributed to St. Cyprian: *aequitas* is justice tempered by the sweetness of mercy (Barton 1973, 143). A later elaboration by the fifteenth century Christian theologian, Jean Gerson, in a noble effort worthy of Aquinas, unsuccessfully attempted to combine the Christian and Aristotelian emphases: "[*aequitas*] is justice [which] having weighted all the particular circumstances is tempered with the sweetness of mercy" (Reuger 1982, 11). We should notice here that there is a decisive difference between the secular *mercy* of Aristotelian επιείκεια and the Christian *mercy* of *aequitas*. In Aristotle, the *mercy* element is political, and requires the arbitrators—low level judicial officials—to take into account human weaknesses. That is, they should consider mankind's passionate nature, which is one of the circumstances to keep in mind in individual cases. This reminder is appropriate in the case of the arbitrators, since they consist solely of men aged 59.5 years of age, who, so the theory goes, no longer feel the passions so strongly.[15]

In contrast to this political mercy, in pre-Reformation Christian thought, humans must freely render mercy to each other solely because God has freely rendered mercy upon them, not on account of the failings of human nature. Thus, while the mercy element in Aristotelian επιείκεια is founded on the specific circumstances of a case, the Christian mercy element of *aequitas* is supposed to be rendered regardless of the circumstances. Human mercy, in the Christian context, is simply a reflection—or echo—of divine mercy. Christian mercy is not the mercy dictated by political prudence—the mercy of Aristotelian επιείκεια. Rather it is a "gift," one that at the divine level is beyond human comprehension. Later in this chapter, I will provide an overview of the key role mercy plays in the transformation of the meaning of equity in sixteenth century England, as it is devolves from the progressively narrowing concept of equity.

Another formulation of *aequitas* which carries forward to the early modern period in the English term equity is the one deriving from the adage "*summum ius, summum iniuria*" (the greatest legal justice, the greatest injury), which was proverbial even in Cicero's time (*De Officiis* i, 10, 33).[16] This formulation highlights that there is a problem with legal justice, but it fails to point out *why* there is a problem or *what* the nature of the problem is. Aristotle's warning that law is inherently defective because it fails, and cannot but fail, to take into account the specific circumstances of particular cases, had begun to be forgotten or ignored.

Since equity is such a multi-faceted concept when viewed from the history of the concept, and since some of its parts do not interact in close concert with others, before turning to equity in sixteenth century England, I will for present purposes focus on just two of equity's critical facets. The first of these involves equity as the essence of justice and connects equity to a transcendent natural law. The second deals with equity in its own right—that is, without any transcendent sense—as the element that acts to address the problem of the laws being too strict, rigorous, and inflexible.

The role of equity as the defining element of a broad conception of justice flows from Cicero's identification of *aequitas* with the Roman notion of justice—of the *aequum et bonum*. As noted, Cicero appears to be responsible for reversing the traditional formulation which placed *bonum* first, thereby elevating the importance of equalness, of equality (Van Zyl 1986 , 61–65). The association of *aequitas* with *aequum et bonum* carries forward directly into the Christian era by its incorporation at the outset in Justinian's code. The very first provision of the Code, Section 1.1.1, describes jurisprudence, the art relating to justice, as consisting of the *ars aequi et boni*. The Code retains the Ciceronian placement of "*aequi*" before "*boni.*" Placing the "equal" before the "good/fair" appears to change to some extent what is generally considered to be good and fair—it roots the good and fair in a foundation of equality. So while "equity" may be at the heart of justice even at the outset of the early modern era, at the core of equity, at least that part of equity derived from the Roman Latin *aequitas,* lies equality of a sort.

What then is equitable from the Ciceronian perspective? A particularly useful formulation for purposes of this analysis was *quod videtur aequum omnibus* (what appears fair—in the sense of equal—to all) (Maclean 1992, 175). While this formulation might be adequate in loose terms for adoption by Christianity, further refinement was necessary. Not surprisingly, there was often a significant disparity between what actually appeared fair to "all" and what Christian clerics and princes thought everyone would consider fair. Consequently, the Canon Law formulation of this principle was more specific—*quod videtur aequum omnibus, vel pluribus, vel saltem sapientibus* (what appears fair to all, to some, or at least to the wise) (177). During the broad span of the middle ages, generally speaking, the "wise" in Christendom were those learned in matters of natural and divine law.

But a crisis eventually developed. A gulf continually existed between how people acted and how the few "wise" said they should act. Often the wise did not act in accordance with their own principles, or they permitted, or at least seemed to permit others to do so. The divisiveness of this gulf led, at the time of the Reformation, to the revolution in thought for which Niccolò Machiavelli is generally given credit. He rejected the notion that people's actions should be governed by religious or philosophic ideas, which he considered to be idealistic, or "utopian" notions. Instead, he suggested people should be governed more realistically—rulers should use as their starting point not how people "should" behave in the abstract, but how people actually behave in the real world.

Machiavelli's "revolution" required a reconceptualization of justice. It was not the few wise who should decide what was equal or fair—according to natural and divine law, or to otherwise idealistic or utopian models. What was equal and fair needed to be abstracted from the way people actually behaved; that is, it needed to be determined based on what everyone generally considered to be equal and fair.[17] The roots of the modern more "scientific" approach to laws and politics began to become visible a this point.

Machiavelli's revolutionary thinking leads almost directly the to the Hobbesian teaching that the essential things we hold in common with our fellow human beings are fear of violent death and a desire for self-preservation. Locke changes the emphasis somewhat to "comfortable" self-preservation—which accounts for his focus on another essential, greed, and ways to harness it. Particularly intriguing for present purposes is the change in the way equality is perceived. The few "wise" no longer decide what is equal and fair for everyone. What is equal and fair gets decided by everyone in effect. One consequence of this, in the context of the Hobbesian social contract, is that everyone must acknowledge a radical equality with everyone else in order for the social contract to be entered. The differences in wisdom, strength, virtue, etc., formerly highlighted by the wise, are no longer relevant—a radical leveling has occurred.

Unfortunately, Machiavelli paints with a very broad brush—one that covers not only religious, idealistic, and utopian schemas, but also more pragmatic concepts like Aristotelian επιείκεια. Aristotelian επιείκεια, at first glance, may seem to fit into one of the idealistic/utopian schemas by virtue of the fact that a few "wise" persons decide what result is dictated by επιείκεια. However, these "wise" statesmen or arbitrators do not impose a decision based on idealistic factors of what should or should not be the case. Instead they decide based on the actual circumstances of the case before them—based on what actually happened, and the facts and circumstances surrounding the event and/or person in question. What is relevant is the way people have actually acted, and who they are. Also relevant, of course, is what the common good might require. The result fashioned by the statesmen or arbitrators is quite practical in that it needs to meet the expectations of the people of what is fair in a given case. After all, the overarching objective of επιείκεια is to preserve the authority of the laws and thereby help maintain the rule of law. These few "wise" persons do not decide based on a transcendent notion of natural or divine law, but based on the intellectual virtue of prudence.[18] By painting with such a broad brush, Machiavelli effectively blocks recourse to Aristotelian επιείκεια to help overcome the shortcomings of the conception of equity based on natural and divine law. According to Machiavelli, there are no viable classical alternatives that adequately address how people actually act.

Equity's meaning as something that works to soften the rigor and strictness of law, preserves something of Aristotelian equity in that it acknowledges that there is a problem with laws and seeks to address it. But the problem of the laws being too rigorous does not make the laws "defective," as it did for Aristotle. After Cicero, laws can be considered rough and inflexible by nature, not defective. Equity, which makes the laws less vigorous, is considered to "follow the law;" it does not entirely set aside the laws—effectively making a new law for each case—as Aristotelian equity quietly did. Presumably, though, the nature of the problem with over-strict laws is the same as the "defects" identified by Aristotle. People are more likely to rebel against the laws unless equity acts to make the results the laws produce fit the circumstances of specific cases. That is, without the operation of equity, the rule of law, and derivatively the regime itself, are in danger. Thus, the recharacterization of laws as non-defective may have far-reaching and very undesirable consequences.

Under Christianity, the nature of the problem with laws is somewhat different from the Ciceronian formulation. The strictness of laws, rather than being simply one of their inherent characteristics, is a reflection of the strictness of divine law. If divine law were strictly applied, Christian doctrine provided that no person would be saved under pre-Reformation Christianity—no one could possibly satisfy the requirements of divine law. Only through an act of divine mercy could anyone expect to achieve salvation. This act of mercy, in a certain sense, can be conceived as softening the requirements of divine law. This grant of mercy is a gift—it is not necessarily tied to any merit on the part of the recipient. Human law, when viewed as a reflection of divine law, also has the problem of being extremely strict. Like divine law, it also needs to be softened by acts of mercy. People should be merciful, the reasoning goes, not to achieve fitting outcomes in legal cases, but in order to merit divine mercy. However, the reasoning behind this parallel seems to defy logic since divine mercy is purely a gift, and not based on the merit of any individual. Consequently, whether or not we act mercifully to others should not impact whether or not we receive divine mercy.[19] While the rendering of human mercy in the pre-Reformation Christian schema might take into account the circumstances of particular cases, the underling theory certainly does not require it. Instead, the rendering of human mercy becomes associated with equity—in line with Aristotle's formulation.

The mercy related component of equity had a profound impact on the notion of justice in pre-Reformation Christianity. Justice was no longer conceived of as *aequum et bonum,* the Classical Roman ideal. Instead, Aristotelian equity is mixed in. Equity becomes the soul of justice, and in St. Cyprian's definition, equity is simply justice tempered by the sweetness of mercy. In pre-Christian Roman jurisprudence, as we saw, a version of the equality principle was employed in large part to avoid *summa iniuriam.*[20] But Christian thinkers considered the equality principle insufficient to avoid harsh consequences—specific circumstances in individual cases still needed to be addressed to achieve fair results.

Interestingly, in pre-Reformation Christian reasoning, specific circumstances in individual cases should have become theoretically irrelevant, since they do not impact the granting of mercy. The problem of this theoretical inconsistency does not get addressed adequately until the very end of the middle ages, when Jean Gerson amended the St. Cyprian formulation.Equity, according to Gerson, "is justice (which) having weighed all of the particular circumstances is tempered with the sweetness of mercy." Equity, under this formulation returns largely to how Aristotle envisioned it.

As this study begins to approach the sixteenth century, two large problems are apparent with equity's association with mercy. The first is the political problem: Can rulers exercise mercy pursuant to the Christian formula and still rule effectively?[21] Clearly the rulers could not, if the rule of law and the regime are to be maintained. They would need to be merciful to everyone to assure they themselves would receive divine mercy. Rulers faced another problem: Is the proper object of mercy a particular offender or the rest of a ruler's subjects? The issue is whether pardoning an offender constitutes acting unmercifully towards the rest of one's subjects.[22] There is no clear guidance how mercy should be dealt with in the political arena.

Secondly, a fundamental problem arises specifically in English Christian thought respecting mercy at the time of the Reformation. Under the doctrine of pre-destination, set forth in article 11 of both the "42 articles" and the "39 articles," and thus the official doctrine of the Church of England after 1553 (except during Mary's rule), mercy was no longer a link in the chain of salvation. Whether or not you were saved was pre-ordained from the beginning of time. Consequently, the need for a gift of divine mercy dissapeared. Moreover, there was no longer any need in the human sphere to render mercy onto others. "Good acts" had become irrelevant to the question of salvation. There was no longer a religious mandate for acting mercifully.

SIXTEENTH CENTURY THEORY AND PRACTICE

Prior to the sixteenth century, the predominant view in the West, in terms of political philosophy, was that theory was superior to practice and should guide and control it. The fundamental theoretical concern of politics was not with existing regimes, with the rulers of any given regime, or with the behavior or character of the citizens of any given regime. Instead, it was with the theoretically best regime, rulers and citizens, which of course did not, and could not exist. Particular regimes, rulers and citizens were to be viewed and critiqued by how they should behave using the ideal regime, rulers, and citizens as the touchstone. The fact that the actual behavior of particular regimes, rulers and citizens inevitably fell considerably short of how they should behave was beside the point.

Accordingly, both the Christian and pre-Christian theoretical positions could be viewed in some sense as extreme in that they did not easily accommodate problems associated with practice—of how regimes and people actually behaved as opposed to how they should in theory behave. Plato's "unconcern with, or even contempt for the merely historical truth"—of what actually takes place in practice—is reflective of this extreme position (Tarkov 1987, 911). Plato's overriding concern was with moral virtue—how people should act, not with how they actually happened to act from time to time.[23] The Christian theoretical position was even more uncompromising since it was less concerned with the dictates of prudence, relying as it did on the absolutes of divine law. Christianity's primary concern was with the salvation of people's immortal souls. This overarching objective leaves little or no room for compromise with merely "human" practice, and resulted in the excesses of the Inquisition.

At the outset of the sixteenth century, the view that "theory should govern practice" suffered an attack from which it has not recovered, an attack instituted by Nicolò Machiavelli. Machiavelli disagreed that theory should govern practice. He considered that the

> [c]oncern with the salvation of men's immortal souls seemed to permit, nay, to require courses of action which would have appeared to the classics, and which did appear to Machiavelli, to be inhuman and cruel . . . [Machiavelli] seems to have diagnosed the great evils of religious persecution as a necessary consequence of the Christian principle, and

> ultimately of the Biblical principle. He tended to believe that a considerable increase in man's inhumanity was the unintended but not surprising consequence of man's aiming too high (Strauss 1988, 44).

Consequently, Machiavelli rejected completely that theory should govern practice. He considered this position to be based on unfounded idealism—on a utopian vision. Machiavelli chose not to distinguish pre-Christian classical positions from Christian ones. He painted them both with the same broad brushstrokes—they were both fundamentally utopian—the city of men of Plato's *Republic* was as irrelevant in key respects as Augustine's *City of God.* Machiavelli had some basis for not distinguishing between the Classical and Christian ideals. After all, philosophy, the guiding light of the pre-Christian western world, had been nothing more than the handmaid of Christianity for more than 1000 years. After rejecting the pre-Christian and Christian views on the significance of being guided by an ideal, Machiavelli chose for his foundation, the way people actually behave.

> [S]ince my intent is to write something useful to whoever understands it, it has appeared to me more fitting to go directly to the effectual truth of the thing than to the imagination of it. And many have imagined republics and principalities that have never been seen or known to exist in truth; for it is so far from how one lives to how one should live that he who lets go of what is done for what should be done learns his ruin rather than his preservation. (*The Prince*, ch. 15)[24]

Machiavelli's foundation of how people actually act intentionally lowers the goals of society, of political life, "so that we shall not be forced to commit any bestialities which are not evidently required for the preservation of society and of freedom"(Strauss 1988, 44). Machiavelli considered the idealistic approaches as far more likely to result in greater evils than his pragmatic alternative. Given the harsh experiences of Machiavelli and his fellow Florentines in the early Inquisition, it is difficult to blame him.

It should be noticed, however, that Machiavelli's assertion that practice governs theory is as extreme as the theory over practice position it seeks to replace. Intriguingly, Machiavelli presented the choice as a dichotomy—he required the selection of one position to the exclusion of the other. It is unclear why he did not choose to present the problem as a continuum with theory preeminent at one end and practice at the other end. Unlike Thomas More in his *Utopia*, Machiavelli, in his *Prince*, does not appear to offer intermediate options.

Thomas More, writing at virtually the same time as Machiavelli, perceived both the problem and the solution differently. Like Machiavelli, More saw that there were problems with theory governing practice. But unlike Machiavelli, he did not reject theory outright. More explored possible hybrid systems—some nearer the "theory should govern practice" end of the continuum, some nearer the "practice governs theory" end. More's *Utopia*, according to the interpretation advanced in this book, appears to be rather nearer the "theory governs practice" end of the continuum than the "practice governs theory" end. In his *Utopia*, More does not just expound a vision of a utopia. Instead, he encloses his utopian vision within a dialogue addressing practical issues and problems; the entire dialogue in Book I involves practical real world issues. At the end of Book II, following Raphael's description of Utopia, the text briefly resumes the real world dialogue.

Utopia's structure suggest that More's and Machiavelli's positions may be closer than one would expect based on Machiavelli's rejection of theory governing practice. One key difference between Machiavelli and More is that Machiavelli identifies the problem with theory as religious—as the inhumanity that results from religion's paramount concern with the salvation of people's immortal souls. More, identifying more with classical thought,[25] felt that theory helped to address the fundamental political problem, which was the uneven distribution of wealth in regimes. It is difficult to escape the conclusion that More's "solution" to the problem of the uneven distribution of wealth, the portion of his *Utopia* actually devoted to utopia, ultimately elevates theory above practice. To summarize, More's position is more moderate than Machiavelli's. Rather than adopting practice as the foundation of theory as Machiavelli had done, More carefully insulates theory within a cacoon of practice. His exploration of utopian theory both begins and ends with the real world concerns of practical politics.

More's "solution," of course, had a serious problem. Pre-Reformation Christianity did not allow room for such a compromise with practice. Divine law, and derivatively natural law (from which equity and human law were considered to flow), required an unadulterated position of theory governing practice.[26] More neatly sidesteps this problem by imagining a utopian state that was not Christian.

Unlike More, Hugo Grotius, in the early seventeenth century, refused to sidestep this issue.[27] He addressed Christianity directly and concluded that it did not allow room for such a compromise. But he, like More, desired to avoid Machiavelli's all or nothing position. He too sought some middle ground between the extremes of theory or practice dominated systems. But after a century of divisiveness due to the Reformation, the only middle ground he saw required the complete severance of natural law from divine law. Consequently, Grotius conceived of a natural law that "would still have great weight, even if we were to conceive what we cannot grant without wickedness, that there is no God . . ." (*De Jure Belli et Pacis*, "Prologema" Par. 11).

But in order to sever natural law from divine law, Grotius had to drastically narrow the scope of natural law.[28] These two factors—disconnection of natural from divine law, and the narrowing of natural law's scope—undermined much of what equity had come to mean after Aristotle's time. In 1500, equity's meaning ultimately depended on its relation to a natural law derived from devine law. Equity had largely ceased to be matter of practical consequence. Aristotelian equity had been largely subordinated since Cicero's reformulation of equity some 1500 years before. By the time Grotius wrote, more than a century after More, he was fighting a rearguard battle. The balance he attempted to strike on the practice-theory continuum was closer to the practice end, whereas More's was nearer the theory end. Grotius' complete severance of natural from divine law seems to require such a shift. Consistent with a shift in the direction of practice controlling theory is Grotius' increased focus on the individual—on the first steps that would lead towards a theory of individual rights. This focus on the individual originates, among other places, in Machiavelli's political emphases, especially his implicit rejection of the notion that people are naturally social beings, and Luther's emphasis on the fundamental liberty and equality of all Christians.[29] In short, by the beginning of the seventeenth century, any middle ground compromise position between a theory dominated position and a practice dominated one was going to be closer to the practice end of the continuum.

By the early seventeenth century, natural law had become "an unstable category of thought which must collapse back into" either a system looking ultimately to divine positive law or a system of man made positive law (Hochstrasser 2000, 7).That is, Machiavelli's view of the situation as a dichotomy of two extremes rather than a continuum eventually predominated. Despite efforts by those like More and Grotius, there was less and less room for compromise positions between these two extremes.

Many factors contributed to the success of the Machiavellian position. Important among these was the initial view of the Protestant reformers Luther and Calvin that their followers had a duty of political obedience to their secular rulers (Hopfl 1991, xvii). That is, in practical affairs, man made positive law trumped divine law. Another element in the triumph of practice over theory was the rise in the late sixteenth and early seventeenth centuries of the scientific method and the raw beginings of the push to replace religious faith with what has been termed faith in technological progress. The scientific method, of course, is based on experiments, and proceeds to formulate theories based on actual occurrences. Viewed in this way, it operates in a fashion perfectly consistent with Machiavelli's position of "practice governs theory." Consequently, it is not surprising that Francis Bacon, frequently associated with the rise of the scientific method, "appeared to accept Machiavelli's formulation that political philosophy ought to concentrate on what men do and not on what they ought to do. Like Machiavelli, he took as his starting point the extreme situation" (Strauss and Cropsey 1987, 367). For Bacon, the highest things depended "upon human construction," upon an "elevation of the man-made, the artificial, over the natural" (367). Consequently, Bacon's "utopia," the *New Atlantis*, effectively attempts to redefine the term. We should not be surprised, given his starting point, and combined with his "faith in technological progress," when he makes the rulers of his utopia scientists, and these scientists are the ones who identify the true religion for the people of New Atlantis.[30]

In sum, the developments during the sixteenth and early seventeenth centuries with respect to the relation of theory and practice invite us to see a struggle between what I will term the "Machiavellian" view of a dichotomy—a clear choice between two (extreme) viewpoints with no middle ground possible—and a continuum flowing between these two extremes and offering the option of various compromises, of mixed possibilities, some closer to one end of the spectrum, some closer to the other.

At the extreme where theory governs practice, equity is the very essence of justice. Where practice governs theory, equity becomes a largely irrelevant concept that continues in greatly reduced form as a series of maxims, or rules of interpretation.[31] A "continuum" position—where there are intermediate possibilities between these extremes—preserves the possibility for the continuation, or perhaps even the rediscovery of a viable form of equity deriving from classical Greek επιείκεια.[32] More presented a continuum position in his *Utopia*, one in which theory continued to guide practice, but in a less rigorous way than formerly—the vicissitudes of everyday life, of practice, were to some extent acknowledged and taken into account. But, More's continuum position did not prevail, Machiavelli's position of practice governing theory did. Consequently, equity eventually meant little more that a series of maxims and rules of interpretation.

The picture I have painted of equity's transformation in England is too bleak in one respect due to unique circumstances there. Ironically, in the short term, the decreasing influence of the theory that had controlled equity's meaning for so long had the odd effect of elevating jurisprudential equity into a tremendously powerful political tool. In fact, in 1616, the equity rendered by the Chancery court in England reaches its apex in terms of political importance. Francis Bacon, as James I's Attorney General, could advise his king that the Chancery court, because of its equity jurisdiction, was the court of James I's absolute sovereignty. This meant, remarkably, that James I was more sovereign in his Chancery court than anywhere else in the realm, even the royal court, because in the Chancery court he could exercise Chancery's equity jurisdiction—a legal jurisdiction which trumped all others and from which there was no appeal. Given James I's expansive views on the extent of royal sovereignty and prerogative, views with which Bacon was intimately acquainted, the significance of such a statement cannot be overestimated.

The unique circumstance in England that led to the elevation in political importance of equity, as applied by the Chancery court, involved the curious division of the legal and equity jurisdictions. Beginning in the twelth century, and accelerating over time, a growing rift developed in English jurisprudence between equity and law. It is difficult to describe the rationale behind the split both because no records exist explaining the shift, and it is hard to conceive of a notion of equity divorced from law. After all, equity's source in Aristotelian επιείκεια appeared to bind equity inextricably to law. Cicero's reformulation of equity continued this connection—albeit in a less dramatic fashion. The primary function of equity, from both these perspectives, was to respond to an inherent problem with laws.

But this almost unthinkable separation of equity from law is in fact what occurred in England. In the twelfth century the Common Law courts began to consider equity less and less in their deliberations and judgments. These courts began instead to rely more and more on precedent and strict application of statute in deciding cases. This course of action was easier than sorting through and assessing the specific circumstances of individual cases. Also, this course appeared to be good for commerce and trade, since it added predictability to the outcomes of commercial litigation (Baker 1978, 37–38). Of course, disregarding equity did not solve the underlying problem with laws as being defective or overly strict, depending on whether one takes the Aristotelian ror Ciceronian view, respectively. Many litigants were unhappy with Common Law court judgments, considering them to be over-rigorous and unfair. Some of these litigants complained to the Crown about Common Law court judgments they considered unfair. The Crown referred these matters to the Council, which in turn referred them to the Chancery, which was then the Crown's only administrative resource with the bureaucratic staff to handle such complaints. Over time, the Chancery's handling of these and other matters began to be considered a separate legal entity—a court in its own right, and a portion of this court's jurisdiction was eventually termed its "equity" jurisdiction. Thus, laws eventually became subject again to adjustment by equity in England, but the unique English circumstances severed the former unity which disguised equity's operation of veiling the problem with laws.

The Chancery court, when acting pursuant to its equity jurisdiction, operated as a kind of extra-ordinary appellate court. By the late sixteenth and early seventeenth centuries the Chancery court could seize a case from the Common Law courts, or even revisit what the Common Law courts considered to be final (i.e. unappealable) decisions. Understandably, Parliament and the Common Law lawyers and judges were not at all content with this state of affairs, and extreme tension developed between the two court systems.

This perplexing separation of equity from law that developed in response to the Common Law system in England was unique. The civil law based legal systems on the European continent did not separate equity from law, nor would such a separation have made sense to them. The core of equity's meaning was inextricably tied to law—equity separate from law was virtually inconceivable in civil law systems.

The curious developments in England leading to the separation of law and equity would have wide-ranging implications for equity once its theoretical foundation came under attack in the sixteenth century. Prior to this time, equity in England remained connected to its theoretical foundation in spite of its artificial separation from law, because Chancery's equity jurisdiction remained under the control of clerics, with limited exceptions, until the fall of Cardinal Wolsey in 1529. Consequently, directly or indirectly, the connection between equity and natural law as well as the derivative connection to divine law was preserved in spite of the split. However, the artificial separation had set the stage for conceiving of an independent, free-standing equity—an equity divorced from its theoretical foundation. Thomas More well understood the danger of the detachment of equity from its theoretical underpinnings in the English legal and political system. Such an equity, rather than correcting the inherent problem with laws, might be used simply as a tool to circumvent the laws. In 1516 More could have his *Utopia* character, Raphael Hythlodaeus, anticipate the possibility of the Crown circumvention of the laws utilizing equity. Hythlodaeus observes that there would always be a "pretext" available to judges to decide in the Crown's favor regardless of what the laws might provide. One such pretext he explicitly identified was equity.

More was keenly aware of the potential dangers and near incomprehensibility of an equity divorced from the laws. Consequently, soon after he became Lord Chancellor in 1529, he invited the Common Law judges to dinner and offered to turn over Chancery's equity jurisdiction to them, provided they use it. They, however, refused to accept it. Perhaps this was not entirely unexpected. After all, accepting it back and using it would require them to closely examine the facts and circumstances of individual cases, and to exercise their discretion, which would, of course, make their jobs more difficult. Also, the Common Law judges did not then foresee, as More apparently did, the full extent of the impact that the misuse of the Chancery court's equity jurisdiction would have on the Common Law courts. This lack of foresight is understandable during the tenure of such a conscientious Lord Chancellor as More—More's actions as Chancellor gave them no cause to worry.

Within just a few years, however, soon after More's downfall, Thomas Cromwell intervened in a copyright dispute on the side of Christopher St. German, the author of *Doctor and Student*, a dialogue between a doctor of divinity and an English student of the Common Law. Cromwell apparently realized the political potential of the equity jurisdiction and felt that St. German's book might advance this cause. St. German's text discusses equity in the English jurisprudential system at length. Moreover, it can be read in a way that would provide support for Henry VIII's imminent Act of Supremacy. Once the Crown possessed the final word in England in matters of religion, it could effectively disregard equity's theoretical underpinnings. Understandably enough, equity quickly thereafter became politicized.

Over the course of the sixteenth century, as its theoretical foundation eroded, and as the equity jurisdiction of the Chancery (and other courts) became politicized, equity became both a theoretically bereft concept and a supremely powerful political tool—not an unlikely combination, as More foresaw. Possibly as early as the mid-1590's, Thomas Hake could describe the Chancery court as the court of the Crown's supreme power because of its equity jurisdiction—a formulation repeated by Bacon to James I in 1616. By the early seventeenth century, John Seldon, apparently drawing on similar previous observations, could quip that the Lord Chancellor's conscience varied by the length of his foot, a saying that became proverbial.

J.H. BAKER: "ENGLISH LAW AND THE RENAISSANCE"

Contemporary scholars examining the intersections of literature, rhetoric, and law in the early modern period in England have relied heavily on J. H. Baker's 1975 Yorke prize winning essay entitled "English Law and the Renaissance," presenting his critique of F. W. Maitland's 1901 Rede Lecture of the same title.[33] Near the beginning of the essay Baker describes his motivation for re-examining early modern English legal history:

> The rebirth of the common law made it capable of adapting, without further radical alteration, to the needs of many generations of Englishmen, not to mention the new world and an empire. The period in which this transformation occurred—the same period in which theology, medicine, astronomy, history, philology and most other sciences were either reborn or first created—ought, therefore, to be one of the focal points of English legal history. (23)

The central question Maitland pursued in his essay, Baker notes, was

> [h]ow, in an age when 'old creeds of many kinds were crumbling and all knowledge was being transfigured,' did the medieval common law of the year books persist with such vigour that Coke in 1629 could describe Littleton as 'the most perfect and absolute work that ever was written in any human science'? (24)

After noting that Maitland's essay, until Baker's time, was the "starting point for all later discussion" of English Renaissance law, Baker points out that of all Maitland's work, this essay was "more widely questioned and controverted than most" (25). It was therefore time, according to Baker, for a new study with a somewhat different emphasis. Baker thought "[attention] ought now to be turned to the changes [in English law of the period] and their causes"(28). Accordingly, the central question of Baker's essay was quite different from Maitland's: "to what extent was there a sixteenth-century Reformation of English law?" (28).

Part of Baker's essay is devoted to the refutation of the position that the "new learning" of the humanists sparked any of the changes in sixteenth-century English law. The reason for this, according to Baker, "as might have been predicted, [was that] English lawyers were more inclined to discuss practical solutions to real problems than to speculate on principles of moral or political philosophy"[34] (29). Baker suggests that there are "five features of the law in Henry VIII's time which might point to some link with the new learning" (29). The third and fourth of these features are respectively

> (iii) the pursuit of the utilitarian ideal of the 'common wealth,' and
> (iv) an 'equitable' approach to the variety of individual cases[.] (29)

Before briefly addressing Baker's treatment of these two features, I want to point out two underlying themes of Baker's analysis. The first involves his complete confidence that practice governs theory. For Baker, that which derives from theory is "not reality," and that which is not real cannot "give any help to the solution of actual problems" (36). Baker sees both "common wealth" and the sort of equity rendered by the Chancery court[35] as having "the same dangerous propensities" in that he considers them both to be based on theory rather than practice.

Baker does not explicitly state what the *danger* is of theory governing practice. But the tenor of his presentation makes abundantly clear that the danger he sees in theory is that it might lead to the practice of communism.[36] Written in 1975, Baker's critique is to some extent a relic of a cold war mentality. Baker is fashioning a revisionist history that advances the cause of "the new capitalism which [in the early sixteenth-century] threatened to undermine the traditional social order" (34). The real threat, Baker advances, was not nascent capitalism, but the possibility "that preferring the common wealth to private wealth might encourage the view that all wealth was common" (36).[37]

Baker's all or nothing approach is similar to Machiavelli's and is equally problematic. Near the outset of his treatment of "common wealth" Baker summarily dismisses More's *Utopia* as irrelevant as a practical matter because it "was not reality" (34). Baker overlooks the fact that More chose to situate the discussion of the ideal place called Utopia within a framework of real world issues and practical concerns. Baker also neglects More's subtle but profound treatments of equity in *Utopia*, including his classically oriented connection of the notion of "common wealth" with equity. More's concern, like that of Plato and Aristotle, was translating theory into practice. Baker's, on the other hand, whether consciously or not, appears to be advancing the agenda set by Machiavelli, by discounting all theoretically oriented approaches to law and politics.

Baker's specific concern relating to equity is to advance the "certainty of a known rule" over "the uncertainly of an arbitrary decision by a single judge" (40). He seeks, with John Hales, to "distinguish between the "kind of equity which kept law on the right course, and the kind of equity which was administered in Chancery" (42). The sort of "equity" Baker promotes is one that he suggests never left the Common Law, one that continues and "operate[s] through the 'increasingly detailed consideration of facts" (42). However, what Baker is in fact describing is not equity in any traditionally accepted sense, but a reconception of law as sufficient to "inquire as far into the facts of a case as justice required" (40). What justice requires must "be balanced against convenience" (40). From this standpoint, Baker's argument is remarkably similar to the reasoning of the Common Law judges in severing equity from the Common Law. Effectively, the equity Baker associates with the English Rennaissance has lost its most compelling characteristic, its flexibility, a characteristic Baker finds troubling.

Baker's treatment of sixteenth-century English legal history, I argue, is somewhat distorted because of his anti-communism revisionist approach. Baker, in his partisanship, has downplayed the potential influence of humanist learning, including the rediscovered classical corpus. This leaves the work of scholars who rely on Baker's interpretation of sixteenth century law as the basis for understanding equity open to question. In Chapter Three I will set forth an interpretation of More's *Utopia* that suggests a much more expansive classical influence and a much greater reliance on theory than Baker allows. My interpretation will to some extent contradict Baker's argument against the practical influence of the idea of commonwealth, and it will highlight a connection between the idea of commonwealth and equity that involves the translation of theory into practice.

Chapter Two

Equity (*Επιείκεια*) in Aristotle and Plato

INTRODUCTION

In this chapter I examine the roots of equity in Plato and Aristotle's treatments of the Greek concept of *επιείκεια*. My impetus for this examination was to account for perplexing uses of the concept of equity by certain English Renaissance authors such as Thomas More, Edmund Spenser, and Thomas Hobbes—uses that were inexplicable in terms of the standard treatments of equity in their respective eras. As I examined Plato's and Aristotle's accounts of *επιείκεια*, I gradually realized that the scholarly discussions of *επιείκεια* in Plato and Aristotle did not adequately address the range of meanings I found in the original texts. Consequently, I considered a fresh treatment of the topic to be warranted.

OVERVIEW

In the next chapter I will establish that the uses of equity in Thomas More's *Utopia* draw upon many significations of equity, some deriving from Greek *επιείκεια*, others from Roman Latin *aequitas*, and still others from Christian Latin *aequitas*. I will also establish that a full understanding of these uses of equity was critical to understanding various difficult elements in the *Utopia*. In my analysis of the uses of equity in *Utopia*, and my explications of a possible solution to these problems, I will rely heavily upon the way *επιείκεια* is treated in the works of Aristotle and Plato. My study of More's *Utopia* revealed that More appeared to be drawing directly on Aristotle and Plato for his understanding of various significations for equity, significations that are now obscure and not adequately treated in texts dealing with the history of ideas or the history of law. Like Thomas More, I felt compelled to learn Greek to enhance my understanding of classical authors like Aristotle and Plato. This chapter contains the results of my research into equity's origins in Aristotle's *Rhetoric*, *Ethics*, and *Politics*, and Plato's *Laws*. Where I considered it necessary, I have provided my own translations of particularly significant passages.

For the purposes of this chapter, I am going to suggest that the various uses of *επιείκεια* in these works forms a large-scale, multi-perspective picture of a single idea. For the sake of convenience, because the contexts in which the term is used warrant it, and because a long tradition in English equates a portion of these perspectives with the concept English translates as "equity," in this chapter I will translate *επιείκεια* as "equity," "equitable"—when describing something or someone, or *the* "equitable"—when referring to a group of persons.

Equity, as developed in these works, is essentially of three sorts. The first two kinds pertain to *city* matters—they are very practical and of use in virtually all legal cases, among other things. When I refer to *city*, I mean a particular political unit. Today we typically refer to a country or nation as the large-scale political unit, in classical Greece, however, the relevant political unit was the city state—the *polis*. The laws of the *polis* and its regime dictated the horizon for the practical sorts of equity. These two kinds of equity are employed either to judge and assess completed actions or events, or to consider what is or is not expedient for the *polis*. The third kind of equity is not practical in the same way as the first two sorts. It is not limited by the laws or the regime of any particular *polis*, since it involves what is and is not expedient as regards the improvement of regimes and their laws generally. This third sort of equity is little concerned with the day-to-day affairs of the *polis* and the application of the *polis'* laws.

Aristotle, in his *Rhetoric*, treats the first kind of equity—the more limited of the two practical sorts. This equity is clearly defined, and Aristotle even provides a specific example of how it should be employed. This equity is clearly subordinate to laws. Any application of it must "follow" upon the laws. In Aristotle's example, a law is posited that prohibits striking another person with iron objects. Aristotle notes that in the case of a person striking another while wearing an iron ring, a technical violation of the law would occur. According to Aritstotle, equity would be employed to exonerate this person. Equity thus corrects the problems associated with the necessarily general statement of the law. This sort of equity must only be rendered by "arbitrators"—citizens who have reached fifty-nine and a half years of age. This restriction appears to relate to the danger inherent in being able to circumvent the strict letter of the laws, even in rather clearly defined circumstances. This power to circumvent the laws cannot be entrusted to ordinary jurors because of the great temptation to abuse this power. It must be reserved for older persons—those long habituated to the laws, who, because of their age and experience, in theory possessed considerable moral virtue, and in whom the sharp desires of youth presumably have been blunted.

In his *Ethics*, Aristotle describes the second sort of "practical" equity. Like the first sort of equity, this second sort deals with the problems associated with the necessarily general statement of laws. However, rather than being carefully defined and circumscribed, this second sort is almost infinitely flexible. Consequently, its relation to laws is far more ambiguous. Rather than following upon the laws, as the first sort of equity does, this equity appears to be parallel or in partnership with them. Aristotle compares it to the flexible leaden measuring device used by the Lesbians to determine which unevenly shaped paving stones will best fit together—traditionally known as the "Lesbian Rule." Only the statesmen, persons who possess the intellectual virtue of prudence, are entrusted to render this equity. Only they have sufficient practical and deliberative intelligence to respond appropriately to all of the infinitely variable particulars of day-to-day matters in the city. This equity is both forensic and deliberative. Its only limits are those of the statesmen themselves. The statesmen's chief limitation is that they tend "to take for granted the naturalness and permanence of the regime that is here and now" (Strauss and Cropsey 1987, 133).

There is a third sort of equity which is of a character different from the two types of "practical" equity just mentioned. The concern of the first two sorts was the preservation of the rule of law in existing regimes. This third type of equity is concerned exclusively with the improvement of regimes. This sort of equity is clearly above regimes and their laws. In fact, its ultimate purpose is to shape and reshape regimes and their laws. Necessarily, it is also concerned with destroying existing regimes—albeit so gradually as not to be noticed. This third sort of equity is rendered by those Plato calls "reformers," and Aristotle the "equitable." These persons, out of a sense of equity, gradually—over a period measured in generations—work to reduce the disparity in terms of wealth between the rich and poor by sharing a portion of their wealth with the poor. Effectively, they create a middle-class of sorts. In this way they erect "the sort of sturdy foundation upon which someone can later build whatever political order befits such an arrangement"—presumably the rule of a true aristocracy (Plato, *Laws* 736e).

EQUITY IN PLATO'S *LAWS*

There are ten distinct uses of *επιείκεια* in the *Laws*. The most significant of these are the fourth, fifth, and eighth uses, which occur in Books V and VI.

After briefly addressing all ten uses, I will return to examine the fourth, fifth and eighth in more detail. I provide the following list for the reader to refer to as they read the descriptions of these ten uses of *επιείκεια* in the *Laws.*

Ten Uses of Επιείκεια in Plato's Laws

1. Kleinias says it is *equitable* for three elderly gentlemen such as he, Megilius, and the Athenian Stranger, to discuss what is praiseworthy and blameworthy in the laws of Crete and Sparta. (635a)(related to #'s 3, 6, 7, &10)

2. The Athenian Stranger describes as *equitable* the drinking party he propses in order to test the characters of potential citizens for the new colony. (649a-650b)(related to # 9)

3. The old men who are in charge of selecting laws for the new colony are described as *equitable*—the specific context involves laws relating to the education of children. (659d)(related to #'s 1, 6, 7, & 10)

4. The flexible quality of the "woof" of fabric (a weaving term) is *equitable,* as are the sorts of people who have qualities similar to the "woof." The Athenian Stranger compares here the sorts of people who will fill ruling offices in a regime to the woof and warp of fabric. The warp is strong, but rigid and inflexible. (734e-735a (related to #'s 5 & 8)

5. The reformers who improve regimes slowly—over the course of generations—are said to act out of a sense of *equity.* (736c-e)(related to #'s 4 & 10)

6. Certain old men are described as *equitable* because they recognize the goodness of the laws being established for the new colony. (741d)(related to #'s 1, 3, 7, & 10)

7. The system of setting up thirty seven-old men as Guardians to ensure that the laws of the new colony will be protected and preserved is described as *equitable.* (753b)(related to #'s 1, 3, 6, & 10)

8. *Equity* is contrasted with the "precision of exact justice" in the context of a polis' necessary blurring of distinctions between people of preeminent virtue and less virtuous people by positing a natural equality of both groups. (757d-e)(related to #'s 4 & 5)

9. Certain laws of the Cretans and Spartans are described as *equitable.* (836b)(related to # 2)

10. Old men who have composed laws in other places, which laws are selected to be adopted by the Guardians of the Laws, are described as *equitable.* (957a-b)(related to #'s 1, 3, 6, & 7)

The first, third, sixth, and tenth uses of *επιείκεια* all appear related in that they all refer to the character of the old men in charge of selecting and modifying the laws of a regime. All of these uses suggest that such men need to have an ingrained decency that has been tested by time and experience.[1] The seventh use appears to be somewhat related to the first, third, sixth and tenth in that *επιείκεια* is used here by the Athenian Stranger to describe the system in the new colony adopted to protect and preserve the laws that are adopted: the appointment of the thirty-seven Guardians of the Laws (753b).[2] The description of the system involving the Guardians as most equitable is appropriate since it involves the exclusive appointment as Guardians of old men who are themselves considered equitable, having become experienced and decent through habituation.

The second and ninth uses of *επιείκεια* also appear related. Both describe elements of the Athenian, Spartan and Cretan regimes that might be useful in establishing the laws of the new colony.[3] The fourth, fifth, and eighth uses of equity, discussed below, are very different from the other uses in that they are intimately related to the problem of distributive justice, and the proposed resolution to this problem.

At the center of Book V of the *Laws*, the fourth and fifth uses of equity occur in close conjunction.[4] The passage in which they occur constitutes a digression from the text as a whole. The digression begins when the Athenian Stranger states:

> And on the one hand, here ends the prelude to the statement of the laws, and on the other hand, after the prelude must follow the design of the laws of the polity.[5] (734e)

But rather than immediately proceeding to the exposition of the laws, the Athenian Stranger begins to speak cryptically, distinguishing between the sort of virtue possessed by persons whom he compares to the "warp" in fabric—which consists of the long, straight, tense threads—and the different sort of virtue possessed by persons he compares to the "woof" in fabric—the threads which interweave the warp together, and therefore are softer, more flexible and have "a certain [equitable], yielding quality" (734e-735a).

> And so, just as in a certain kind of weaving or other plaited work, it is not possible to produce both woof and warp each expressed perfectly in themselves, but rather the strength of the firm twistings of the warp must be transferred by the woof to produce excellent cloth; the warp must be subject to the softer, flexible quality of the woof, a quality that can be described as a certain just equitableness.[6] 734e-735a

The Athenian Stranger then says that in the same way one discriminates between woof and warp, so also one must discriminate between those persons "who are to fill the ruling offices" and "others who have been tested by only a small education." The Athenian Stranger ends this portion of the passage with a third distinction, which obviously relates in some fashion to the prior two. This third distinction contrasts the "two fundamental parts" of a "political regime." The first part relates to the *appointment* of persons to fill each ruling office. The second consists of "the law[s] that are given to the ruling offices."

The Athenian Stranger, then digresses even further by discussing the two kinds of purges that are necessary prior to the implementation of a regime with good laws. These purges, of course, are not obviously relevant to the current situation where a new colony is being established and no purge is necessary. The "best" method of purging can only be accomplished by a "tyrant" who is also a "lawgiver." This method of purging is "harsh" and involves the killing or exiling of that portion of the population that constitutes "the greatest offenders, those who are incurable and who represent the greatest harm to the city"(735d). The Athenian Stranger then distinguishes the Greek "method [of purging]," which is one of the "gentler" methods. This "gentler" method is described in the following way:

> Those who, because they lack food, show themselves ready to follow men who lead the have-nots in an attack on the property of the haves will be looked upon as a disease growing within the city; they will be sent away in as gentle a manner as possible, in an expulsion that bears the euphemistic name "colonization." (735e-736a)

The Athenian Stranger then notices "the problem [for the new colony] happens to be rather unusual," in that "there isn't any need to devise a colonizing expedition or purgative selection at present" (736a). They simply need to ensure that those who are selected for the new colony are appropriate.[7] At this point the Athenian Stranger digresses still further by discussing how to address the improvement of existing regimes—a topic which seems to be entirely irrelevant to the task at hand.

The Athenian Stranger opens the digression by, in effect, highlighting its irrelevance, by commenting on their own good fortune at being able to construct a colony virtually from scratch:

> It does not escape my notice the good fortune born for us—it is like the good fortune of the colony of the Heraclidae, which fled away from the dangers and strife caused by laws requiring the cancellation of debts and redistribution of land and money. (736d)[8]

Then, without explanation, and as if to emphasize its apparent irrelevance, the Athenian Stranger begins to discuss the situation in cities that do not possess the good fortune of the Heraclidae colony or the new colony being created:

> When a *polis* of ancient lineage must frame laws concerning debt cancellation and wealth distribution, it is neither [safe] to attempt to frame such new laws, nor is it [safe] to simply do nothing. All that remains for such a *polis* is to pray for small changes that occur over long periods of time. Among the persons who set these changes in motion there must arise a supply of reformers possessing much land and many debtors. These reformers must wish, in accordance with equity, to share their wealth with the neediest of their debtors. By making these distributions they are acting moderately, and revealing that poverty does not consist of reducing one's wealth but rather increasing one's greediness.[9] (736c-e)

Who are these remarkable people who, at their own expense, are willing to effect a large-scale redistribution of wealth incrementally over the course of generations? Unfortunately, the Athenian Stranger gives no further hints as to who they might be, or what they are like.[10]

The Athenian Stranger emphasizes the critical importance of the reformers to existing regimes in no uncertain terms. Their presence "is the most important source of a city's preservation, and provides a sort of sturdy foundation upon which someone can later build whatever political order befits such an arrangement" (737a). Their presence is the only way of "escape" from the problems engendered by the "money-loving that goes with justice"

(737a). The Athenian Stranger ends the digression by returning to the subject of the new colony and stating: "Let [the device instituted by such reformers] stand now as a kind of buttress for our city."[11] He does not explain, however, why the device that improves existing regimes is necessary for the new colony, which presumably will not be in need of improvement.

Several things should be pointed out about this fifth use of *επιείκεια* in Plato's *Laws*. First, this *επιείκεια* is indispensable for improving an existing regime in regards to debt cancellation and wealth distribution. Second, *επιείκεια* needs to continue to be present in a *polis* that has achieved good laws to insure it does not regress.[12] Third, *επιείκεια* is critical to resolving the fundamental problem that prevents existing regimes from improving their laws: namely private property—or more specifically, the large disparity between the amount of property owned by the wealthy and by the poor.[13]

The eighth usage of equity, and the final one remaining to be discussed, occurs in Book VI (757e). The context is the Athenian Stranger discussion of the selection procedure for the annually elected Council that will rule the colony. This discussion raises the problem of distributive justice, and suggests that a city is "compelled" to blur the distinction between the sort of equality that is "most just," and the sort of equality which is required by conventional or strict justice—justice according to the laws of the city (757a-758a). Absent such a blurring, the consequences are severe; the city will face "civil war in some of its parts." *Επιείκεια* is raised at this point:

> Every city is sometimes compelled to [blur the distinction between those with more virtue and those with less by positing a natural equality of those who are unequal in terms of virtue], if it does not intend to set up factions in its parts. For equity and pardon, wherever they occur, are set beside the precision of exact justice.[14] 757d-e

While on the surface the wording seems to depict *επιείκεια* in a negative fashion, we must remember that that which *επιείκεια* "enfeebles," strict justice, is the lesser, conventional sort of justice. Implicitly, then, *επιείκεια* empowers that which is "most just"—the higher, less conventional sort of justice. Further development of this point will occur later in the chapter in the passages dealing with Aristotle's treatment of *επιείκεια* in his *Politics* and *Ethics*. It suffices here to notice that the conventional justice of the *polis* is not equitable. There is a problem with this third sort of equity functioning too openly—while this third sort of equity is necessary to achieve a more comprehensive justice, it must be used discreetly since the consequences of its open application can be as severe as civil war.

ARISTOTLE'S *RHETORIC*

Aristotle's explains equity in his *Rhetoric, Ethics* and his *Politics*.[15] Aristotle's most extensive *direct* treatment of equity occurs in his *Rhetoric*, while one almost as long, though emphasizing different aspects, occurs in the *Ethics*. Aristotle's treatment of equity in the *Politics* is of an entirely different order. It is more *indirect*, more profound, and highlights an altogether different kind of equity than those addressed in the *Rhetoric* or *Ethics*. The treatments in the *Rhetoric* and *Ethics* are the ones commonly cited as a root source for the Latin *aequitas*, and as the ultimate source of English equity.

Aristotle's *Rhetoric* raises the issue of equity at its most basic level. Rhetoric is the art of speaking, and according to Aristotle's *Politics*, speech

> serves to reveal the advantageous and the harmful, and hence also the just and unjust. For it is peculiar to man as compared to other animals that he alone has a perception of good and bad and just and unjust and other things [of this sort]; and partnership in these things is what makes a household and a city. (1253a1.2.11–12)

While speech "serves to reveal" the just and unjust, and therefore is related to politics, its method is to persuade. Since most men are more moved by compulsion than persuasion, rhetoric can only represent a part of politics. "A greater part of politics must be concerned with compelling men, and through repetition habituating them, to do without thought what they could never be persuaded to do" (Arnhardt 1981, 6). Nor is speech primarily concerned with ethics—since speeches are insufficient to make most men virtuous. "Most men, especially in their youth, live by passion and the pleasures of the body" (*Ethics* 1179b-1180b; Arnhardt 1981, 5).[16] Such persons can only be controlled by force—not argument.

Since rhetoric is based on enthymemes, and enthymemes are derived from common opinion, which typically is partly true and partly false, rhetoric is also insufficient to move persons whose opinions have already been refined by philosophic examination. The lower starting point of rhetoric explains why "Aristotle treats certain subjects," such as equity, "differently in the *Rhetoric* than in the [*Ethics* or] *Politics*" (Arnhardt 1981, 7). It also explains why the most basic sort of equity is dealt with in the *Rhetoric*.

Aristotle's treatment of equity in the *Rhetoric* arises in the context of an examination of forensic rhetoric. Forensic rhetoric deals with the "sort of things [from which] it is necessary to construct syllogisms concerning accusation and defense" (1368b1–3). Part of this examination involves making "a complete classification of just and unjust actions" (1373b), which in turn involves looking at the laws relating to these.[17] These laws are of two kinds, written and unwritten. One of the two kinds of unwritten laws, according to Aristotle, is equity, the purpose of which is to make "up for the defects of a community's written code of law" (1374a).

The reason equity is necessary, we are told in the *Rhetoric*, is to make up for defects in laws. Laws then are in some critical sense defective. Presumably, this is not the sort of fact to which you want to draw the attention of the multitude, who need to acknowledge the authoritativeness of laws, and be "coercively habituat[ed]" to them (Arnhardt 1981, 5). Equity then, in the *Rhetoric*, helps to preserve the authority of the laws by correcting, or rather concealing their defective nature.

The underlying problem is that the multitude, while they cannot be persuaded by reason regarding what is fair, as deduced by rhetoric, do have an innate sense of fairness, though as in everything else, their passions drive even this. They can vaguely sense, based on their own experience with passions, what sorts of persons and conduct deserve punishment or leniency in particular circumstances. In perhaps the majority of instances it will suffice if the laws are equally applied to all, in spite of their rigor and any special circumstances relevant to specific cases. But, frequently, equity must be resorted to in order to adjust the outcome dictated by the laws to the facts and circumstances of a particular case, so as not to violate this passion-based sense of fairness, and thus to undermine the laws' authority.

But resorting to equity endangers the authority of laws unless equity is carefully controlled. The passionate multitude cannot be entrusted with a tool, which if misused, could undermine the laws—the very device by which the passions are kept in check. Consequently, jurors, selected from the multitude, must strictly follow the laws, and not have access to equity. Aristotle reserves the equity of the *Rhetoric* specifically for the arbitrators, a more refined group.

Arbitrators can be trusted with equity, while the multitude cannot, for two reasons, both relating to the requisite age of an arbitrator of fifty-nine and a half. First, they have been habituated to the laws for their whole lives. Consequently, they are amenable to rhetorical reasoning (Arnhardt 1981, n.6, ch.1). Secondly, they are older and, presumably, their passions have calmed. Even so, Aristotle is extremely careful to set forth explicitly the sorts of things the arbitrators are to consider, and to emphasize in what way equity follows the laws, even as it goes "beyond" them. These things include taking into account the intentions of people, the weaknesses of human nature, the broad circumstances of an occurrence—including the character of the perpetrator apart from the occurence. All of these clearly respond to the element of fairness sensed by the multitude.

Given the importance of this Aristotelian formulation in the *Rhetoric* to the tradition of equity, I quote it in full:[18]

> The second kind [of unwritten law] makes up for the defects of a community's written code of law. This is what we call equity; people regard it as just; it is, in fact, the sort of justice which goes beyond the written law. Its existence partly is and partly is not intended by legislators; not intended, where they have noticed no defect in the law; intended, where they find themselves unable to define things exactly, and are obliged to legislate as if that held good always which in fact only holds good usually; or where it is not easy to be complete owing to the endless possible causes presented, such as the kinds and sizes of weapons that may be used to inflict wounds—a lifetime would be too short to make out a complete list of these. If, then, a precise statement is impossible and yet legislation is necessary, the law must be expressed in wide terms; and so, if a man has no more than a finger-ring on his hand when he lifts it to strike or actually strikes another man, he is guilty of a criminal act according to the written words of the law; but he is innocent really, and it is equity that declares him to be so. From this definition of equity it is plain what sort of actions, and what sort of persons, are equitable or the reverse.[19] Equity must be applied to forgivable actions; and it must make us distinguish between criminal acts on the one hand, and errors of judgment, or misfortunes, on the other. (A "misfortune" is an act, not due to moral badness, that has unexpected results: and "error of judgment" is an act, also not due to moral badness, that has results that might have been expected: a "criminal act" has results that might have been expected, but *is* due to moral badness, for that is the source of all actions inspired by our appetites.) Equity bids us be merciful to the weakness of human nature; to think less about the laws than about the man who framed them, and less about what he said than about what he meant; not to consider the actions of the accused so much as his intentions; nor this or that detail so much as the whole story; to ask not what a man is now but what he has always or usually been. It bids us remember benefits rather than injuries, and benefits received rather than benefits conferred; to be patient when we are wronged; to settle a dispute by negotiation and not by force; to prefer arbitration to litigation—for an arbitrator goes by the equity of a case, a [juror] by the strict law,[20]

> and arbitration was invented with the express purpose of securing full power for equity.[21]
>
> The above may be taken as a sufficient account of the nature of equity. (1373a24–1374b-23)

This passage contains Aristotle's sole example of a law applied to a situation that requires correction by equity. This example serves as the transition point in the passage from the problem of law's necessarily general statement, to the specifics of that to which equity must and should be applied. Intriguingly, Aristotle does not tell us what the law says that is violated in his example. As a practical matter, this forces us to step into the shoes of the legislator in order to determine what was intended—that is, we must act as arbitrators. It also makes us realize more profoundly the necessary shortcomings of laws and the need for equity.

This passage also raises an issue which anticipates the treatment of equity in the *Ethics*, but which seems out of place here. Aristotle refers to persons who are "equitable or the reverse." However, nothing in the *Rhetoric* passage suggests who these persons might be.

ARISTOTLE'S *ETHICS*

The *Ethics* presents us directly with a new variety of equity, the almost infinitely flexible sort rendered by the statesman, a figure who combines moral virtue with *practical* intelligence, experience, and deep knowledge of the things pertaining to the city (Strauss and Cropsey 1987, 131). The statesman, in brief, acts with the kind of political prudence needed to adequately deal with the day-to-day ruling of the city.[22] In addition to the "infinitely flexible" equity of the statesman, the *Ethics* also prepares the foundation for an even more profound level of equity, the kind rendered by the "legislator." Legislators' equitable actions transcend the regime—such persons possess *theoretical* knowledge about the "legal and customary institutions and practices that define a city's regime" (132)[23] Their concerns are not constrained by the regime under which they live; and this is altogether appropriate since their objective is to improve the regime. To put it somewhat differently, their actions are informed by philosophy, while those of the statesman are not (123). While the building blocks for the sort of equity rendered by legislators are in the *Ethics*, we must wait for the *Politics* for the concept's full development.

Before proceeding to the treatment of equity in the *Ethics*, it will be useful to clarify the nature of the *Ethics* generally, and its relation to the

Politics. Formally, the *Ethics* is not an independent treatise, its ending is explicitly the prologue to the *Politics*:

> Is it not, then, out next task to examine from whom and how we can learn to become legislators? Is it not as always from the experts, in this case the masters of politics? For, as we saw, legislation is a part of politics.
>
> . . .
>
> Accordingly, since previous writers have left the subject of legislation unexamined, it is perhaps best if we ourselves investigate it and the general problem of the constitution of a state, in order to complete as best we can our philosophy of human affairs. (*Ethics* 10.9.1180b29–31, 1181b13–15)

To understand the connection between the *Ethics* and the *Politics*, we need to see that Aristotle's conception of political science is quite broad—it includes what we would term ethics and economics, not to mention the matters we typically associate with the governance of a political community (Strauss and Cropsey 1987, 121). The reason why ethics is included is that the city, for Aristotle, "must be understood as existing for the sake not of living, but of living well, nobly, or happily" (Strauss and Cropsey 1987, 137; *Politics* 3.9.1280a24–1281a6). To help its citizens achieve this objective, the city enacts laws and otherwise educates its citizens so that they will develop the habit of acting in accord with the city's conception of the moral virtues.

Aristotle's treatment of the moral virtues, however, takes up only about two and a half of the ten books of the *Ethics*, all in the first half of the work. Consequently, Aristotle's seeming emphasis on the moral virtues is misleading. Taken as a whole, the *Ethics* traces an upward movement away from the *practical* moral virtues, which are defined as "disposition or habit . . . inclining a [person] in a certain way" (Cropsey 1977, 259). The moral virtues, it seems, are not "essentially rational" (Strauss and Cropsey 1987, 125). The movement away from the moral virtues culminates in the *theoretically* informed intellectual virtues. Given this progression, one would expect to be quite removed from practical political matters by the end of the *Ethics*. Instead, after raising us above the political to the apparent highpoint of the *Ethics*—to the point where we are philosophically informed, Aristotle forces us back down to the political sphere—albeit not to the politics of any particular regime.[24] He does this by drawing our attention to the problem of politics and the question of "how we can learn to become legislators," the ones who *know* about political matters (*Ethics*, 10.9.1180b25–29).

The final moral virtue Aristotle treats before raising his sights to the intellectual virtues is justice, the discussion of which occupies all of Book V.[25] Justice is the "peak of moral virtue from the view of the city," and, consequently, "virtually identical with law-abidingness" (Strauss and Cropsey 1987, 127). Justice alone among the moral virtues is "held to be the good of another"; Aristotle does not even try to "demonstrate that justice . . . is in fact choiceworthy for its own sake" (127). Instead, Aristotle makes a critical distinction between two notions of justice: one kind is general, and constitutes justice from the city's point of view (law-abidingness), the other kind is specific (sometimes described as "precise," or "partial" justice) and involves a "disposition to give or take only a fair or equal share of good things."[26] The distinction between varieties of justice will have an analogue in equity, to which we now turn.

The discussion of equity in the *Ethics* occurs at the very end of Book V, as the ending point of the discussion of justice (Stewart 1892, 526).[27] Its placement makes equity the transitional topic with which Aristotle moves from his discussion of the moral virtues to the discussion of the intellectual virtues. This is altogether appropriate since it does not fit neatly into either category, but partakes of both depending upon which of its meanings is under consideration. However, equity's presence here at first appears to be problematic. It seems as though the transitional topic to the intellectual virtues should be the one which immediately precedes equity, the problem of distributive justice.[28] This problem involves the question of "in what is it that men are to be held to be either equal or unequal?" (Strauss and Cropsey 1981, 109). This has been called the "supreme" political problem, one that requires political philosophy to address (109). It is clear that by raising this issue Aristotle has an immediate need to turn to the intellectual virtues—the moral virtues are clearly inadequate to address the overarching problem. It may also explain why he needs to return to political matters at the end of the *Ethics*. What remains obscure is why equity is inserted between Aristotle's raising of the problem of distributive justice and his treatment of that which is required to address it, political philosophy.

The resolution to this obscurity, naturally enough, is that there is a sense in which equity—or as will be discussed below, the "equitable" person—both is associated with, partakes of, or is informed by political philosophy, and is in some way integral to the resolution of the problem of distributive justice. We are prepared for this by the "drift" in Aristotle's argument about justice away from law as a sufficient guide to justice that precedes the introduction of equity (Cropsey 1977, 263).[29] His argument also highlights the fact that justice, in the *general* sense, only holds good for people for whom "the things good in themselves are only good to a certain extent" (Cropsey 1977, 264; *Ethics* 5.9.1137a27–29). There is another group for whom there are no such limits (Cropsey 1977, 264–65; *Ethics* 5.9.1137a27–29).[30] This group, or a subcategory of this group, constitutes the "equitable" described at the end of the equity passage, reproduced below.[31] The equitable are also the "legislators," or a subcategory of the legislators, a group Aristotle describes in the second half of the *Ethics*.

The core of the treatment of equity in the *Ethics* corresponds with its treatment in the *Rhetoric*. This core relates to the universality of laws—that is, to the necessarily general treatment that laws give to their subject matter. However, that is where the similarity between the treatments ends. In the *Rhetoric* Aristotle carefully ties this core concern of equity to very specific considerations, and he only allows equity to be rendered by the arbitrators, not by just any citizen. In the *Ethics*, Aristotle's emphasis is completely different. Instead of tying down equity, he frees it to a remarkable extent. Since the situations to which equity will be applied are infinitely variable, equity needs to be infinitely flexible.[32] The sole example associated with equity in the *Ethics* compares equity to the leaden rule used by the Lesbians in construction. Its flexibility allows it to measure precisely each stone so that they can be fit together with other unevenly shaped stones. We should be reminded here of the sort of equity in the fourth usage of *επιείκεια* in Plato's *Laws*, and of its comparison to the flexible "woof" of fabric.

The rendering of such an equity cannot be left to arbitrators (as is done with the limited equity of the *Rhetoric*); it requires the practical experience and intelligence of the statesman. This intelligence represents the '"practical and deliberative" prudence which is concerned with the particulars of day to day politics"' (Strauss and Cropsey 1987, 131).[33] Aristotle signals the need for the intellectual virtue of prudence (as opposed to the moral virtue of the arbitrators) by posing the relation of justice and equity as a logical problem.

> But at other times, when we follow the logical consequences, it appears odd that the equitable should be distinct from the just and yet deserve praise. If the two terms are different, then either the just is not of great moral value, or the equitable is not just. If both are of great moral value, they are the same. (*Ethics*, at 5.10.1137b2–5).

Aristotle further highlights the need for logic when he claims, perhaps ironically, that "there is no inconsistency" in his presentation of equity (1137b6). The reason more talented persons are needed, of course, is because equity no longer is closely following the laws, or being clearly defined with precision, since that would reduce its flexibility. Aristotle even acknowledges that "not all things are determined by law[s]" (1137b27). While other laws may provide guidance in such a case, by analogy, it is clear that the persons rendering this new sort of equity will need to move beyond the existing laws. The general trend in the treatment here is for equity to begin moving further and further away from the laws—precisely the reverse of the trend in the *Rhetoric* passage. The arbitrators, whose capacities are no better than the laws which have habituated them, are clearly not to be entrusted with this sort of equity.[34]

The drift away from laws points towards the third and highest component of equity. This component is obliquely raised in the *Ethics'* passage on equity, but we must wait for the *Politics* to appreciate its full significance. If the *Politics* is fundamentally concerned with reforming regimes, and if such reform occurs in small incremental steps, as seems best, then three things are evident (Strauss and Cropsey 1987, 133, 143).[35] First, the statesman is not the one to improve the regime, for he is shaped by it. Second, the statesman will be inadequate to prevent small incremental changes made by those whose business it is to improve regimes. For the statesman "is insufficiently sensitive to apparently insignificant developments that, over time, can dramatically affect the political makeup of a city and thereby its governing arrangements" (133). Finally, there must be a class of persons "who 'rule' in a stronger more precise sense" (139). These persons are the ones who will institute the incremental changes that will reform regimes—who will address "the central political task" of blunting or eliminating the political conflict between the rich and the poor" (144). These persons are the equitable, and the equity associated with them is the most profound sort.

Aristotle closes his passage on equity in the *Ethics* with an obscure reference to these equitable persons. This reference has no obvious relation to the long description of equity in either the *Ethics* or the *Rhetoric*, except it bears a certain similarity to the sort of equity rendered by statesmen in that it certainly points beyond legal justice. Aristotle leaves us, all too abruptly, with a picture of a group who "choose" to perform equitable acts of the sort that are better than the just, who, therefore, are no "stickler[s] for [legal] justice," and who are "satisfied with less than [their] share even though [they have] the law on [their] side" (*Ethics*, at 5.10.1137a35–1138a3). This last characteristic is especially perplexing. It is not entirely clear what Aristotle means by equity here—it only begins to become clear after we have examined the role of the group of equitable persons in the *Politics*. Even then, we will need to pursue clues Aristotle leaves which ultimately direct us back to the treatment of equity in Book V of Plato's *Laws*.

As with the equity passage in the *Rhetoric*, the treatment of equity in the *Ethics* is seminal for the development of equity in the Western tradition—consequently I reproduce it here in full:

> The next subject we have to discuss is equity and the equitable, and the relation of equity to justice and of the equitable to what is just. For on examination they appear to be neither absolutely identical nor generically different. Sometimes we go so far in praising a thing or a man as "equitable" that we use the word in an extended sense as a general term of praise for things in place of "good," and really mean "better" when we say "more equitable." But at other times, when we follow the logical consequences, it appears odd that the equitable should be distinct from the just and yet deserve praise. If the two terms are different, then either the just is not of great moral value, or the equitable is the better of the two. What causes the problem is that the equitable is not just in the legal sense of "just" but as a corrective of what is legally just. The reason is that all law is universal, but there are some things about which it is not possible to speak correctly in universal terms. Now in situations where it is necessary to speak in universal terms but impossible to do so correctly, the law takes the majority of cases, fully realizing in what respect it misses the mark. The law itself is none the less correct. For the mistake lies neither in the law nor in the lawgiver, but in the nature of the case. For such is the material of which actions are made. So in a situation in which the law speaks universally, but the case at issue happens to fall outside the universal formula, it is correct to rectify the shortcoming, in other words, the omission and mistake of the lawgiver due to the generality of his statement. Such a rectification corresponds to what the lawgiver himself would have enacted if he had known (of this particular case). That is why the equitable is both just in general, but better than the mistake due to the generality (of the law). And this is the very nature of the equitable, a rectification of law where law falls short by reason of its universality. This is also the reason why not all things are determined by law. There are some things about which it is impossible to enact a law, so that a special decree is required. For where a thing is indefinite, the rule by which it is measured is also indefinite, as is, for example, the leaden rule used in Lesbian construction work. Just as this rule is not rigid but shifts with the contour of the stone, so a decree is adapted to a given situation.
>
> [And it is clear from this what sort of person the equitable man is; he is practical and chooses not to make exact justice more severe. Instead he accepts as helpful even great disadvantages to himself imposed by

> law. This is what it is to be equitable, and what holds for equity itself; that is, it is a certain kind of justice and not something else.] [36] (5.10)

As I indicated before, we must turn now to Aristotle's *Politics* in order to pursue his otherwise obcure reference to the "equitable man."

ARISTOTLE'S *POLITICS*

Equity arises in two ways in the *Politics*. First a new kind of equity tacitly emerges, an equity that clearly does not follow the laws. Second, Aristotle describes the nature of equitable persons more fully than in the *Ethics*, and he states what their role in the *polis* is, or at least should be.

In *Politics* 3.11 Aristotle clearly alludes to equity in terms almost identical to portions of his treatment of equity in the *Ethics* and *Rhetoric*, in that the nature of the problem with laws is explicitly identified. Responding to the question of what the authoritative element in the *polis* should be, Aristotle indicates that

> . . . nothing [is] more evident than that it is laws—correctly enacted—that should be authoritative and that the ruler, whether one person or more, should be authoritative with respect to those things about which the laws are completely unable to speak precisely on account of the difficulty of making clear general declarations about everything. 3.11.19

At first glance, the aspect of this passage referring to equity—"those things about which the laws are completely unable to speak precisely on account of the difficulty of making clear general declarations about everything"—seems to be perfectly in accord with his prior treatments of equity, except that here his treatment is tacit in that no reference to *επιείκεια* occurs. In context, it is evident that Aristotle is pointing towards a new sort of equity, one that does not follow the law. We know this because immediately following this passage, Aristotle presents a radical critique of all laws by pointing out their derivative and hence questionable character (Strauss 1988, 34).[37]

> But as to what the quality of the laws should be if they are to be correctly enacted, it is not at all clear, and the question that was raised previously remains. Laws are necessarily poor or excellent and just or unjust in a manner similar to the regimes [to which they belong]: if nothing else, it is evident that laws should be enacted with a view to the regime. 3.11.20–21.

Moreover, Aristotle has already implicitly drawn attention to laws' shortcomings. Laws are static and do not and cannot encompass the peculiar virtue indispensable to the ruler(s), at least of correct regimes, prudence (*Politics* 3.4.17). They cannot react appropriately to specific events or persons, taking into account the particular circumstances involved. In short, laws do not possess the necessary flexibility of the Lesbian rule.

But why does Aristotle not explicitly mention equity, and why is his critique of laws so obscure here? Upon examination, it is apparent that Aristotle's careful method of presentation here is absolutely critical—after all, he is addressing his "reservations" about law and "legality" (Anastaplo 1992, 23–24). Being too explicit about such a topic would make him "irresponsible in his teachings" (23–24). As Plato's Athenian Stranger reminds us in the *Laws*, also in a passage involving equity, the questioning and critiquing of laws needs to be reserved to the older, more experienced elements of the *polis*, and even then, discussions involving such questioning or critiquing must be conducted in a way so that they will not be overheard by any younger persons (*Laws* 635a). Aristotle's care in not explicitly referring to equity is therefore warranted, since Aristotle's tacit treatment of equity in *Politics* 3.11&15 suggests a radical critique of laws and legality.[38]

The second passage dealing tacitly with equity underscores the reasons for Aristotle's careful presentation. In *Politics* 3.15, after suggesting that the "best regime is not one based on written laws," Aristotle goes on to say

> [t]hat [the ruler] must necessarily be a legislator, then, and that laws must exist, is clear; but they must not be authoritative insofar as they deviate [from what is right], though in other matters they should be authoritative.[39] 3.15.6

When this passage is contrasted with the previous equity passage alluded to, 3.11.19, it becomes clear that Aristotle is pointing far beyond the sorts of equity of the *Rhetoric* and *Ethics*, which both involve, in the final analysis, an equity that follows laws. Instead, the sort of equity described here in the *Politics* surpasses laws—it leads rather than follows them—and its touchstone is not the regime, but what is right. Aristotle, immediately following this passage, poses the question of who should rule "as regards the things that [laws are] unable to judge either generally or well?" This question is related to a prior question raised by Aristotle, one which is not expressly answered in the *Politics*—a question which provides a useful transition to the discussion of the nature and role of equitable persons in the *Politics*.

The question is: who should be in charge of changing laws—of changing the very character of the regime itself? (*Politics* 2.8.25).

The equitable persons described in the *Ethics* equity passage reappear explicitly in the *Politics*.[40] In the *Ethics* we learned that these people were not overly concerned with legal justice, and, oddly, that they were satisfied with less than the laws otherwise allowed them. We learn in the *Politics* that their characteristics additionally include that they do not wish to "aggrandize themselves" in terms of property ownership (2.7.20). Moreover, they are "adequately educated with a view to the qualities" of good persons (2.9.25). Remarkably, Aristotle explicitly states that they are the group "capable of ruling best." That is, they are the group that should rule, if possible. When they rule, care should be taken that they are "well off" in terms of property, or at the very least they should enjoy considerable leisure (2.11.12).[41] When the equitable rule, the regime is only then properly called an "aristocracy"—a regime characterized by "the distribution of prerogatives on the basis of virtue" (4.8.7). In such a regime the equitable persons are the "rulers" in the ordinary sense of that word; in the lesser forms of aristocracy, which for all practical purposes appear to be varieties of polity, their role is less clear (4.7–4.8).

Strangely, Aristotle does not focus on the regime that truly deserves to be called aristocracy—the one ruled by equitable persons. Rather he focuses on a lower form of regime, the one which he elsewhere describes as a polity with a "tendency to incline more towards oligarchy" (2,6,16–18; 4,7,5).[42] Aristotle apparently allows himself to call this a kind of aristocracy because of the presence in it of equitable persons, mixed together with democratic and oligarchic elements (4.8.9). What Aristotle does not explicitly state is the precise role of equitable persons in this regime. It is evident that they are intended to play some "ruling" role because of their mysterious presence at the very center of a list of possible answers to the fundamental question of "what the authoritative element of the [*polis*] should be?" (3.10.1).

This question, it has been observed, is the "supreme political question" (Strauss and Cropsey 1981, 104). It is posed at the outset of a passage which encompasses *Politics* 3.10–3.15—a passage described as the "culminating theoretical analysis" of both Book 3, and the *Politics* as a whole (105). The question begins "the most fundamental discussion of the *Politics*"; this discussion, which occupies 3.10–3.11, has been characterized as "almost a dialogue between the oligarch and the democrat" (Strauss 1964, 21).[43] Aristotle has led us to expect that the group of equitable persons would play a critical—even a commanding role—in the *polis* at this juncture. However, what role the group plays in the *polis* is never even addressed—the silence is deafening.

Instead the discussion in 3:10 & 11 focuses exclusively on the ruling roles of the democratic and oligarchic elements in the form of polity we are descrbing as an oligarchic aristocracy. The most striking aspect of these chapters, leaving aside the unexplained appearance of equitable persons at the center of the list, is the presence of the only two oaths uttered in the entire Aristotelian corpus (Strauss 1989, 4; Strauss and Cropsey 1981, 105). These oaths demand our attention—they highlight the passage, if possible, evenmore than the content of the passage, which itself is of central significance not only to Aristotle's text but also to the entire art of political science. Both oaths, in context, underscore the questionable nature of allowing the passionate multitude to participate in ruling the *polis*: the first oath, occurring right after the list of possible rulers at the beginning of 3.10, seems to "[justify] the extreme of injustice," which is characteristically committed by the radical democracies; the second oath, occurring near the middle of 3.11, right before Aristotle begins restricting the kind of offices the democratic element can hold, "insists that [the multitude] are sometimes bestial" (107–08).

As one might expect, after the second oath, Aristotle's concern is with limiting the role of the democratic element to the lesser offices. But rather than assign the greater offices to the members of the equitable group, who are best qualified to hold them, he instead assigns them to the oligarchic element. By so doing, Aristotle moves the polity away from democracy and in the direction of oligarchy, much the same way as he reports Plato does with the regime in the *Laws* (*Politics* 2.6.18–21). This movement causes us to wonder whether Aristotle is describing a lower level of aristocracy, rather than a polity. But, if it is an aristocracy, Aristotle tells us that an aristocracy of this lower sort involves authoritative roles for not only the oligarchic element and the democratic element, but naturally for the equitable as well. We are told in 3.11 what the roles of the oligarchic and democratic elements are to be. They appear to split between them all of the regime's ruling roles, at least all of those provided for or anticipated by the regime's laws. Aristotle is careful to provide that both the oligarchic and democratic elements are subject to the rule of law. The oligarchic element, with its occupation of the higher ruling offices, to be sure, will have some flexibility in this regard in its use of the infinately flexible sort of equity described in the *Ethics*, though still a sort of equity that follows the laws. If all of the ruling offices of the regime, both the lesser and greater, are occupied by the democratic and oligarchic elements, it remains to be determined what unconventional ruling role remains for the equitable.

To determine what role the equitable persons play, we must return to the earlier unanswered question of who should be authoritative with regards to changing the laws. Who can be entrusted to change the nature of a regime's laws, to change the fundamental structure of the regime? The answer must be the group of equitable persons. We know their role must be outside the established regime and its laws—since all of its conventional ruling offices are already taken by the democratic and oligarchic elements. Aristotle has previously indicated that the members of the equitable group are not sticklers for the sort of justice associated with established laws. Moreover, in order to change the regime, they must necessarily move outside the parameters of the regime because the regime's laws will certainly prohibit changes to the regime that are not authorized by the its laws.[44]

If indeed, the equitable group's role in the "oligarchic aristocracy" is to improve the regime in unauthorized, and therefore necessarily discreet ways, it remains to discover *how* they will do it and what precisely constitutes improvement. Unfortunately, Aristotle does not address this issue at all in the *Politics*—although he does leave us clues as to where we should look to find the answer. When Aristotle raises the issue of changing a regime's laws, he indicates that since obedience to laws is largely a matter of habit, changing the laws is inherently problematic. In order for the laws not to lose their indispensible majesty and authority, thereby endangering the rule of law, any changes must be made gradually, over long periods of time. So while we may not know the equitable group's precise method of proceeding, we do know that it will be so gradual that the members of the oligarchic and democratic elements either do not realize that changes are taking place, or fail to appreciate their wider significance.

Of course, our investigation has now come full circle to that analogous situation in Plato's *Laws*, the Platonic work that corresponds most closely to Aristotle's *Politics*. Aristotle is cryptically alluding to and creating an intertextual connection with the master "political" work of his own teacher, Plato, a work in which Plato carefully addressed the role of the group of people he calls reformers, and Aristotle chooses to call the equitable. The primary purpose of the reformers in the *Laws* is to improve existing regimes. The similarities between these reformers and Aristotle's group of equitable persons are striking. Both groups work outside the regime's existing legal framework with the objective of gradually improving the regime—that is, they are, to paraphrase Aristotle, not overly concerned with following the laws of the regime as they pursue their paramount objective of improving these laws. Both groups are satisfied with less than their share—that is, their entitlements under the existing laws—and both groups are either equitable or acting out of a sense of equity. For purposes of the present analysis, the groups appear in all significant respects to be identical.

The key difference between Aristotle's and Plato's accounts is that in Plato's, the Athenian Stranger describes what Aristotle fails to tell us in the *Politics*: what the reformers must do to accomplish their objective of improving the regime—that is, he tells us precisely what their ruling role is. Aristotle merely hints at what this role might be when he says in the *Ethics* that the group of equiable persons must be satisfied with less than the share of property and honors to which they might otherwise be entitled to under the laws of their regime. Plato fleshes this point out when he elaborates that the reformers, out of a sense of equity, will take from their share of property and redistribute it to those who are poor. Of course the efforts of any single reformer, or even a group of contemporary reformers, will be insufficient to accomplish much regime-wide change. A group of reformers must work in concert, and there will will need to be a series of reformers who continue these efforts over the course of generations. Existing reformers will need to nurture the next group of reformers and ensure that they will be in an appropriate social and fiscal position to continue the work. By acting gradually, these generations of reformers will avoid "the terrible dangerous strife occasioned by [the quick] redistribution of land, canceling of debts, and redistribution," such as is alluded to in the context of Aristotle's first oath in *Politics* 3.10 (*Laws* 736c-d). The reformers' principle objective appears to be to reduce the disparity in wealth between the oligarchic and democratic elements.[45] The ratio the Athenian Stranger mentions as the goal of the new regime being established in the *Laws* is 4:1 (*Laws* 744e). Aristotle, curiously citing Plato as his authority, refers to a slightly higher ratio of 5:1.[46] The nature of the laws that would emerge from this redistribution of wealth would presumably approach those of the regime to be formulated in Plato's *Laws*; the particular laws elaborated there could be consulted by the reformers for guidance.

Thomas More, I will argue in the next chapter when I analyze his *Utopia*, appears to have appreciated the subtleties of Aristotle's and Plato's treatments of *επιείκεια*. More, that is, appreciated the both the theoretical and practical possibilities of an equity possessed of its full range of classical meanings.

In conclusion, I would like to briefly mention the contemporary relevance of reintroducing the full range of the classical meanings of equity into the contemporary jurisprudential and political arena. As described in the Introduction, certain vexing problems encountered in recent Anglo-American jurisprudence could be solved by equity as formerly conceived. For instance, many of the widely identified problems associated with zero tolerance schemes, three strikes laws, and mandatory judicial sentencing guidelines could be readily addressed by reintroducing classical notions of equity into Anglo-American legal systems.

To my great surprise, I discovered that the more profound sort of equity described in Plato's *Laws* and Aristotle's *Politics*, the kind practiced by Plato's reformers and Aristotle's group of equitable persons, in some fashion exists in contemporary times. On Sunday, February 18, 2001 the *New York Times* published on its editorial page a petition from an organization called "Responsible Wealth" opposing ongoing political initiatives, including proposed legislation to repeal the United States' estate tax (this petition is reproduced on page 117). Remarkably, the signatories to the petition included some of the nation's wealthiest individuals—persons whose families could certainly be expected to benefit financially from the repeal of the estate tax. The key point in the petition is that the repeal of the estate tax "would leave an unfortunate legacy for America's future generations" because it would "enrich America's millionaires and billionaires while hurting families who struggle to make ends meet."

Chapter Three

Equity (*Aequitas*) in Thomas More's *Utopia*

In this chapter I analyze the meanings of Thomas More's references to equity (*aequitas*) in his *Utopia*. In three uses of the word and one clear allusion to the concept More offers one of the most profound treatments of equity in English Renaissance writing.[1] The first usage of equity occurs in a passage from Book I, in which More dramatically presents the interplay among the various elements beginning to transform equity.[2] These elements change equity from a jurisprudential concept of the first order into a very narrowly conceived idea largely severed from its former meanings and role, though curiously, with an enhanced raw power in the political arena.[3] Meanwhile, as More anticipates, the concept of mercy, the political manifestation of which is the Crown's pardon power, begins to be used to perform equity's former jurisprudential function. However, the attempt to substitute mercy for equity generally leads to unsatisfactory results, since the concept of mercy, though related to equity, is not capable of performing equity's critical role in the legal process.[4]

My analysis also positions More's treatment of equity within the political-historical context of the momentous changes involving the Court of Chancery's acquisition and employment of the equity jurisdiction. These changes would ultimately justify Francis Bacon's comment to James I in 1616 that the Court of Chancery, because of its equity jurisdiction, was the court of his *absolute* power.[5] More's treatment of equity also needs to be located within the larger context of his humanistic and legal education, and his most perplexing act as Lord Chancellor: his unsolicited offer to return the Court of Chancery's equity jurisdiction back to the Common Law courts.

Concentrating upon the references to equity in *Utopia* helps to uncover the complex of meanings that constituted early Renaissance English equity. An appreciation of these meanings in turn permits a more probing treatment of equity—in all its historical complexity—than modern commentators of

Utopia have allowed. References to equity reveal, among other things, More's awareness of the concept's essential role in maintaining and preserving the rule-of-law in a regime.[6] These references also reveal More's sensitivity to the changing role of equity in England, and his understanding that because of these changes, equity might well become incapable of performing the essential role the ancient philosophers had assigned it. This failure, in turn, could lead to a political and social crisis, whether because of the potential abuse of equity used simply as a political tool, or because the concept of mercy, replacing equity, was insufficient to perform the indispensable role of classical equity.[7] Analyzing More's references to equity also highlights the way in which More's text resists the new tendency in political thought—a tendency associated with Machiavelli—to render political counsel based solely on pragmatic rather than idealistic principles.[8] Finally, using equity as a touchstone invites a reexamination of Guillaume Budé's introductory letter to *Utopia*, which in turn sheds considerable light on how we should understand More's treatment of equity at its most profound level—its association with communism.

MORE AND BUDÉ

Budé's letter draws attention to the curious association of equity with communism in Book II of *Utopia*. This association is absent from other Renaissance treatments of equity, and is today nearly incomprehensible. But, as Budé hints, equity and communism were linked in classical thought, albeit quietly. The fact that More draws upon the link between equity and communism invites a reevaluation of modern interpretations of *Utopia* that read its communist element as either wholly ironic or quite serious. As detailed below, my analysis of the text in terms of the references to equity allows a reading that avoids this binary opposition. My reading sees the work as ironic in that More is not *really* suggesting that the absolute communism of the Utopians is workable in practice; however, I also see More as highly serious in his implicit argument that there is a crucial link between equity and communism.[9] More's text suggests that this link is important to any effort to achieve the best *possible* state of a commonwealth since this state would represent the regime closest to absolute communism within the restrains imposed by human nature.[10]

My reading of *Utopia* presumes that More was familiar with the classical link between equity and communism, as well as the various meanings associated with equity in his own time, including how it was practically applied in English courts. More's familiarity with equity (as *aequitas*) would have begun in his grammar school education, probably when he encountered Cicero's uses of *aequitas* in the *De Finibus*, the *Topica* and the *Pro Murena*, texts typically drawn upon for rhetorical exercises and translation practice. Later, during his placement as an adolescent in Lord Chancellor Morton's household (circa 1490–92), More would have had his first exposure to what was soon to be described as the Chancery Court's "equity" jurisdiction (Haskett 1996, 250–53). Then, at Oxford (circa 1492–94), he would have read Aquinas' treatment of *aequitas*,[11] which was heavily indebted to Aristotle as well as to treatments by Medieval Christian thinkers, since the humanist educational reforms had not yet been instituted.[12] At New Inn, one of the Inns of Chancery, where More lived and studied from 1494–96, he would almost certainly have encountered Fortescue's treatment of equity in the *De laudibus legum Anglie*, and he would also have learned Chancery practice as it related to both the Canon and Civil Law, including the portion of that practice that soon became explicitly associated with the term "equity" (Guy 1980, 128). More next attended Lincoln's Inn, one of the less specialized Inns of Court, where his education continued. During his time at Lincoln's Inn, he set aside his study of Latin in order to begin his extra-curricular study of Greek under Grocyn and Linacre.[13] Linacre had just returned from Italy where he had helped publish the complete works of Aristotle in Greek. More read portions of Aristotle in the original Greek, and it is quite possible he read portions of Plato in Greek as well.[14] Portions of *Utopia* reflect a clear knowledge of Plato's *Republic* and *Laws*, as well as Aristotle's *Rhetoric*, *Ethics* and *Politics*, the relevant texts for identifying the various ways in which Plato and Aristotle treat *επιείκεια* (Jayne 1995, 87; White, T. 1982, 329).

The aspect of More's education and experience pointing most clearly to a familiarity with equity as conceived of and used pragmatically on the Continent is his admission in 1514 to Doctor's Commons, an institution similar to an Inn of Court, but more refined in that it was reserved almost without exception for practitioners of Civil and Canon Law who possessed degrees either of Doctor of Civil Law from Cambridge or Doctor of Law from Oxford. Since More possessed neither of these degrees, scholars suggest that More's philosophical, theological, and legal knowledge must have been quite remarkable to warrant the honor of being admitted (Schoeck 1972, 19).

I have collected here the available historical evidence that bears upon the extent of More's knowledge of equity in 1515, when he began writing *Utopia*. This knowledge appears to include some familiarity with equity's derivation from the Latin *aequitas* and the Greek *επιείκεια*, and an appreciation of the nuances of their respective similarities and differences. Of the early humanists, perhaps only Guillaume Budé, who had earlier explored the

Latin and Greek roots of equity in his *Pandectus* (1508), appreciated them as deeply. I turn now to Budé's relation to *Utopia.*

While no modern scholar, to my knowledge, has examined the issue of equity in More's *Utopia*, More's correspondent Budé (1468–1540) certainly concentrated on the crucial passages in which the equity usages occur and suggested ways in which they relate to each other. An older contemporary of More's, Budé had a career that mirrored More's in many respects.[15] Budé had an exceptional capacity for understanding the themes and issues dealt with in More's *Utopia*. In fact, many at the time considered Budé's intellect to be on par with Erasmus'; remarkably, Budé knowledge of Greek surpassed even Erasmus'—Budé was the preeminent western Greek scholar of his time. [16] It was Erasmus who solicited Budé's famous introductory letter to *Utopia*, for inclusion in the 1518 Froben edition.

I approach Budé's letter with more attention than is usually paid to *parerga*. However, as a complex rhetorical performance, the letter requires no less care than More's *Utopia* itself. More himself provides guidance as to the degree of care with which Budé's writings must be approached:

> I never skim any of your works, but study them seriously as works of the first importance. To your treatise on Roman Measures [*De Asse*] I gave a very special attention such as I have given no ancient author.[17] For that it cannot be understood in any cursory way, you have provided by your careful choice of words, your well-balanced sentences, the studied gravity of your diction, and not least by the serious and difficult nature of the matters you treat of—matters almost lost in antiquity, and requiring the deepest research. But yet if anyone will turn his eyes to what you have written and give it careful and continued attention, he will find that the light you have thrown upon your subject brings the deepest past to life again. (*Selected Letters*, 108) (August 1518)

Budé's letter, addressed to Thomas Lupset, the person who provided Budé with a copy of *Utopia*, is 169 lines long as reproduced in the *Yale Edition*. At first glance, the letter appears loosely structured. It opens with references to persons other than More and works other than *Utopia*; the first half of the letter does not even directly address the contents of *Utopia*.[18]

The keys to understanding the letter, I propose, are to treat it seriously by complicating the nearly 500 year-old assumption that Budé is simply praising *Utopia*, and to remain open to the possibility that Budé is simultaneously praising and also profoundly critiquing the work.[19] Budé's insights are particularly valuable because they are made by one of More's contemporaries, one who appears to have drawn upon similar authorities to More and generally to have shared More's perspective on matters like the significance of equity. His insights help to situate *Utopia*—to place it squarely within an historical context in a way that most modern interpretations do not.

The structure of Budé's letter hinges on the placement at the letter's precise center of the passage quoted below, just before Budé specifically begins to address the *Utopia*. In this passage Budé mentions something he carefully describes as the "law of communion" (*communionis legem*). Budé alludes here to the communist community of the disciples described in *Acts* 5.1–11, where the story of Ananias and his wife Sapphira, and their ill fated attempt to join the disciples' community, is related. The "law of communion" is the requirement of the disciples' community that its members sell all of their possessions and give the proceeds to the community.[20]

> Yet Christ, the founder and supervisor of possessions left among His followers a Pythagorean communion and charity [sanctified] by [shining] example when Ananias was condemned to death for breaking the law of communion. Certainly by his own arrangement, Christ seems to me to have abolished, among His own at least, the whole arrangement set up by the civil and canonical law of fairly recent date in contentious volumes. This law we see today holding the highest position in jurisprudence and controlling our destinies. (*Yale Edition*, Vol. 4, 9–11)[21]

Before he explicitly turns to *Utopia* in the next paragraph, Budé implicitly identifies the central element of Book II of *Utopia* (and perhaps of the *Utopia* as a whole), as the "Christian" ideal of communism from *Acts*. Budé also implicitly identifies that the most critical element of Book I is the imposition of the death penalty in situations that do not warrant it. By combining these central elements, Budé not only suggests that they are related, but also shows the way in which they relate. The critical issue upon which Budé focuses in his discussion of *Utopia* Book I is the peculiarly "English problem" identified by Raphael in his story within the story (the Lord Chancellor Morton passage). The problem Budé refers to involves the English practice of imposing capital punishment for theft—even what we today would consider to be relatively petty theft—and even though in some sense, the broader society is responsible for driving people to take desperate measures such as stealing food to avoid starving. The specific problem leading to this sort of thievery, as Hythlodaeus famously puts it, is "your sheep"—a humorous and provocative way of referring to the vexing problems of enclosure practices (65). Put differently, the "core" problem of Book

I is that there is an imbalance between the dictates of laws, which mandates the imposition of capital punishment for theft, and the individual cases of theft to which the laws are applied, cases such as the theft of food to avoid starving which clearly do not warrant so severe a penalty.

As I will establish, both of these elements are intimately connected to equity, though in different fashions. While Budé's overall critique of *Utopia* is fascinating in its own right, for present purposes Budé's apparent area of agreement with More is most pertinent.[22]

Budé's letter suggests that he agrees with Raphael, and it should be noted also with Aristotle and Plato, that the most critical problem of existing regimes is the large disparity between the wealthiest and poorest segments of society. Budé pointedly addresses the wealth disparity problem immediately preceding the letter's central passage, which, as we just observed, highlights the primary New Testament passage that arguably is supportive of communism.

> This [problem of wealth disparity] happens in every age, under any customs and institutions and among any peoples who have decided that a man should have supreme power and authority in the degree that he has built up the biggest possible private fortune for himself and his heirs. And the process is cumulative, since his descendants and their descendants strive to build up their inheritance by one gigantic increment after another—meanwhile cutting off stringently all their connections and relatives by marriage, birth and blood. (Logan, Adams & Miller 1995, 13)

Budé points out in this passage that avariciousness is a characteristic of human nature, and that its presence tends to promote wealth disparity regardless of the governing regime.

In the corresponding paragraph that immediately follows the one at the letter's center, Budé implicitly dismisses communism as a solution to the problems of avariciousness and wealth disparity by indicating that More's nation of Utopia is also called "Udepotia" (13). Utopia, the nation famed for its communism, in Greek literally means "no place;" that is, no such place actually exists. Budé's name for the place, Udepotia, in Greek literally means "never place;" that is, it can never come to exist—a temporal possibility which More's name did not foreclose.[23]

Between the one extreme of the problem of human avariciousness, and this characteristic's practical manifestation in the wealth disparity present in existing regimes, and the other extreme of the impossible goal of political theory, absolute communism, both Budé and More create space for a practical compromise that draws upon the theory of absolute communism without advocating it as a practically realizable goal. More's resolution is described later in the chapter. Budé's proposed compromise involves the "Pythagorean" communion celebrated in Erasmus' very first adage.[24] Budé alludes here to the group of humanists for whom absolute communism has some meaning: to the very group of humanists for whom it is possible to conceive all things being in common. It does not appear accidental that at the very heart of Bude's letter, he deals both with communism and the group who, according to Plato, can achieve the betterment of existing regimes by gradually reducing wealth disparity.[25]

UTOPIA, BOOK I

To fully appreciate the first equity reference in *Utopia*, it must first be contextualized. As J. H. Hexter persuasively argued, Book I, as originally formulated, did not contain the passage in which the first usage of the term equity occurs. This passage describes Raphael Hythlodaeus' circa 1498 visit to England and a conversation that took place there between Raphael and Lord Chancellor Morton at the latter's residence. According to Hexter, this passage (the "Lord Chancellor Morton passage") was written shortly after Erasmus' August 1516 visit with More, and presumably after Erasmus had read and discussed with More the then existing draft of the work (Hexter 1965, xv-xxii).[26]

What is intriguing about the order of composition is that before the addition of the Lord Chancellor Morton passage in Book I, Raphael's statements about how ineffective he would be as a royal counselor, and also how dangerous such an activity would be for someone like him, are quite persuasive. Also intriguing is how difficult it is to distinguish Raphael's position from that of Machiavelli's; he argues that royal counselors who base their advice on ideals rather than practicalities will be ruined. Arguably, in the absence of the Lord Chancellor Morton passage, this might be a primary message of the *Utopia*. But with the addition of the passage, Raphael's actions clearly belie his words. As will be discussed below, Raphael succeeds in producing positive change in the English regime by utilizing the fictional example of the Polylerites—a "utopian" society—and it is clear that he is not ruined in the process.

The first explicit use of equity in Book I occurs in the passage in which Lord Chancellor Morton specifically asks Raphael to describe his alternative solution to the problem of how best to punish thieves. Raphael responds by asserting that if equity has any meaning, then the capital punishment of thieves—England's solution to its thievery problem—is unjust because it equates theft with murder since both crimes receive the same punishment. Reproduced below is this first use of equity in context, beginning with Morton's request to Raphael to present his alternative proposal for how to deal more humanely with the thievery problem, and continuing with the relevant portion of Raphael's response:

> [Morton] "But now I am eager to have you tell me, my dear Raphael, why you think that theft ought not to be punished with the extreme penalty, or what other penalty you yourself would fix, which would be more beneficial to the public. I am sure that not even you think it ought to go unpunished. Even as it is, with death as the penalty, men still rush into stealing. What force and what fear, if they once were sure of their lives, could deter the criminals? They would regard themselves as much invited to crime by the mitigation of the penalty as if a reward were offered."
>
> [Raphael] "Certainly," I answered, "most reverend and kind Father, I think it altogether unjust that a man should suffer the loss of his life for the loss of someone's money. In my opinion, not all the goods that fortune can bestow on us can be set in the scale against a man's life. If they say that this penalty is attached to the offense against justice and the breaking of the laws, hardly to the money stolen, one may well characterize this extreme justice as extreme wrong. For we ought not to approve such stern Manlian rules of law as would justify the immediate drawing of the sword when they are disobeyed in trifles nor such Stoical ordinances as count all offenses equal so that there is no difference between killing a man and robbing him of a coin when, if equity [(*aequitas*)] has any meaning, there is no similarity or connection between the two cases."
>
> "God has said, "Thou shalt not kill," and shall we so lightly kill a man for taking a bit of small change?" (28–29)

Several elements in this passage deserve comment. The characterization of "extreme justice as extreme wrong" was a very old idea—as I noted in Chapter One, Cicero cites the related maxim "extreme law" (or justice), extreme wrong" (*summum ius, summa iniura*) in his *De Officiis* (I.x.33). "Extreme justice" occurs when the terms of laws are strictly applied to specific cases for which such strict application is clearly not intended or warranted. The results of such strict application, naturally enough, are widely perceived as harsh—as unjust in some crucial sense. It is in precisely such a situation that Aristotle indicates the application of equity is necessary: otherwise, such harsh results erode the authority of the laws.[27]

The reference to "Manlian" law alludes to an incident in Roman history which became the stereotypical example of extreme justice as extreme wrong. Titus (Torquatus) Manlius, a Roman general and consul, first became famous for his success in single combat with an enemy champion. Later in his life he became infamous for condemning his own son to death for violating his command prohibiting such single combats in a subsequent war, after his son had successfully defeated the enemy champion. The extreme wrong consists in the failure to make exceptions in cases where the circumstances—and even human nature—a father's love for his son—cry out for exceptional treatement.

The reference to the problematical "Stoical ordinances" is best summarized, and critiqued, by Cicero in his description of the Stoic system in which "[a]ll sins are equal, [and] every peccadillo is a deadly crime. He commits no less a crime who unnecessarily strangles a cock, than the man who strangles the father" (*Pro Murena* xxix. 61). Stoical ordinaces differ from, and in some sense are even more extreme than Manlian laws in that *all* offenses are assigned the same extreme penalty, without regard for circumstances.

The sequence Raphael creates in this passage begins with the quite practical concern of a specific example of a harsh pagan law—the "Manlian" law. Then he proceeds to critique the misguided pagan philosophical position that treats all offenses as equal—the "Stoical ordinances." He first proves that both the Manlian type of law, and then the Stoical ordinances are faulty because they are inequitable—both fail to account for the circumstances of individual cases. Stoical ordinances additionally fail to distinguish in degree of punishment for offenses of varying severity. Raphael later buttresses his position with a different sort of proof drawn from Judeo-Christian scripture, which culminates in the notion that the New Testament law of mercy should override such harsh human laws as are in effect in England:

> Finally, the law of Moses, though severe and harsh—being intended for slaves, and those a harsh breed—nevertheless punished theft by fine and not by death. Let us not suppose that God, in the new law of mercy [*clementiae*] in which He gives commands as a father to his sons, has allowed us greater license to be cruel to one another. (30)

Thus, Raphael proffers both equity and mercy as overlapping solutions to the problem of over-harsh punishment. Mercy addresses this problem from a distinctly Christian perspective, that is, it does not appear to draw upon the sort of classical mercy Aristotle incorporated into his formulation of equity in his *Rhetoric*. Aristotle's *Rhetoric's* merciful elements are connected exclusively with considerations for human frailty:

> Equity bids us to be merciful to the weaknesses of human nature; . . . [it bids us] not to consider the actions of the accused so much as his intentions; [it bids us to consider not] this or that detail so much as the whole story. . . . (1374b)

The Christian mercy Raphael mentions also appears distinct from what can be called "political" mercy—a kind of mercy that is rendered on the basis of political rather than religions considerations, or Aristotle's considerations of human frailty.[28] Raphael's presentation places equity in an intermediate position in the text between the "harsh" pagan law, and the softer, paternal position of Christian mercy. Raphael's formulation of equity thus encompasses both the classical pagan and the Christian response to the problems of rigorous laws and over-harsh punishments.

The argument and action of Book I of *Utopia*, in which the first use of equity occurs, has been described as a "debate on counsel." The fictional More persona of the dialogue, together with Peter Giles, attempt to persuade Raphael Hythlodaeus that because of his experience and learning he should join a king's retinue as a counselor. Raphael responds that it would be worse than useless to do so—as a counselor he would produce no positive good and his actions quite likely would prove harmful to himself. However, the only "real" as opposed to "hypothetical" example Raphael draws upon to prove his point—an example in which he once gave advice in England to its effective ruler, Lord Chancellor Morton—in fact defeats his point by showing that his advice had a positive effect and that he suffered no harm as a result of rendering the advice. It is in the context of the portion of the "debate on counsel" where Raphael offers his "real" life example that the first usage of equity occurs in *Utopia*.

According to the More persona, Book I consists entirely of "the talk which drew and led [Raphael] on to mention [the commonwealth of Utopia]," together with the introduction to that "talk." The description of Utopia is self-contained in Book II. Peter Giles opens this introduction—the dialogue portion of the work—with the following observation:

> Why, my dear Raphael, I wonder that you do not attach yourself to some king. I am sure there is none of them to whom you would not be

> very welcome because you are capable not only of entertaining a king with [your] learning and experience of men and places but also with furnishing him with examples and of assisting him with counsel. (16)[29]

Giles adds that such a course of action would be profitable for both Raphael and his relatives and friends. Raphael, however, feels he has already satisfied his duties to his relatives and friends, and indicates that being in the service of a king—in effect, a king's slave[30]—is is not worth any salary he might receive. The More persona then joins the discussion, recognizing the truth in Raphael's assertion that for a person without worldly ambition, serving a king had no personal benefit:

> [I]t is plain that you, my dear Raphael, are desirous neither of riches nor of power. . . . But it seems to me you will do what is worthy of you and of this generous spirit of yours if you so order your life as to apply your talent and industry to the public interest, even if it involves some personal disadvantage to yourself. This you can never do with as great profit as if you are councilor to some great monarch and make him follow, as I am sure you will, straightforward and honorable courses. (17)[31]

Raphael disagrees, and by way of illustrating the "ridiculous and obstinate prejudices" that would prevent him from being able to "promote the public interest," he introduces the example of his trip to England and his efforts there to counsel Lord Chancellor, Cardinal Morton on an English domestic problem (18).

Raphael then directs Morton's attention to the problem previously mentioned—the harsh punishment allotted to convicted thieves in England; they are put to death. At Morton's request Raphael suggests an alternative, reduced form of punishment that he claims would be no less effective in deterring thievery. The punishment would not only continue, or begin to deter persons from theft, but it would also conform to the dictates of equity, which clearly include the propositions that not "all offenses [are] equal," and that "there is no similarity or connection" between "killing a man and robbing him of a coin . . ." (29).

Raphael's proposed solution draws upon the customs of the fictional nation of the Polylerites,[32] a people who inhabit a place seemingly even more idyllic than the island nation of Utopia. Particularly striking is their ability to be "completely free of militarism" by virtue of their isolation, satisfaction with their lot—no imperial tendencies, and willingness to pay tribute to the padishah of Persia, whose nation partially or possibly completely surrounds theirs (31).[33] Raphael's description clearly illustrates the ideal quality of this nation:

> They are far from the sea, almost ringed round with mountains, and satisfied with the products of their own land, which is in no way infertile. In consequence they rarely pay visits to other countries or receive them. In accordance with their long-standing national policy, they do not try to enlarge their territory and easily protect what they have from all aggression by their mountains and the tribute paid to their overlord. Being completely free from militarism, they live a life more comfortable than splendid and more happy than renowned or famous, for even their name, I think, is hardly known except to their immediate neighbors. (31)[34]

Morton takes Raphael's example seriously—so much so that he indicates that he will conduct an experiment to determine whether a method like that employed by the Polylerites might work in England. As indicated above, Raphael offers the story of his visit with Morton specifically to demonstrate that he would not be an effective counselor—that he would not be taken seriously. However, the example instead establishes that Raphael is a successful counselor. Moreover, the counsel Raphael succeeds in rendering to the most powerful political figure in England after the king is based upon an "imagined" nation—that is, upon a kind of pure political theory.

This first usage of equity further reveals its complexity when we correlate it with Raphael's own understanding of equity. Peter Giles describes Raphael in Book I of *Utopia* as a much-traveled Portuguese gentleman of great learning, particularly with respect to the Greek philosophers. We can safely presume, then, that Raphael approaches equity from a continental rather than English perspective. The difference between the continental and English perspectives on equity is essential to appreciate the significance of equity in the Lord Chancellor Morton passage. The basic difference is that on the contintent the political theory which governs equity continues to influence its practical application, while in England the development of the Common Law system has created a rift that has separated the political theory of equity from its practical application.[35]

On the continent, at least in those nations with Roman Law based legal systems, the political theory informing equity can be summarized as follows:

> *Aequitas* may be taken . . . as being a prudent moderation of the written law (*lex scripta*), transcending the exact literal interpretation of the

> latter; and in this sense, *aequitas* is spoken of in the *Digest* (xxxix.iii.2, Sec. 5) as being opposed to *ius* in its strict meaning. So, also, Terentius Clemens has said: "Between *ius* and *aequitas*, there is this distinction: *ius* is that which exacts that all things be strict and inflexible; whereas *aequitas* to great extent abates the rigour of *ius*." [citations omitted]. [T]he judge [in such cases] is said to act, not according to law (*iure*)—not at least, according to the letter of the law as it stands—but in accordance with what is equitable and good [*aequum et bonum*]. . . . Such is the view expressed in the *Code of Justinian* (*Code*, I, xiv.5): "There is no doubt but that he attacks the law (*lex*) who, while accepting its words, labours against its spirit." And therefore, it is possible that jurisprudence has been called the art of the good and the equitable because, in the interpretation of the laws, the good and the equitable should always be regarded; even if it be needful at times to temper the rigour of the words, in order not to depart from what is naturally equitable and good. (Francisco Suarez, *De Legibus*, Ch. 2, Sec. 9.1) [36]

The critical feature of this description is that equity is inseparable from the laws; equity's design and function are exclusively to address a specific problem with human laws—equity has no meaning in its jurisprudential sense if removed from the laws. Suarez's analysis of equity explicitly relies on the *Digest* and *Code*, which were influenced by Christian thought—the *aequitas* described in these texts is not identical to the *aequitas* of Cicero. In its most profound Christian manifestation, equity was considered to flow from divine law and be the very essence of human justice (St. German 1974, 13; Landau 1997, 130). The association of equity with divine law, though, would become a distinct liability for the concept as notions of human law began to be reconceived as entirely separate from divine law by the early seventeenth century. But in the early sixteenth century, this trend was still only in a nascent stage.

In England there existed an additional complication, equity was isolated from its theoretical underpinnings by the physical separation of equity from the Common Law—the principal source of England's laws. Equity of a sort continued to be applied in England, but it was necessarily a bastardized sort since it was not integrated with the laws. The reason for this separation was due to the Common Law judges desire to save themselves

> from the embarrassment of having to reach decisions. . . . [J]udges tended to avoid beoming too involved with the variable facts of paricular cases . . . Legal principles could thus remain elementary, which was in the interests of clarity and certainty. (Baker, *Spellman* 37–38)

It was far easier for the Common Law judges to rigorously apply existing laws than to take the time and effort actually to deal with the "variable facts of particular cases" and to use the discretion and flexibility of equity to help fashion fitting results.

As we can see from the following segment, excerpted from the larger passage quoted above, Raphael probably is not aware of the different status of equity in England:

> For we ought not to approve such stern Manlian rules of law as would justify the immediate drawing of the sword when they are disobeyed in trifles nor such Stoical ordinances as count all offenses equal so that there is no difference between killing a man and robbing him of a coin when, if equity [(*aequitas*)] has any meaning, there is no similarity or connection between the two cases. (29)

In effect, for the Common Law judges in England, equity does not have meaning—it has been relinquished or discarded.

Raphael's proposition that for equity to have "any meaning," there must be a distinction between the punishment for theft and murder presupposes that first equity is associated with the laws and second that equity's meaning involves making such a distinction betweem disparate degrees of offenses. But neither presupposition is true in England, and consequently, we find that Lord Chancellor Morton's attempt to resolve the issue of the capital punishment of thieves is not based on this understanding of equity.[37]

Fortunately, Raphael is not operating simply from a then-contemporary continental understanding of equity. He is also a classical scholar.[38] Raphael provides a clue that he is dealing with an additional layer of equity's meaning when he characterizes the problem. Instead of addressing a single case of theft, which clearly fits into the contemporary understanding of equity, Raphael chooses to frame the issue in terms of an entire class of cases—those which involve theft. The difficulty here is that equity typically only intervened between the laws and a specific case—equity was applied on a case-by-case basis. A convenient presumption associated with equity, apparently originating during the middle ages, and based on what appears to be a misreading of Aristotle, posited that the legislator, if faced with a particular case in which the circumstances did not warrant the penalty assigned by the laws, would decide not to enforce the letter of the laws (Aquinas, *Summa* 283ae. 60, 5.). [39] The reasoning is that laws are framed in general terms and are not intended to address the facts and circumstances of any specific case.

But this presumption clearly does not apply to the situation described by Raphael, where the problem is that a law is deemed unfair in terms of its general application to a class of cases. For here the law is performing precisely the function for which it is designed: the necessarily generally stated law is operating with respect to a general class of situations. There is no gap here between the law and its application to a specific case—between the general and the specific—for equity to fill. Any problem with the law at this level could not be addressed by equity. The legislator would need to address such a problem directly—at least according to Aristotle's treatments of equity in the *Rhetoric* and *Ethics*.

Remarkably, what Raphael appears to be suggesting is that equity in some sense can be called upon not only to intervene between laws and their application to specific cases, the traditional Aristotelian formulation, but also, on occasion at least, to work to improve the laws themselves—even in their general sense. The implications of this are far-reaching, since equity, in this sense, would be circumventing the ordinary legal processes of the regime. Viewed from the perspective of the regime, such a notion must be seen as subversive—even treasonous.

I will now examine the wonderfully ambiguous, possibly even subversive way Morton elects to understand Raphael's suggestion of an "equitable" solution. On the surface, Morton appears to ignore Raphael's suggestion that he deal with the problem of excessive punishment for theft in terms of equity. Instead he responds by proposing an experiment imitating the Polyleritean system, in all relevant respects, *except* that the vehicle for the experiment is the king's prerogative power of pardon—a power theoretically based on mercy rather than equity. Morton's solution is to conduct an experiment in which

> . . . after pronouncement of the sentence of death [for a thief], the king [orders] the postponement of its execution and, after limitation of the privileges of sanctuary, [tries the system employed by the Polylerites], then, if success proved its usefulness, it would be right to make the system law. In case of failure, then and there to put to death those previously condemned would be no less for the public good and no more unjust than if execution were done here and now. In the meantime no danger can come of this experiment. Furthermore, I am sure that vagrants might very well be treated in the same way for, in spite of repeated legislation against them, we have made no progress. (34–35)

Unlike equity, which quickly fashions the actual result or verdict based on the facts and circumstances of the particular offense and offender, and creates the illusion that the laws themselves were flexible enough to achieve the fitting outcomes, the pardon power is typically drawn upon only after the laws have been rigorously applied and an unfitting verdict has been rendered. Pardons usually set aside all or a portion of the verdict after the fact on the basis of mercy. Morton expands the traditional scope of the pardon power when he creates this hybrid notion of a "conditional" pardon.

Morton's solution appears to draw upon a more esoteric form of Aristotelian equity, one which sidesteps both the laws and the legislative process, with the objective of improving the laws.[40] Morton is forced to move beyond most of the regime-bound restraints of the more traditional equity alluded to by Raphael both because it is not an available option in England and because, even if it were, the situation Morton faces is not the typical one in which laws are being applied strictly to a specific case, rather they are being applied to a general category of cases. The sort of equity Morton employs is available to great statesman like Morton in this situation because he is faced with a law that is defective in its general application. For great statesmen, as Aristotle notes, the laws "must not be authoritative insofar as they deviate [from what it right]" (*Ethics* 3.15.6)[41] Morton, therefore, employs a more profound kind of equity to fashion a remarkable and creative solution utilizing the king's prerogative power of pardon.[42]

Morton's solution completely disregards—even undermines—the existing law of the regime, and rhetorically models a legislative change while circumventing the ordinary legislative channels. Morton, moreover, is well aware that his proposed solution is in some fundamental way extra-legal. He is driven to adopt the experimental measures because of "repeated failures of legislation" (35). He realizes that for some problems laws are simply insufficient.

We should notice, however, that Morton's implied solution of using the royal power of pardon rather than the ordinary sort of equity, the tool specially designed to address the shortcomings of laws, is not an ideal one: it is problematic in at least two respects. First, the early modern royal power of pardon lacked the incredible flexibility of classical equity. Consequently, the results it produced by the granting of a pardon—even a conditional one—would be far less "fitting" than those custom-tailored by equity. The sole focus of the power of pardon is whether to extend "political" mercy or not; its only application, after all, is the granting of such mercy. It is impossible to design customized individual outcomes within the limits of these constraints. Second, the power of pardon is extra-ordinary. It is not intended to be used frequently. If the crown regularly pardons offenders, the rule of law also will be undermined. Equity, on the other hand, is designed to be in use—or at least potentially in use—in every individual case. Finally, the power of pardon's crude results cannot effectively disguise the defective nature of laws. Equity only succeeds in concealing their defective nature by producing results fitting to particular cases; the laws are thereby rendered to appear as though their application accomplished the right results. The royal power of pardon fails to disguise the "unfitting" results produced by the laws—which, according to Aristotle, was the reason ordinary equity was even necessary. In most cases, the pardon power can only crudely modify these results in some fashion after a judgment is publicly rendered, leaving the deficiencies of laws in plain view. Regularly resorting to the pardon power to correct the problems with law inevitably will produce an eroding effect with respect to the rule of law.[43]

One consequence of the shift away from equity towards the royal prerogative power of pardon and its underlying principle, mercy, as reflected by this passage in *Utopia*, is that it renders invisible the Aristotelian insight that laws, because of their necessarily general statement, are incapable of dealing with specifics. Appreciating this insight requires a thorough understanding of equity and its derivation from Aristotelian *επιείκεια*. This invisibility leaves a gap in which laws can be reconceived as non-defective—as sufficiently refined to be able to address adequately the specific circumstances of individual cases. In fact, the notion of the sufficiency of laws quickly rose to prominence in the early modern era, and continues to be a bedrock principle of modern Anglo-American jurisprudence.

The final perspective from which I would like to examine the *Utopia*'s first reference to equity, is from that of More the author. The critical problem in unraveling the significance of any single element in *Utopia*, such as the use of equity, is the "sphinx-like" ambiguity of the work caused by More's use of "a whole series of devices—fictionality, dialogue, paradox, . . . irony [and] litotes." Every position in the text seems to be either unreliable, cancelled out or unfounded (Wooten 1999, 23–27). However, I am suggesting that we are able to reconstruct important aspects of the work's historical meaning by recontextualizing it from the perspective of the uses of equity. My reading of these uses of equity sheds new light on the structure and composition of the work—especially the relationships of Book I and II to the work as a whole.

By the way he deals with equity in the Lord Chancellor Morton passage, More reveals what I take to be his firm conviction, in accord with Aristotle, that the ordinary sort of equity belongs with the laws. This conviction is evident not only in the text of *Utopia* but also in More's unprecedented act as Lord Chancellor, as reported by his son-in-law Thomas Roper. Shortly after becoming Lord Chancellor, More invited the Common Law judges to a dinner at which he offered them back the equity jurisdiction which they had relinquished centuries before. The judges refused, as More probably expected they would.[44] But the fact that he made the offer is what is so remarkable. The offer reveals, I suggest, More's profound understanding of equity's relation to the laws. Equity's separation from laws made little sense theoretically. Practically, it represented a danger to the regime since an independent equity could bypass the guidelines and controls which typically restrained and controlled its use, and effectively disregard or overrule the laws. In this regard More's offer reveals a high degree of prescience: the real dangers of equity separated from laws—dangers which actually materialized in England later in the century—were arguably quite obvious to him.[45]

The dangers that More foresaw with respect to a power of equity independent of the Common Law can be seen as directly and substantially contributing to the political crisis and civil disorder of the interregnum period more than a century later.[46] But if the application of the laws without the intervention of equity presented one kind of danger to a regime, the separation of the power of equity from the Common Law presented an entirely different one. Such a power, once disassociated from the Common law, could be used simply as a tool of raw political power by whoever controlled it—a tool that could, if abused, as it perhaps inevitably would be, subvert the legislative and constitutional processes. Eventually, this separation ended; approximately 300 years after More's offer, and 600 years after the beginnings of the separation of equity from the Common Law, England finally reunited the two with the passage of the Judicature Act of 1873. Of course the scope of equity had by this time been circumscribed for the most part to a series of maxims. The reunion seen in England has yet to occur in America.

Finally, I would like to focus briefly on the specific nature of the pardon that More has his character Lord Chancellor Morton devise to experiment with Raphael's proposed solution to the thievery problem—it is a *conditional* pardon. This constitutes the very same solution which later would be adopted by the crown in England to alleviate the nation's overreliance on capital punishment for relatively minor offenses. Conditional pardons became the backbone of the system of "transportation," which over the course of the three centuries following the writing of *Utopia*, became the more humane way the English dealt with convicted thieves, and most other felons. While an actual law authorizing deportation was eventually passed by Parliament, the relevant legislative body, in 1597, the transportation system continued to rely on the crown's conditional pardon until English courts finally were fully empowered to impose a sentence of transportation with the passage of the transportation act of 1717 (Sebba 1977, 224). By the begining of the nineteenth century, the "transportation" system had become pervasive: of 1254 defendants sentenced to death in 1818, for a remarkable 220 capital offenses, only 97 were actually executed (Moore 1989, 17). More foresaw in the *Utopia* the legal and extra-legal maneuvers that would by necessary, in the absence of equity, to address the English over-reliance upon capital punishment.

I turn now to address the main elements of the second explicit use of equity in Book I as well as one implicit use there. The second explicit use of equity in Book I is contained in the "original" structure of Book I, and presents equity in a highly critical way simply as a tool that can be used by judges to circumvent the laws in order to consistently rule in the king's favor regardless of the merits of the cases. The passage occurs in the context of the second hypothetical situation posed by Raphael in the original structure of Book I. In this second hypothetical case, a king's counselors are advising on ways the king can increase his revenue, presumably to finance the imperial plans kings characteristically pursue, such as the ones critiqued in the first hypothetical. One of the ways of raising revenue suggested by the counselors is to "persuade [the king] that he must bind to himself the judges, who will in every case decide in favor of the king's side," especially if they are requested "to debate [cases involving] his affairs in his presence" (44). The judges will not be lacking a "pretext . . . for deciding on the king's side" since

> it is enough that either equity [(*aequitas*)] be on his side or the letter of the law or the twisted meaning of the written word or, what finally outweighs all law with conscientious judges, the indisputable royal prerogative[47] be used as the basis for the decision. (45)

As I will show below, by the end of the sixteenth century, there was in fact little to distinguish equity from the royal prerogative.

This particular usage of equity serves above all to reveal the potential power of equity as a political tool, at least if its power is abused. More appears to predict the dangerous developments that will result in England if equity is not reunited with the Common Law. Particularly troubling is the overriding emphasis in this passage on the king's prerogative power. Certainly, the extent of this power in England in the early sixteenth century, while broad, was not as extensive as in France, for instance, where the king "could legislate through his own unimpeded will" (Lander 1989, 6). In the early sixteenth century, the English king's power arguably was little different than it had been when Fortescue wrote in the fifteenth. Fortescue had indicated that the king of England "cannot at his pleasure change the laws of his kingdom;" rather, English laws "are established not only by the prince's will but by the assent of the whole kingdom" as reflected in Parliament (Lyon 1980, 589). Fortescue adds that the coronation oath binds kings before God to the observance of the laws (588). But if equity were to become simply another of the king's prerogative powers, as the development of the Chancery court's equity jurisdiction made likely, then the king's prerogative power indeed would "outweigh all laws" as a practical matter. England's monarchy would become much more absolute, and begin to resemble that of France.

Francis Bacon's (in)famous message to James I a century later begins to make sense when read in light of this history: following James' 1616 ruling in favor of the Chancery Court's equity jurisdiction over the jurisdictions of the Common Law courts, Bacon told James that the Chancery Court, with its equity jurisdiction, was the court of his *absolute* power—a power which could even "outweigh all law." Even during Henry VIII's reign, possibly as early as 1534, there is evidence that equity was being considered in this vein. A copy of the coronation oath exists from Henry's reign, marked up in his own hand, making changes to reflect that the required "equytee" of his judgments shall be "according to hys conscienc[e]." The markup also qualifies the king's duty to maintain peace and civil order to those situations in "which honor and equite do require it." Certainly Henry's insertion of the "according to hys conscienc[e]" qualification reflects a simultaneous focus both on the Chancery's equity jurisdiction, and on his desire to expand his own discretionary prerogative powers.[48]

The sole implicit reference to equity in *Utopia* occurs in Book I later in Raphael's second hypothetical. This implicit reference also presents equity in a negative light. Here equity is alluded to in Raphael's critique of the More persona's advocacy of the "indirect" method of counseling kings. Raphael compares the More persona's position to the infinite flexibility of the Lesbian rule, and condemns More's method as being the same sort of thing clerics do to circumvent the true teachings of Christ:[49]

> [Christ] forbade us to dissemble [his doctrines] to the extent that what He whispered in the ears of His disciples He commanded to be preached openly from the housetops. . . . But preachers, crafty men that they are, finding that men grievously disliked to have their morals adjusted to the rule of Christ and following I suppose your advice [of indirection], accommodated His teaching to men's morals as if it were a rule of soft lead that at least in some way or other the two might be made to correspond. (51)

Raphael draws upon the classical tradition of thinking about equity when he describes the "rule of soft lead," which is a clear allusion to the "Lesbian Rule" that Aristotle uses to characterize equity in the *Ethics*.[50] Notice that this implicit reference to equity seems to emphasize flexibility in terms of method rather than content. But, we should also keep in mind that the underlying content—Christ's "teaching" that he whispered to his disciples—relates to living communally, at least in Budé's view. We will begin to appreciate better the dual significance of equity, both as method and content, when we revisit Lord Chancellor Morton's method of addressing the over-severe punishment of thieves issue that Raphael posed as a problem of equity. As we turn to the use of equity in Book II, we will confront another dual significance—one which is foreshadowed by the passage we have just examined, and one in which the communal content of equity becomes clearer.

To determine the narrative significance of this allusion to the "Lesbian rule"—an allusion whose connection to equity originally derives from Aristotle's treatment of equity in the *Ethics*, we need to return to the larger context of Book I, and to consider the significance of equity to the "debate on counsel." In the original design of Book I, we are seemingly left on the one hand with a "pure" position viz-a-viz "counsel," that of Raphael, who asserts, on the authority of Christ, that all counsel should be forthright.[51] On the other hand, we have the More persona's "impure" position that "wise" counselors must employ an indirect approach and that their goals are limited[52] to making things as little bad as possible rather than, for instance, producing positive changes for the better like Raphael accomplished in the Lord Chancellor Morton passage. [53] So, when we consider together Raphael's and the More persona's explicit positions, we are faced with the dilemma that wise counsel is either "pure" and ineffective—and quite dangerous to the counselor—or it is "impure" and safe for the counselor, but also largely ineffective because it accomplishes so little.

But Book I's original design contains hints towards a possible solution to this dilemma—or at least a partial solution. The first clue is embedded within Raphael's description leading up to the implicit equity reference of the "Lesbian rule":

> Yet [Christ] forbade us to dissemble [his doctrines] to the extent that what He whispered in the ears of his disciples He commanded to be preached openly from the housetop. (51)

There is an obvious problem with Raphael's reliance on this example to buttress his argument for a "pure" approach to wise counsel. Far from clarifying that Christ demanded forthrightness, the example instead suggests both that there are teachings that are not meant for the ears of the multitude and that these teachings are not intended to be passed on in a "forthright" fashion.[54] Raphael's employment of this "proof" seems to fall squarely within More's "impure" approach of counsel by indirection. It certainly does not partake of the "pure" approach Raphael advocates; indeed, Christ can be seen in this example operating according to the precepts of infinite flexibility—of equity. He is being both subtle and guarded in his teaching. Implicitly this passage suggests that following Christ's "example" means siding with More's position of using indirect counsel.

What then is the significance of an example which tends to prove a point opposite to the one for which it is offered? The answer is contained in the text which More later added to Book I—in the Lord Chancellor Morton passage. In this passage we encounter Raphael employing a less "pure" form of counsel than he argues for later in Book I. One need point no further than the way Raphael succeeds in enticing Morton into a dialogue about the English domestic problem of rampant thievery; he suggests that thieving is necessary because of the unique English problem of their "sheep," a cryptic, amusing, and most importantly, irresistibly tantalizing way of drawing Morton into a serious discussion (24). By using these "indirect" means Raphael effectively contradicts his later assertions that he would be ineffective as a king's counselor; he succeeds in achieving a change in domestic policy by utilizing a complex rhetorical strategy.

Moreover, Raphael succeeds in achieving positive change to a far greater extent than the More persona suggests is possible by using the "indirect" approach, the stated goal of which, according to the More persona, is to reduce as much as possible the evils that otherwise would occur. Raphael in fact succeeds in persuading Morton to reverse a domestic policy so that the result is more in conformance with the dictates of political theory. Raphael produces an outstanding positive change in the regime, in part, at least, because he employs an indirect approach. One message conveyed in these passages, when examined from the context of equity, is that the sort of equity of the "Lesbian rule" variety is associated with the indirect approach. Such flexibility is necessary to produce positive change in a regime. Moreover, the indirect approach is the correct way to proceed, even, or perhaps especially, if we approach things from the standard of Christ's conduct and the conduct of his disciples.

To summarize, we have observed that equity, broadly conceived, has a double significance in the Lord Chancellor Morton passage, a late addition to Book I of *Utopia*. First it represents the "theory" that Raphael is drawing upon and towards which he is trying to influence a change in English domestic policy. In the first Book I use of equity, equity demands that distinctions be made between murderers and thieves with respect to their punishments; in Aristotelian terms, equity must intervene between the laws mandating capital punishment and the specific cases to which they are applied, and for which they are patently too strict, in order to ensure fitting outcomes based on the specific facts and circumstances of each case. We might also notice in passing that equity, in the context of "theory," is here applied to an issue of domestic concern; there is some question as to whether equity has any relevance to other areas such as foreign relations.[55] The most obvious reason for this is that the theory that underlies equity relates, by and large, to that portion of a regime's laws which regulate domestic matters.

The second significance of equity to the Lord Chancellor Morton passage, as we have seen, regards method. The type of equity associated with the "Lesbian rule" represents a means or method for achieving outcomes in accordance with the underlying theory of equity. Because of the sensitivity of the theoretical problem underlying equity—the absolute necessity of preserving and maintaining the rule of law, which equity accomplishes by veiling the defective nature of the laws—infinite flexibility is required at the level of counsel seeking to produce change in accord with equity theory. Wise counsel rendered in order to achieve ends comporting to theoretical equity cannot be constrained to follow a "pure," straightforward approach; indirection must often be at least an option, if not the rule. Because of the seriousness of the consequences of a breakdown in the rule of law—civil unrest or war—the "end" of avoiding these does in some essential way justify such "impure" methods.[56]

UTOPIA: BOOK II

The preceding summary of how the equity allusions in Book I should be viewed will help us to address the most critical question with respect to the single use of equity in Book II: why is "the principal foundation [of the Utopian state's] whole structure," its communism, described by Raphael as equity? (151). This association raises an additional question that has perplexed readers of *Utopia*: is there any practical, that is, politically useful lesson intended by the example of Utopian communism?

The passage in Book II where the word "equity" occurs actually employs the word twice—once in each element of a comparison. The passage occurs just after Raphael finishes his description of the Utopian nation, and as he returns and completes his dialogue with the More persona and Giles that occurred in Book I. Equity is referred to as Raphael is comparing what he considers the essence of Utopia—its communist system—to the systems of existing European regimes:

> Now I have described to you as accurately as I could the structure of that commonwealth which I consider not only the best but indeed the only one that can rightfully claim that name. In other places men talk all the time about the commonwealth, but what they mean is simply their own wealth; here, where there is no private business, every man zealously pursues the public business.
>
> . . .
>
> At this point, I'd like to see anyone venture to compare [1] this equity of the Utopians with [2] the justice that prevails among other nations—[3] among whom I'll be damned if I can discover the slightest trace of justice or [equity].[57] (Logan, Adams, Miller 1995, 241 & 243)(my emphasis and numbering)

Before beginning to make a detailed examination of this passage, it will be helpful to first make a more general observation about it. Raphael speaks this soon after he returns to the dialogue with the More persona and Giles; his oration on Utopia has ended. Put differently, Raphael has returned from the world of the ideal to the "cave" of European politics. We need to be sensitive to the possibility that, like the philosophers of Book VII of Plato' *Republic* who return to the cave from the outside where the sun shines, Raphael will be blinded by his discussion of Utopia, and be unable to perceive clearly the world of practical affairs. Consequently, he will also be unable to see clearly the practical applications and manifestations of the ideal notions he has been contemplating. Therefore, in Book II we cannot rely on Raphael as our guide to what the practical applications or manifestations of equity might be. Nor, obviously, can we expect him to provide us with an explicit example of a practical application, like the one he provided for Lord Chancellor Morton in Book I, before he had been blinded by his discussion of Utopia.

Closer examination of Raphael's comparison shows that the terms of the initial comparison shift enigmatically. In the first element of the comparison we encounter equity describing the essence of the Utopian system—or, since the Latin is ambiguous, it could also be describing the characteristic quality of the Utopian people. Either way, it clearly refers to an extreme form of communism.[58] This is evident both in Raphael's brief comments preceding this usage of equity, in which he extols the virtues of the Utopians' communist system, and in the More persona's later comment in which he independently identifies the most important characteristic of Utopia and the Utopians as "their common life and subsistence—without the exchange of money" (151). Raphael for some reason clearly intends to associate equity with the extreme communism of the Utopians.

Raphael then compares this ideal equity with the practical, real-world justice associated with existing European nations. It is a debased justice that no longer conforms to Christ's teachings and represents a kind of "conspiracy of the rich" who make laws and palm these "off as justice" when they are really directed at protecting and furthering "their own interests under the name and title of commonwealth" [59] (148). Raphael does not explain why he is comparing an ideal kind of equity with debased real-world justice. This lack of explanation is puzzling since it is not at all clear that the terms can be compared in the way Raphael proposes—they have no evident relation if one only considers the generally accepted significations for equity. In order to determine what Raphael means by using the word equity here, we need to return to Aristotle's discussion of equity in the *Ethics*, where he attempts to clarify equity's relation to justice. But, while Aristotle tries to clarify the relation there, it remains confusing, and certainly without any evident association with communism. In fact, equity's treatment in the *Ethics* on the surface appears to treat it solely as a practical, applied concept tethered to the laws, without any ideal component. Two points remain unclear: why does Raphael associate equity with the ideal concept of extreme communism; and how does this ideal communism relate to real world justice?

As we continue with the comparison, an extraordinary rhetorical flourish occurs. Raphael, who has become increasingly emotional since finishing his oration, becomes angry and frustrated and utters his first oath: "I'll be damned," or more literally, "may I perish."[60] Those familiar with Aristotle, as humanists such as More and Budé were, would recognize that Aristotle employs just two oaths in his entire corpus. Both occur, not in his idealistic *Ethics*, but rather in his most practical of works, the *Politics* (3.10). I will turn to the significance of Raphael's oath, and its relation to the Aristotelian oaths, shortly. For the moment it is sufficient to notice that Raphael is becoming emotionally upset over his difficulty relating the ideal situation of Utopia to the real world of European politics.

Immediately after his oath, Raphael, without explanation, shifts the terms of the already problematic comparison he just finished expressing. Instead of the original comparison contrasting the ideal equity of Utopia, representative of extreme communism, with the real-world justice of the existing European nations, Raphael compares the ideal equity of Utopia with real-world justice *and equity*. This change suggests that Raphael is looking for a real-world analogue to ideal equity—a practical manifestation of the ideal equity of Utopian communism. But he does not see any, either or both because he has been blinded by his "Utopian" discourse, or because what he is searching for is hidden from view.

The problematic relation of equity and justice again compel us to return to Aristotle, only now we come armed with two additional insights to consider. Raphael's oath may well be related to Aristotle's oaths in the *Politics*; and we now know we are searching for a practical manifestation of equity that relates to or flows from the ideal of Utopian communism.

An additional consideration that draws our attention to Book 3.10 of the *Politics*, comes not from Raphael, but from the More persona and his rejection of Utopian communism:

> When Raphael had finished [recounting this],[61] many things came to my mind which seemed very absurdly established in the customs and laws of the people described . . . most of all in that feature which is the principal foundation of their whole structure. I mean their common life and subsistence—without the exchange of money. This . . . alone utterly overthrows all the nobility, magnificence, splendor, and majesty which are, in the estimation of the common people, the true glories and ornaments of the commonwealth. (151)

The problem with the More persona's position here, of course—at least from an Aristotelian perspective—is that the "common people," who are traditionally considered to have limited education and understanding, are the very ones who *seem* to advocate for extreme communism, at least initially. Their prime objective, however, as we learned in Book 3.10 of the *Politics*, is to "distribute among themselves the things of the wealthy" (1281a1, 3.10.1). Aristotle's first oath emphasizes this point. Aristotle points out that those who object to communism, and probably any other kind of restriction on wealth, are not the common people, but the "refined" (χαρίεις)—the beautiful people, the wealthy few. More the author causes the More persona to say something that his humanist readers and anyone else familiar with the relevant passages from Aristotle's *Politics* will notice. His critique of Utopian communism, at leat in this respect, appears ironic.

At the opening of Book 3.10 of the *Politics* Aristotle presents a list of the five contenders to be the authoritative element in the *Polis*.[62] The list includes, of course, the wealthy few (χαρίεις), and the many poor—the common people (πληθος). But at the center of the list, as was noted in Chapter

Two, is the critical clue that reveals the connection between equity and communism. As previously noted, the central group consists of the persons Aristotle describes as the equitable (επιεικες)—those persons who are "capable of ruling best" in what Aristotle describes as the best achievable regime, the regime in which "the distribution of prerogatives" occurs "on the basis of virtue" rather than on wealth or numerical superiority. The critical characteristic of this group is that they are no "stickler[s] for justice in a bad sense," and that they are "satisfied with less than [their] share" even though the laws authorize or allot them a larger share.[63]

The connection between equity and communism is clear. Equity, in terms of political theory, looks to extreme communism, which itself is the ideal political order that escapes the "harsh poverty" and/or "extreme wealth" that "breed civil war and faction," and also avoids "the money loving that goes with justice" (*Laws* 737a).[64] We must recognize that this meaning of equity is, from a political perspective, extremely dangerous for anyone to propound openly because it will inevitably work against the perceived interest of those typically in political power.[65] Even in political treatises the doctrine must be carefully handled as we witness in the delicate ways Aristotle and Plato treat it.

To be more precise, though, the extremely dangerous part of the doctrine of equity—in its sense associated with communism—is not the expounding of this concept as an ideal model, for there is a long tradition of this. Rather it is the explicit expounding of what practical steps need to be taken to move a regime in the direction of this ideal, and the identification of the persons who will initiate and pursue these steps.[66] These practical steps, and the identity of those who will take these steps, must be expressed with the utmost care so as to avoid detection by the rulers of the regime and those who advise them. For all practical purposes they must be invisible, for if they are detected, such persons would inevitably be eliminated, their wealth confiscated, and wealth sharing practices prohibited.

In the light of the implications of the esoteric sort of equity advanced in Plato and Aristotle, we can understand why More does not hide the fact that communism is identified by some in theory as the ideal political situation in a regime, while still appreciating his efforts to distance himself as much as possible from this position.[67] And, we should no longer be surprised at the extraordinary lengths to which he goes to disguise what practical steps need to be taken, and by whom, to change existing regimes in the direction of Utopian communism.

Enough has been said about the relation of communism and equity, as well as the practical manifestation of this sort of equity. Now, I will return for a moment to Book I to see whether in hindsight there was any foreshadowing of what we have discovered by reading *Utopia* Book II, in light of the way equity is dealt with in Aristotle's *Ethics*, *Politics* and Plato's *Laws*.

In Book I, before Raphael became "blinded," we encounter him summing up his argument in favor of Utopian communism in his discussion following the second hypothetical—a discussion in which Raphael qualifies that certain ameliorating measures can be taken to improve existing regimes *short* of adopting the communism of the Utopians:

> I admit that this burden [of poverty and misfortunes] *can be lightened to some extent*, but I contend that it cannot be removed entirely. A statute might be made that no person should hold more than a certain amount of land and that no person should have a monetary income beyond that permitted by law. Special legislation might be passed to prevent the monarch from being overmighty and the people overweening; likewise, that public offices should not be solicited with gifts, nor be put up for sale, nor require lavish personal expenditures. Otherwise, there arise, first, the temptation to recoup one's expenses by acts of fraud and plunder and, secondly, the necessity of appointing rich men to offices which ought rather to have been administered by wise men. By this type of legislation, I maintain, as sick bodies which are past cure can be kept up by repeated medical treatments, *so these evils, too, can be alleviated and made less acute*. There is no hope, however, of a cure and a return to a healthy condition as long as each individual is master of his own property. (54)(emphasis added)

Significantly, Raphael allows that these evils "can be alleviated and made less acute" by enacting legislation that reduces wealth disparity—by legislation that closes the gap between existing regimes and the ideal regime of Utopian communism.

The qualifications contained in this passage create a space in which political theory has room to affect practical affairs. This space lies between Raphael's absolute position "I am fully persuaded that no just and even distribution of goods can be made and that no happiness can be found in human affairs unless private property is utterly abolished" (53), and the More persona's equally absolute "Life cannot be satisfactory where all things are common . . . [f]or . . . individual[s] do[] not have the motive of personal gain and [are] rendered slothful by trusting to the industry of others" (55). Occupying the space between these two positions is the practical application of communism such as occurs in Plato's *Laws*.

Further examination of Book I might reveal how More's practical equity distinguishes itself from Plato's. For instance, we might hypothesize that the "wise" counselors, liberally employing indirection in their counsels pursuant to the sort of equity Aristotle associated with the "Lesbian rule," are in fact the early Renaissance equivalent of the "equitable" persons identified by Aristotle and Plato.

Budé first reveals an appreciation that More's "wise" counselors were in fact the humanists—those persons whose friendship was informed by the only extreme communism existing in practice. These humanists, as idealized by Erasmus, practiced the Pythagorean communion described in Erasmus' first adage "*amicorum communia omnia*," or in its Greek rendering, "*τα των φίλων κολνά*." (*Works*, Vol. 31, p. 29). Many of these humanists, such as More and Budé, were well off, and they to some extent at least aspired to a kind of Pythagorean communion. Certainly they understood in a profound way the political theory of the classics, and were capable of unfolding its practical implications.

Chapter Four

Equity in Book V of Spenser's *The Faerie Queene*

In a central and critical passage of Book V of *The Faerie Queene*, the Book devoted to the virtue of justice and its representative knight, Artegall,[1] the Goddess Isis is reported to represent "That part of Iustice, which is Equity," while her husband, the God Osiris, is said to represent justice itself (V.vii.3.4).[2] The text presents Isis as equity ruling over Osiris as justice. This surprising presentation shows a female monarch ruling over her male counterpart in direct contrast to conventional expectations of the era. Equally surprising is how this presentation shows equity, a constituent part of justice, as ruling over justice as a whole. As discussed in Chapter One, by the end of the sixteenth century the English concept of equity was considered to be subordinate to law. Accordingly, equity's significance to justice was greatly reduced.

I will show in this chapter that the enigmatic way in which Spenser's text treats equity reveals a profound appreciation for Aristotle and Plato's treatments of *επιείκεια*, as well as a complex understanding of the ways in which the meanings of *επιείκεια* continued to influence the English concept of equity. On a more pragmatic note, I will also demonstrate that Spenser's treatment of equity in Book V of *The Faerie Queene* constitutes a kind of lesson for a select segment of Spenser's audience, gentlemen such as Sir Walter Raleigh. This lesson consists of the subtle attempts of these gentlemen to influence Queen Elizabeth in favor of James VI of Scotland on the succession issue. In order to demonstrate this, I will show that one way Spenser reacts in *The Faerie Queene* to the crisis of feminine authority in late sixteenth century England (also frequently called the "women's rule" issue) is by dividing the concept of equity between two of its principal meanings and assigning each meaning a set of stereotypically gendered qualities. In the central passages of Book V, Spenser rejects as feminine the infinitely flexible sort of equity deriving from the Greek *επιείκεια*.[3] Instead he promotes the stereotypically more masculine concept of classical Roman equity, which is an equity based upon a kind of equality.

By focusing on Spenser's division of equity, I hope to show the narrative and rhetorical strategy behind the guileful persuasion of Britomart at Isis Church that equity based on *επιείκεια* really constitutes a secret sort of power women can exercise over men. The secret component requires women publicly to subjugate themselves to male rule—to make it appear to men that men are in control. Behind the scenes women then "over rule" men's decisions and judgments utilizing equity based on *επιείκεια,* which the text presents as being firmly under the control of women. I argue that this interpretation explains Britomart's otherwise perplexing subjugation of women to men's rule. Britomart herself must perform the subjugation because she is the premier female warrior and, as Katherine Eggert notes, only Britomart can subdue herself (Eggert 2000, 41). Consequently, men must persuade her—they must give her a reason to subdue herself, to subjugate women to men. The principal reason they give her—or rather entrap her with—is the artificially constructed controlling female power associated with equity based on *επιείκεια.*

The narrative of Book V functions at multiple levels in its central passages. At one level, as Eggert argues, Spenser completes his defeminization of *The Faerie Queene*'s poetry with Britomart's subjugation of herself and other women to the rule of men—an enterprise begun with Guyon's destruction of the Bower of Bliss in Book II. Eggert maintains that Spenser can now shift to the less poetically powerful, but more straightforward mode of historical allegory with which he completes Book V.

Another of these levels, I argue, involves the "ensample" presented in these digressive, "feminine" central passages of Book V, the entrapment of Britomart by the priest of Isis. This "ensample," I will establish, involves the succession issue. Spenser is showing gentlemen like Raleigh "by ensample" that Elizabeth, like Britomart, must be persuaded to subdue Elizabeth; she needs to be nudged in the direction of settling the succession on James, just as Britomart was influenced at Isis Church to settle the succession of the Amazon realm on Artegall.

My project complements and builds upon the work of Eggert and others, who seek to explain—and to bridge—the gap between the central and final episodes of Book V of Spenser's *The Faerie Queene.* This gap separates the "feminine" literary genre of romance, a genre which disappears from *The Faerie Queene* in the middle of Book V with Britomart, and the "masculine" literary genre of historical allegory which dominates Book V's five remaining Cantos. Eggert explains the shift in terms of Spenser's desire to rescue poetry from feminine authority—from the feminizing influence both of romance and of Elizabeth's long rule. She does not see

Spenser as ultimately successful in creating a de-feminized poetic genre; but she does see his attempt as a bold and influential experiment in poetic form responding to the crisis of women's rule in late sixteenth century England—a response that "engag[es] in as well as submit[s] to improvisations of power" (20). Eggert sees Spenser's experiment itself as positive in result—the reaction to female authority creates texts that are themselves improvisatory, shape shifting, in flux; that is, the texts that are seeking to defeminize themselves are essentially adopting a "feminine," a protean literary mode, and are certainly inspired and shaped by the feminine literary mode of romance they are reacting against.

Eggert observes that Spenser's objective of de-feminizing poetry is analogous to lying "down with Talus," the iron man who is the embodiment of the rigorous justice and its enforcement which were given to Artegall by the goddess Astrea. I argue that "lying down with Talus" in turn involves the elimination or suppression of a certain kind of equity, the flexible equity derived from the Greek *επιείκεια*. Not coincidentally, this flexible sort of equity plays a critical role in the central "feminine" passages of Book V involving Britomart. While Eggert's focus is the gap between the poetic modes of the central and final cantos of Book V, mine is a particular gap within the digression at the heart of Book V, the gap represented by the movement from Isis Church, where Britomart is indoctrinated by means of guileful persuasion into the mysteries of this equity, to her final actions in *The Faerie Queene*—her defeat of Radigund, freeing of Artegall, and reforming of the Amazonian commonwealth by (re)subjugating women to rule by men. In order to explain this gap, let me briefly examine the two principal meanings of equity Spenser draws upon in Book V.

Justice, the overriding theme of Book V, is in many respects the most ambiguous of virtues. It can mean simply the impartial enforcement of the laws of a particular regime, or it can relate to a transcendent sense of fairness that supersedes any particular regime's laws. If the latter, then a regime's laws are always subject to challenge as unjust in some absolute sense—a state of affairs that is in tension with the objectives of quick, convenient, predictable and inexpensive results in legal proceedings.

Equity is introduced in Book V as part of the goddess Astrea's instruction of Artegall in the ways of justice:[4]

For *Artegall* in iustice was vpbrought
Euen from the cradle of his infancie,
And all the depth of rightfull doome was taught

By faire *Astrea*, with great industrie,
Whilest here on earth she liued mortaille. (V.i.5.1–5)

Among the things she taught him was

. . . to weigh both right and wrong
In equall balance with due recompence,
And equitie to measure out along,
According to the line of conscience,
When so it needs with rigour to dispense. (V.i.7.1–5)

At first glance, this sort of equity appears to be consistent with the flexible equity based on *επιείκεια* of the central passages of Book V. Appearances in Book V are deceiving, however. There are at least two clear indications that Artegall's equity differs markedly from the equity that Britomart learns about in Isis Church. First, there is no reference in the Isis Church passage to measuring out equity "according to the line of conscience," as Artegall is taught. Second, Artegall's judging actions in Book V do not in any way reflect dispensing with rigor; in fact, they have much in common with Guyon's "rigour pitilesse."[5]

The reference to equity being measured according to the line of "conscience" reflects the theory in English law that saw equity as flowing from or in accordance with the monarch's conscience.[6] This association with conscience is a remnant of Christian scholastic influence upon equity and can be traced to canon law developments in the middle ages, as noted in Chapter One. The Chancery court, with its equity jurisdiction, had long been known as a court of conscience since the Chancellor was considered the keeper (or delegee) of the king's conscience, in deciding matters of equity. As a practical matter, when the term equity became associated with the Chancery court's special jurisdiction, conscience became associated with the term equity. But the canon law ideal of conscience did not translate well to practical politics. By the late sixteenth century, sayings had become proverbial about how the Chancellor's conscience had become an unpredictable, even arbitrary and biased measure. As John Seldon notes:

Equity is a Roguish thing, for Law we have a measure, know what to trust to, Equity is according to the Conscience of him that is Chancellor, and as that is larger or narrower, so is Equity. 'Tis all one as if they should make the Standard for the measure, we call [a Foot] a Chancellor's Foot, what an uncertain Measure would this be? One Chancellor

> has a long Foot, another a short Foot, a Third an indifferent Foot: 'Tis the same thing in the Chancellor's Conscience.[7] (*Table Talk* 64)

Hypothesizing that Spenser shared Seldon's skepticism, I see irony in Spenser's reference here to Astrea's training of Artegall to measure out equity according to the line of conscience. The "line of conscience" is not principled according to Seldon's description; it is arbitrary or biased, as Seldon notices. This interpretation is amply supported by Artegall's actions in Book V.

Artegall is not an apt student of equity. His first six exploits in Book V, following Astrea's legal instruction and leading up to his submission to Radigund, are illustrations of rigorous (harsh) justice rather than equity (Fowler 44; Phillips, *Justice* 106). Following the digression of the central passages, Artegall's "zeal" for rigorous justice is no less strong than in the earlier episodes (Eggert 45). Therefore, as Judith Anderson has observed, Artegall is "ineffectual" as the hero of a broader form of justice that incorporates equity and is not simply rigor (65). Artegall's leaning towards rigor rather than equity certainly is consistent with his clear literary pedigree as the heir of Hercules, the wielder of the "club of Iustice dread" (V.i.2.9, 3.1–2).

In Canto vii, another sort of equity emerges when Britomart visits the temple of the pagan goddess Isis. As previously noted, Isis is reported to represent "That part of Iustice, which is Equity" (V.vii.3.4). This characterization of course raises the question of what if any relationship to justice Artegall's equity had.[8] The role assigned to Isis' equity is to intervene into the legal process conducted by her husband Osiris, the pagan god of justice, to insure that his judgments are not unduly "sterne" or "cruell" (V.vii.22.9). Implicitly, she is to take into account the circumstances of each case and to intervene where necessary to adjust the outcome to fit the circumstances. This is the sort of equity that derives from *επιείκεια*, and, as already described, is in direct tension with the sort of equity based on equality that Artegall renders.

Isis' equity also differs from the sort Astrea teaches Artegall in that there is no indication that her equity is measured out "according to the line of conscience." Presumably the sort of "measure" Isis is to use when rendering her equity based on *επιείκεια* is the infinitely flexible rule of Lesbos, which, as we have seen, is able to adjust outcomes to the infinite variety of circumstances presented in the individual cases decided by Osiris.[9]

The objective of the following examination of the Isis Church passage (V.vii.1–24) is to explain how Spenser, by associating equity based on *επιείκεια* with the feminine—with Isis and Britomart, renders equity based on *επιείκεια* subordinate to the more masculine type of equity based on equality and associated with Artegall. Equity based on *επιείκεια* certainly shared many of the traits stereotypically associated with Renaissance women: equity based on *επιείκεια* was *dilatory* because it required more time than equity based on equality to reach judgment—its focus on the individual facts and circumstances of specific cases was time and labor intensive (Eggert 45); equity based on *επιείκεια* was considered more *unstable* and *disorderly* because its results were unpredictable since each case was considered unique (9); in the same vein, equity based on *επιείκεια* could be considered *inherently changeable* or protean (21); and finally, equity based on *επιείκεια* could be described as *discontinuous* or *digressive* as compared to the relatively quick and straight forward results achieved by equity based on equality, or to put it another way, equity based on equality was superior at achieving finality—closure (23, 31, 37, 41). In effect, Spenser is gendering equity—he is dividing off equity based on *επιείκεια* as distinctly feminine and equity based on equality as masculine.

Spenser's treatment of equity based on *επιείκεια* occurs at the center of Book V in a narrative digression. This is noteworthy since digression itself is a stereotypically feminine characteristic, and since More also deals with this sort of equity in a digression, as we saw in Chapter Two.[10] Book V's digression begins when Artegall is distracted by Radigund's beauty from his quest to free Irene. Instead of completing his victory over the fallen Radigund, he becomes her captive. The digression ends when Britomart rescues Artegall. In between these two events there occurs an inner digression consisting of Britomart's visit to Isis Church. Spenser's treatment of equity based on *επιείκεια*, occurring in this inner digression, is effectively buried within—veiled by—the narrative structure of Book V.[11]

Spenser introduces Canto vii, in which the Isis Church passage occurs, with the following four-line "argument":

> *Britomart comes to Isis Church,*
> *Where shee strange visions sees:*
> *She fights with Radigund, her slaies,*
> *And Artegall thence frees.*

Britomart, on her way to rescue Artegall from Radigund, happens upon the pagan temple devoted to the ancient pagan goddess Isis,[12] whose main characteristics are first that she represents that "part of Iustice, which is Equity" and second that she is responsible for suppressing "forged guile,/And open force" (V.vii.3.4,7.2–3). What sort of equity is associated with Isis is not immediately explained, though its association with a female suggests equity based on *επιείκεια*. As might be expected at a pagan goddess' temple, Britomart, a woman, is permitted inside, but Talus, her male companion, is barred entry (3.6–9).[13] Britomart is brought to the "Idoll"—a statue of the goddess. The statue depicts Isis standing with one foot on a crocodile, a configuration reported to represent the goddess' suppression of forged guile and open force (V.vii.6.1,7.3–4).

Britomart prostrates herself before the idol in prayer, and as night falls, she removes her helmet and falls asleep on the floor at its foot. There she is visited with a nightmarish dream which is said to secretly express the "course of all her fortune and posteritie" (V.vii.12.9). Many elements of this dream will later appear to be in considerable tension with the Isis' priest's interpretation of it. In the dream, the royally dressed Britomart is suddenly surrounded by a whirlwind of fire that threatens to engulf her and burn Isis Church. As Angus Fletcher notes, such secret flames are appropriate to the celebration of a mystery (271). The crocodile then awakes, swallows the fire, and, "swolne with pride of his owne peerlesse powre," tries to eat Britomart (V.vii.15.1–9). Before it can do so, Isis beats it back. The beaten crocodile then meekly prostrates itself at Britomart's feet.

The dreaming Britomart readily accepts the crocodile's apparent change of heart. She also receives its amorous advances, from which she becomes pregnant. The dream ends after Britomart gives birth to a lion that subdues all other beasts. Not surprisingly, Britomart wakes "full of fearefull fright" and "doubtfully dismayd" at the "uncouth" visions in her dream (V.vii.16.8–9). Indeed, this seems to be a natural and appropriate reaction to a nightmare in which in rapid succession she was almost burned to death, eaten by a crocodile, and impregnated by it. But in the morning, when Britomart consults the chief priest, who has noticed that she seems upset, he interprets the dream for her in a reassuring fashion. His credibility is enhanced when he correctly identifies Britomart in spite of her disguise. He attributes his ability to see through her disguise to the gods' omniscience.[14] The priest's description of Britomart clearly shows that she is intended as a mirror for Elizabeth: "Magnificke Virgin, that in quaint disguise/Of British armes doest maske thy royall blood" (V.vii.21.1–2).

The chief priest begins to interpret Britomart's dream in remarkable fashion by unexpectedly suggesting that the crocodile represents both the god Osyris, Isis' husband, and Artegall—an association not anticipated by the original description of the carved crocodile in the idol. The priest then explains Isis' earlier association with equity:

> For that same Crocodile *Osyris* is
> That vnder *Isis* feete doth sleepe for euer:

To shew that clemence oft in things amis,
Restraines those sterne behests, and cruell doomes of his.[15]
(V.vii.22.6–9)

I argued above that equity based on *επιείκεια* is associated with Isis; now it is also with associated with Britomart. Since Isis and Britomart are both female characters or figures, and since a kind of equity is being introduced in a narrative digression, this is hardly surprising. What is surprising is equity's involvement in the resolution of the crisis of women's rule posed in Book V's central digression. Equity proves to be the bait that catches Britomart and persuades her voluntarily and even eagerly to (re)subjugate women to the rule of men.

Dramatically, the Isis Church passage presents equity as a kind of power with which Isis physically controls—literally "over" rules Osyris. The priest has made clear that this power of control associated with equity also applies to the relationship of Britomart and Artegall. Britomart will rule over Artegall in the same way Isis rules over Osyris. I have found no precedent for Spenser's association of equity with women's power of control over men, or to place it in a political context, of queens over kings.[16] Spenser's device of the priest's dream interpretation amplifies equity based on *επιείκεια*'s meaning here. One clear indication of this is the tension between the priest's interpretation of Isis and the crocodile in the dream and what they represented in the idol—there the crocodile did not represent any particular person, but open force and forged guile. I will return to address this tension in more detail later in the chapter when I discuss what Spenser's political motivation may be in these Book V digression episodes.

The priest's conclusion to his interpretation is designed to calm and reassure Britomart; he continues to downplay and explain away its alarming nature:

[Artegall] shall all the troublous stormes asswage,
And raging flames, that many foes shall reare,
To hinder thee from the iust heritage
Of thy sires Crowne, and from thy countrey deare.
Then shalt thou take him to thy loued fere,
And ioyne in equall portion of thy realme.
And afterwards a sonne to him shalt beare,
That Lion-like shall shew his power extreame.
So Blesse thee God, and giue thee ioyance of thy dreame.
(V.vii.22&23)

Apparently forgetting the earlier association of the crocodile with forged guile, Britomart is "much eased in her troublous thought" (V.vii.24.2). She evidently accepts the priest's interpretation without reservation.

The "mystery" revealed to Britomart at Isis Church is the role equity plays in the relationship of Isis and Osyris, and by association, the role it will play in Britomart's relationship with Artegall. According to the priest's interpretation of Britomart's dream, Isis and Britomart possess a controlling—a ruling—power over Osyris and Artegall respectively. This power is presented as deriving from or at least integrally connected to equity based on *επιείκεια*. Knowledge of this sort, of equity's gendered controlling power, is a mystery, a closely guarded secret, apparently available only to women who learned it at Isis Church. Presumably women's exercise of equity's controlling power would need to be discreet, to preserve the mystery.[17]

The compelling reason for the secrecy surrounding feminine equity involves the narrator's surprising claim that women once were superior to men in battle—in the open display of force. In Book III of *The Faerie Queene*, the narrator reports that:

> . . . by record of antique times I find,
> That women wont in warrres to beare most sway,
> And to all great exploits them selues inclind:
> Of which they still the girlond bore away,
> Till enuious Men fearing their rules decay,
> Gan coyne streight lawes to curb their liberty;
> Yet sith they warlike armes haue layd away,
> They haue exeld in artes and policy,
> That now we foolish men that prayse gin eke t'enuy. (III. ii. 2)

Men, who nonetheless ruled women, rightly fearing that otherwise their rule would be supplanted, enacted laws that subjugated women to male rule in spite of their fighting prowess—presumably by limiting women to domestic activities and preventing their training as warriors. Since men have successfully controlled women's ability to take advantage of their natural superiority as fighters, women instead need to work to preserve the controlling power of equity over men. Women who learn of its existence must keep it secret; its exercise must be discreet lest men recognize and eliminate it for fear of losing their domination of women. The controlling power's dramatic *over-rule* of men's laws can proceed only in secrecy.

It is significant that the narration of Britomart's encounter with Radigund picks up without pause from the end of the Isis Church episode since they appear to be parts of a single episode. Spenser amplifies this impression by ending the Isis Church episode and beginning the Britomart/Radigund one in the same stanza (V.vii.24). This connectedness supports my view that the secret lesson Britomart learns at Isis Church is reflected in her actions in the encounter with Radigund, Britomart's final appearance in *The Faerie Queene*. It is in her actions as ruler of Radigund's former realm that Britomart practically applies her Isis Church lesson:

> So there a while they afterwards remained,
> [Artegall] to refresh, and [Britomart] her late wounds to heale:
> During which space [Britomart] there as Princess rained,
> And changing all that forme of common weale,
> The liberty of women did repeale,
> Which they had long userpt; and them restoring
> To mens subiection, did true Iustice deale: (V.vii.42.1–7)

Thus, the Britomart/Radigund episode presents the paradox of "Britomart, the perfect ruler [and a woman], teach[ing women] to deny women's [right and ability] to rule" (Wood 155). But Britomart's apparently self-undermining ruling actions begin to be understandable if they are considered in light of the mystery she learned at Isis Church. There she learned that her principal ruling role will be behind the scenes, where she will control her husband, king Artegall, by "over" ruling him utilizing the controlling power of equity. She therefore rescues him, publicly declares against women's rule, and in accordance with this declaration, tenders rule to Artegall. All of these actions help to preserve her own ability later to exercise the controlling power of equity over Artegall since Britomart's ruling actions will not give him or any other man any indication that she is reserving a secret ruling role to herself.[18]

Britomart's defeat of Radigund also helps to preserve the controlling power of equity for other women who later learn the mystery of Isis Church. Radigund's error was that she publicly proclaimed her superiority and also acted upon it openly, thereby threatening once again to trigger men's fear of losing their dominance and resulting in women's complete subjugation. Britomart's temporary rule for the limited purpose of restoring male rule over women usurpers implicitly qualifies as an exception to her generally stated principle against female rule—an exception that does not trigger men's fear of losing their dominance over women.

Britomart's role as ruler of Radigund's former realm is about more than simply just the (re)subjugation of women to men's rule—it is about *succession.* Specifically, Britomart's rule is mostly about Artegall succeeding her. Britomart's temporary reign is necessary only because the man who "should" be ruling is temporarily incapacitated. Britomart's rule is an exception to the norm of male rule, and appears to satisfy the moderate Puritan position on women's rule which views women capable of ruling only in exceptional circumstances when God so ordains.

Arguably, Elizabeth's own rule can also be interpreted as an exception to a rule, and consequently as acceptable to the moderate Puritans. She was raised to the throne because Henry VIII lacked male heirs. Until 1587, the principal contender for succession was another woman, Mary Stuart (Queen of Scots). Consequently, for the first thirty years of her reign, Elizabeth's rule appears justified as an exception to a rule. For a while thereafter it could certainly be asserted that Elizabeth should continue to rule while James, Mary's son, was too young and inexperienced to succeed. However, by the early to mid 1590's, when Spenser was writing Book V, James was clearly old and experienced enough to succeed.[19]

Once the passage begins to be viewed in terms of succession, it becomes clear that the gendering of equity at Isis Church is an invention—a device used by men to recruit women to the dubious cause of women's (re)subjugation to the rule of men. That men would need to resort to such a device, a culturally "feminine" conception as outlined above, supports Eggert's claim that this conception of "feminine" is inherently superior to the "masculine" in terms of power—what this conception of femininininity may lack in terms of the masculine characteristics of force and rigidity, it makes up for in its flexibility.[20] Eggert explains that such "feminine" poetic modes are more powerful than "masculine" ones in their ability to captivate and subdue. Radigund captivates Artegall to begin the digression with which Spenser captivates the "most" part of his audience.[21]

The first clue that the Isis Church episode is problematic involves Britomart's failure to persevere in the behavior that proved to be her salvation in her adventure at Dolon's house, where she stayed the night before her arrival at Isis Church. The prior day a seemingly kindly knight, Dolon, befriends her and asked if she needed lodgings for the night. When Britomart goes to her chamber for the evening, Dolon tries to persuade her to disarm before going to bed, but Britomart flatly refuses. She is being faithful to her solemn vow not to remove her armor until she wreaks revenge on Radigund:

> But She ne would vndressed be for ought,
> Ne doff her armes, though he her much besought.
> For she had vow'd, she said, not to forgo

Those warlike weedes, till she reuenge had wrought
Of a late wrong vppon a mortall foe;
Which she would sure performe, betide her wele or wo. (V.vi.23.4–9)

Not only does Britomart remain armed all night, she also remains awake. She refuses even to lie on the bed lest she be tempted to sleep—even though she does not yet have reason to be suspicious of Dolon. Towards morning, her innate watchfulness and care are repaid when Dolon's trick bed fails to plunge her to the dungeon. Thus,

. . . by God's grace, and her good heediness,
She was preserved from [Dolon's] traytrous traine.
Thus she all night wore out in watchfulnesse,
Ne suffred slothfull sleepe her eyelids to oppresse. (V.vi.34.6–9)

Not only is Britomart being faithful to her vow of not disarming in Dolon's house, she also shows that she learned a lesson from her Book III adventure in Castle Joyous, Malecasta's abode, where against her better judgment she disarmed and went to bed. That night Malecasta crept into her room and bed in her mistaken belief that Britomart was a male knight. In the uproar that ensues when Britomart awakes and discovers Malecasta, and Malecasta discovers her error, Britomart is wounded by one of Malecasta's knights, Gardante (III.i.20–67). His name suggests that the cause of Britomart's wound is sensual—it somehow involves sight. Britomart's weakness, apparently, is that she can be subdued by false appearance—by beautiful show, if she is not on her guard.[22]

In a subsequent adventure at the enchanter Busirane's house, Britomart keeps up her guard in spite of her astonishment at the beauty of Cupid's altar:

That wondrous sight faire *Britomart* amazed,
Ne seeing could her wonder satisfie,
But euermore and more vpon it gazed,
The whiles the passing brightness her fraile sences dazed. (III.xi.49.6–9)

But forewarned is forearmed—Britomart is saved from herself because the outward appearance of Busirane's house had put her on guard before she enterred:

But in the Porch, that did them sore amate,
A flaming fire, ymixt with stinking Sulphure, that with grisly hate

> And dreadfull horrour did all entraunce choke,
> Enforced them their forward footing to reuoke. (21.5–9)

Britomart knows in advance, by obvious signs, the peril of what lies within, however beautiful the interior vistas might appear. Nonetheless, her amazement at Cupid's altar in spite of her forewarning reveals a pronounced weakness in her to succumb to the captivating beauty of "fowle Idolotr[ous]" objects (49.5).

Upon her arrival at Isis Church, Britomart does not receive any forewarning of possible danger of the sort she received at Busirane's house. Consequently when she sees the beauty of Isis Church, she is unreservedly captivated by it—she fully and immediately lets down her guard. Her reaction is described in virtually the same terms as her previous reaction to Cupid's altar:

> She wondred at the workemans passing skill,
> Whose like before she neuer saw nor red;
> And thereupon long while stood gazing still,
> But thought, that she thereon could neuer gaze her fill. (Vvii.5.6–9)

Instead of taking care as she did the previous night at Dolon's house, Britomart quickly falls asleep at the very foot of Isis' altar, as though she hadn't a care in the world. Even worse than letting down her guard by falling asleep, she unlaces her helmet, thereby breaking her solemn oath not to do so until she defeats Radigund (V.vii.8.8). In sharp contrast to her conduct at Dolon's house the previous night, at Isis Church Britomart lowers her guard completely—her senses have been captivated by Isis Church's beauty. Consequently, if guile happens to be lurking in Isis Church as it was in Dolon's house, Britomart is defenseless against it.

The next indication that Britomart is not justified in letting down her guard against guile at Isis Church is that she is clearly entering a pagan temple. This should at least be a cause for concern given the clear parallel of her wakeful watch in Dolon's house to *Mark* 14.37–38, the passage relating Christ's three visits to his sleeping disciples (Hamilton 1977, 168, note to V.vi.25). Moreover, the fact that idol worship is practiced and an altar used at Isis Church should raise her guard in light of her experiences at Busirane's house with its altar to Cupid, and its "fowle Idolotree"[23] (III.xi.47.2,49.5; Stump 92). As Richard Hardin points out, the Isis Church setting is at least suspect, if not for its pagan qualities, then for its Catholic overtones. The "quality of the worship in the temple" is "heavily ritualistic, even idolatrous," and "the priests wear elaborate vestments 'linen robes with siver hemd,'" images reminiscent of "the old church" (Hardin 1992, 102).

Another clear indication that the Isis Church passage is problematic is that the reader is informed at the outset that the ancient world had invented—made up—the gods Isis and Osiris.

> Well therefore did the antique world inuent,
> That Iustice was a God of soueraine grace,
> And altars vnto him, and Churchs lent,
> And heauenly honours in the highest place;
> Calling him great *Osyris*, of the race
> Of th'old Aegyptian Kings, that whylome were; (V.vii.2.1–6)
>
> His wife was Isis, whom they likewise made
> A Goddesse of great power and souerainty,
> And in her person cunningly did shade
> That part of Iustice, which is Equity[.] (V.vii.3.1–4)

Whatever occurs in Isis Church is, I argue, at least initially suspect because of its pagan source, its idolatry and priests reminiscent of the "old church," and its fictional goddess. Also suspect, of course, is the product of these, the controlling power of equity, that the priest associates with Isis' control over Osiris. However, the "ornaments" of Isis Church have "beclouded" Britomart's reason, and she is no longer capable of noticing these things—she is completely captivated.[24]

The priest's 'divinely' inspired interpretation of Britomart's dream, not unexpectedly, is also dubious. The interpretation is at least as suspect as the religion that supposedly inspires it. The priest's association of the crocodile with Osiris and Artegall certainly appears forced.[25] In Britomart's dream the crocodile intended to kill her until Isis forcefully beats it back. This fact alone should cause Britomart to doubt the priest's interpretation. After its attempt to kill her using open force fails, the crocodile suddenly acts as though it is tamed:

> Tho turning all his pride to humblesse meeke,
> Him selfe before her feete he lowly threw,
> And gan for grace and loue of her to seeke: (V.vii.16.1–3)

Britomart should be doubly on guard now if she recalls that the crocodile originally stood for both "forged guile,/And open force" and that Isis needed continually to restrain it (V.vii.7.3–4). [26] A far more likely interpretation of the dream is that the crocodile, when its attempt to kill Britomart using open force fails, resorts to its other aspect, forged guile. With this it succeeds in piercing her, since she had voluntarily partially disarmed the previous night before falling asleep. Britomart accepts the crocodile's tender of love, and

> . . . he so neare her drew,
> That of his game she soone enwombed grew,
> And forth did bring a Lion of great might;
> That shortly did all other beasts subdew. (V.vii.16.4–7)

Britomart is impregnated by guile and also gives birth to it. Guile defeats arguably the best warrior in *The Faerie Queene,* just as the lion that Britomart gives birth to is able to defeat all other beasts. Britomart's initial reaction to her dream of being "dismayd through that so uvcouth sight" is the correct one (V.vii.16.9). The reassurance that Britomart feels after hearing the priest's interpretation—"she much was eased in her troublous thought"—is misplaced; she has been taken in by guile.

Because Britomart succumbs to guile, she unquestioningly accepts the chief priest's interpretation of equity as including a secret power of women to control men. Once Britomart accepts the identification of the crocodile with Osiris and Artegall, she also implicitly agrees with the interpretation that Isis—and she herself as Isis' counterpart—is able to control the crocodile by means of the controlling power of equity. According to the dream interpretation Isis and Britomart, by means of this power, literally over-rule Osiris and Artegall, both in a physically dominating sense, and in the sense that Osiris' and Artegall's decisions and judgments are subject to their modification. It is dubious whether there really is such a thing as the controlling power of equity; instead it appears to be an invention created the Isis priest who uses it to fool Britomart into acting on men's behalf to help preserve and maintain men's dominance over women. Certainly Britomart should take care before accepting the idea of a controlling power, since she learns about this secret power from a *man.*[27]

For the reasons I have just enumerated, I argue against the view that accepts the Isis Church passage uncritically. Britomart, I have shown, has let down her guard at Isis Church and is wholly to blame for the consequences. Rather than being cautious, she is amazed by the superficial beauty and craftsmanship of Isis Church: rather than staying awake and on guard, as she did at Dolon's house, she falls asleep: rather than remaining armed, as she vowed to do, she takes off her helmet: finally, rather than continuing to be alarmed at her dream, as is warranted, she uncritically accepts the chief priest's dubious, though reassuring, interpretation. By persuading Britomart of the controlling power of equity, the chief priest disempowers Britmomart, the premier woman warrior—one undefeated by any man, and simultaneously engages her in the men's cause of regaining male dominance over Radigund's realm, which dominance the women of that realm "had long vserpt" from men. Once Britomart is disempowered by her belief in the controlling power of equity, she disappears from the pages of *The Faerie Queene*. The priest has succeeded in getting Britomart to defeat Britomart—the feminine power of the beauty of Isis Church has captivated her, setting her up to be beguiled. As Eggert notes, feminine negates feminine, Britomart negates herself, and both depart the pages of *The Faerie Queene* without further ceremony (27).

Eggert has persuasively related these central Book V passages to the larger shift in poetics that she contends Spenser was attempting in *The Faerie Queene*—a shift from more feminine poetic modes such as romance, to more masculine ones, such as historical allegory or the history play. I have built upon her work by showing how the shift from feminine to masculine poetics impacts the narrative in Book V's central digressive passages, at least from the perspective of Spenser's division of equity along gender lines. I return now to the question of succession as I explore these passages to reveal Spenser's discreet way of addressing perhaps the premier political issue in 1590's England—one stemming from the crisis of women's rule—the problems and uncertainty posed by the Elizabethan succession.

An issue of immense—perhaps unparalleled—political consequence of the early and again the late years of Elizabeth's reign, especially from the late 1580's and early 1590's, was who would succeed her (Phillips 1941, 28). However, unauthorized publication on the succession question was muted because it had been outlawed by act of Parliament in 1571—effectively all publication on this topic was outlawed since none was in fact authorized (Hurstfield 1961, 371). Even earlier, in 1559, Elizabeth had issued an edict forbidding plays dealing with religion or politics—these "being no meet matters to be written or treated upon but by men of authority, learning, and wisdom, nor to be handled before any audience but of grave and discreet persons" (Cauthen xii).[28] The aim of the 1559 edict and the 1571 legislation

> was wholly to remove the question of royal lineage from discussion by subjects, since the discussion itself implied their capacity to render judgment on the legitimacy of monarchs, a dangerous contradiction of the

> Crown's self-representation as immune from all judgments except God's. (Lane 461–62)

Consequently Spenser's treatment of the succession question in *The Faerie Queene* needs to be discreet. It cannot be safely treated in obvious historical allegory like other issues in Book V such as the transparent parallel between Duessa's trial in Mercilla's court and the trial of Mary Queen of Scots in Elizabeth's. After all, James I immediately perceived this connection (Hamilton 1977, 281).[29] It should not be unduly surprising that the passage in *The Faerie Queene* dealing with the Elizabethan succession is not in the form of historical allegory, but in a more ambiguous "feminine" poetic mode like romance.

It is virtually unthinkable that Spenser failed to deal in some way with an issue of such magnitude somewhere in *The Faerie Queene*—probably in Book V, in which "the history of Spenser's own time has an especial importance" (Bieman 156). As William Nelson has noted, "the affairs of the nation play[] a larger role in the Legend of Justice than in the other books of the poem" (174–5). The likely place for Spenser to hide a veiled treatment of the Elizabethan succession would be in the heart of Book V, where it would not draw attention. I argue that the Isis Church and Britomart/Radigund episodes, containing the bulk of the digression at the heart of Book V, contain Spenser's major veiled treatment of the succession issue. As it happens, these passages occur surrounding both the bisection and arithmetic center of Book V (Fowler 45). In all likelihood Spenser consciously placed these passages in the middle of the book, in light of his well established concern with structure in *The Faerie Queene*[30] (Fowler xi, 3).

To appreciate the ingenious device Spenser fashions in these passages to comment on the succession issue, we need to review the key elements of the 1590's succession controversy. Moreover, because Spenser choose to address this controversy in the context of the sixteenth century crisis of women's rule, it will be necessary briefly to consider the three main positions on women's rule held by educated Englishmen during the second half of the sixteenth century.

As I mentioned earlier, Elizabeth prohibited public discussion of the succession. I also mentioned that there were several potential contenders to succeed Elizabeth—the line of succession was murky at best. The point I want to emphasize in this review of the succession possibilities is that of the three leading contenders for succeeding Elizabeth, two were women.

The three contenders were James Stuart, Mary's son, Arabella Stuart (James' English-born cousin), and the Spanish king's daugher, Isabella

Clara Eugenia, commonly referred to as the Infanta. There were serious, and in one case insurmountable difficulties with the claims to succession of each of these contenders. Consequently, the political backing of each contender's faction may ultimately have been more important than the actual merits of their respective claims. Certainly if Elizabeth chose to advance one of the viable claims over the others, that would weigh heavily, perhaps decisively, in the advancement of such a claim—though arguably Parliament ultimately was responsible for deciding the succession, as I explain below.

Parliament's responsibility for the matter in fact lay behind much of the succession controversy. In 1544 Parliament, under some duress from Henry VIII, made law the Succession Act pursuant to which Henry was "empowered to nominate heirs should his own children fail to produce offspring—as they did"[31] (Williams 383). In his will Henry VIII bypassed the succession that would have occurred pursuant to the Common Law—which would have directed the crown to James Stuart, after the death without issue of Henry's own children, Edward, Mary, and Elizabeth, since James was the oldest living descendant of Henry's eldest sister Margaret (Somerset 104). Instead, Henry's will designated that the crown would go to the descendants of his younger sister Mary. Mary's eldest living descendant Mary Grey, had died in 1578.

The problems with the succession claim of James Stuart gave rise to the claims of the other two contenders. James Stuart's succession claim faced three distinct problems. First, his line (deriving, as I said, from Henry VIII's elder sister Margaret) was specifically excluded from succession by Henry VIII's will; I will return to the problem of the will in a moment. Second, James was not born in England, and since foreigners couldn't inherit property in England, James couldn't succeed to the crown, or so argued the anti-James factions. This argument was far from conclusive, however, since the crown might be exempt from the inheritance prohibition—the position that ultimately prevailed (Somerset 104). Finally, James' claim was suspect because his mother, Mary Queen of Scots, had been convicted of treason, a circumstance that could be interpreted as automatically forfeiting James' claim.[32]

Arabella Stuart's succession claim derived from the fact that she was the oldest living relative of Henry VIII's older sister Margaret who happened to be born on English soil. On this basis, her supporters argued, her claim should be preferred over that of the foreign born James Stuart. Arabella's claim derived from Margaret Stuart's second marriage. Her father, Charles Stuart, was a grandchild of Margaret (Somerset 68, 561). However, since Arabella's claim derived from Henry VIII's older sister Margaret, she could only succeed if Henry's will was invalid. If Henry VIII's will was valid, her claim was clearly superior to James'. But, since Henry's will had been stamped rather than personally signed, it was technically invalid (Williams 384).

The claim of the Spanish Infanta, Phillip II's daugher, sidestepped both the Common Law succession issues and the difficulties of an inconsistently applied primogeniture theory, "in favour of a contractual theory of sovereignty" (Axton 92). This contractual theory, developed by Robert Doleman in the early 1590's, purported to trace the royal bloodline from the Norman Conquest forward (Axton 94). Doleman concluded that the Lancastrian royal bloodline flowed to the Spanish descendants of John of Gaunt, through his second wife, Constance of Castille[34] (Axton 92; Somerset 560). The Infanta's claim, in addition to appealing to Catholics, had the advantage of avoiding all of the problems of the other contenders' claims since the Infanta's claim was not Tudor-based.

I have considered the Elizabethan succession possibilities of the early 1590's in some detail in order to establish that Elizabeth would have had an eminently defensible position for advancing two of these claims—the Infanta's claim was not a genuine option given her Catholic faith. With a nod from Elizabeth, any one of the two viable claims would gain a tremendous, perhaps insurmountable advantage over the other. Spenser, I argue, was worried that Elizabeth might choose in favor of the female contender—a possibility in conflict with his views on the appropriate purpose and scope of women's rule.

Spenser's views on the women's rule issue were persuasively characterized by the pioneering work of James Phillips. Phillips argued that of the three main positions on women's rule which had developed since Mary Tudor's reign, Spenser subscribed to the "moderate" Puritan position of "Calvin and [Heinrich] Bullinger, and eventually, when he wished to reconcile with Elizabeth, by [John] Knox himself" (Phillips 1941, 211). The moderate Puritans disagreed with the Puritan extremists such as the early "Knox, Christopher Goodman, and George Buchanon . . . that, according to the laws of God, of nature, and of nations, women have neither the right nor the ability to rule" (Phillips 1941, 211). The moderate Puritans also rejected "the Anglican spokesmen for Elizabeth and [the] Catholic supporters of Mary Stuart[, both of which groups] maintained that women are qualified by nature to govern, and that any woman called upon by God has the right to do so" (211).

The moderates agreed generally with the extreme Puritans "that women in general are not [naturally] equipped to exercise political authority (211). The distinction between these two groups was that the moderate Puritans "claimed that God sometimes sees fit to endow certain exceptional women rulers with the necessary qualifications"[35] (211). According to Phillips:

> There are indications in *The Faerie Queene* that Edmund Spenser was familiar with the arguments in the controversy, and that he, too, considered the theoretical aspects of feminine government in connection with the specific individuals and incidents which he undoubtedly figures forth in the allegory of the poem. It should not be surprising to find evidence of the gynecocratic controversy in a work crowded with the figures of women rulers, and designed to live with the eternity of the fame of the chief representative of feminine sovereignty. (211)

The available evidence, both external and internal to *The Faerie Queene*, Phillips concludes, indicates "that Spenser adopted . . . the [moderate Puritan] position taken by Calvin, and after the succession of Elizabeth, by Knox" (213). It is no coincidence that the moderate Puritan position is the one publicly declared by Britomart as she reforms the Amazon nation in preparation for its return to male rule.[36] Britomart rules only because she is compelled to until Artegall is recovered and ready to assume power. Her rule is geared solely towards preparing the Amazon women for subjection to male rule. Britomart's actions and words in this passage suggest that she views women's rule such as her own as appropriate only in exceptional circumstances, like the one she finds herself in Radigund's realm, where the clearly recognized male ruling figure is temporarily incapacitated.

Spenser's treatment of the succession appears to be directed towards an exclusive category of gentlemen such as Sir William Raleigh and Lord Buckhurst—a category of men whose literary credentials and political acumen would enable them to appreciate the "ensample" of these episodes, and whose positions at court gave them the opportunity discreetly to influence the queen on the succession issue much as the Isis' priest influences Britomart.[37] Spenser discusses his audience in his 1589 Letter to Raleigh describing the plan of *The Faerie Queene*'s early books (Hamilton 1977, 737–38). In this letter Spenser divides his audience between "the most part" of men who "delight to read" for "variety of matters" and others—presumably the "least" part of men—who read for "profite of the ensample" (737).

Spenser emphasizes in this letter the significance of teaching and learning by "ensample;" he argues that "Xenophon [is to be] preferred before Plato," since Plato "formed a commune welth as it *should* be" (emphasis added). Xenophon, however, "fashioned a government such as *might best* be" (emphasis added). Spenser concludes "so much more profitable and gratious is doctrine by ensample, then by rule" (737). Navigating by what can actually be accomplished, according to Spenser, is to be preferred to taking course by what "should" be the case in an ideal world, but which can never be realized in actuality. The "ensample" of the central Book V episodes is concerned with the Elizabethan succession and its object is regime change—a shift from nearly a half-century of women's rule in England back to rule by men.[38]

The character of the change in regime envisioned by Spenser, I suggest, is neither dramatic nor violent. It involves a select group of men close to Elizabeth simply nudging her in a direction towards which she is probably already inclined. After all, the moderate Puritan position on women's rule, the position Elizabeth herself is thought to have endorsed, requires the transfer of power to a male successor once any incapacities the male might be under have been overcome—precisely as Britomart transferred power to Artegall once he recovered.

Spenser has provided a template—an "ensample"—for how these gentlemen might want to proceed. There is certainly precedent for suggesting that women's real power is of the sort hidden and exercised behind the scenes.[39] Be this as it may, there was probably no expectation on Spenser's part, or on the part of his select audience, that Elizabeth would surrender power to James during her lifetime. Certainly there is no historical evidence for this, and Elizabeth's experiences of the 1550's would clearly argue against her doing so. Spenser's poem implicitly counters the possibility that an aged Elizabeth might advance the claims of one of the female contenders for the throne.

In conclusion I want to point out that both Spenser and More appear to possess a profound understanding of equity, its derivation from the Greek *επιείκεια*, and its relation to justice. Their specific treatments of equity seem quite different because of the distinct narrative contexts and modes of their works. However, both of their treatments reveal an appreciation for equity's conceptual status as an intermediary between the unattainable ideal of the perfect, though unachievable best political regime, and the best regime achievable in practice. Their respective treatments can even be reconciled to some extent. More's *Utopia*, as I have argued, is concerned with the application of the *conception* of an ideal regime to practice; it does not advocate the realization of the ideal regime itself. Instead, the object is to move existing regimes in the direction of the ideal regime, while acknowledging that there will always be a gap between the two. Spenser's forthright rejection of the ideal regime as a goal does not necessarily rule out the possible use of the *conception* of the ideal regime in efforts to improve existing regimes.

At the more practical jurisprudential level, Spenser's treatment of equity reflects his awareness of the tremendous changes that had been occurring between his time and More's (and partially predicted by More)—changes reflected in the way equity was becoming the centerpiece in the controversy between the Crown and Parliament (as reflected in the tension between the Common Law courts and the Chancery court over Chancery's equity jurisdiction)—a controversy that would eventually lead to the tumult of 1642 and beyond.

Afterword

A front page *New York Times* article reported in 2003 that

> The 400 wealthiest taxpayers accounted for more than 1 percent of all the income in the United States in the year 2000, more than double their share just eight years earlier, according to new data from the Internal Revenue Service. But their tax burden plummeted over the period.
>
> . . .
>
> The data, in a report that the I.R.S. released last night, shows that the average income of the 400 wealthiest taxpayers was almost $174 million in 2000. That was nearly quadruple the $46.8 million average in 1992 ("Very Richest's Share of Wealth Grew Even Bigger, Data Show." *New York Times*, June 26, 2003, p.A1).

This trend reflects to some extent the capital gains tax cut from 28 percent to 20 percent in 1997.[1] The further reduction of that tax to 15 percent in 2003 only amplified this effect.

The current political situation in the United States appears to be aggravating the situation.

> Supporters of President Bush's tax plan don't deny that it offers little if any immediate benefit to the poorest Americans. Nor is there much doubt that the wealthiest would see the greatest gains. Yet meaningful discussion of the potential widening of inequality—the polarizing of rich and poor—has been sadly lacking ("Efficiency and Equity (In the Same Breath)" *New York Times*, April 20, 2003, Business Section, p. 4).

Another factor widening the margin between the wealthiest and poorest Americans is the initiative to eliminate the estate tax. This initiative led in 2001 to the passage of President Bush's "tax relief" bill that included the gradual phase out of the estate tax until its complete elimination for one year in 2010. It would then automatically return to 2001 levels with the sunset of the 2001 tax relief bill provisions. On Wednesday July 18, 2003 the United States House of Representatives voted 264–163 to permanently repeal the estate tax. On Wednesday April 13, 2005, an updated bill was passed 272 to 162. The United States Senate is scheduled to consider the bill during the spring or fall 2006 sessions.

While the estate tax repeal is currently quite popular in the conservative political sphere—it has become a keynote for Republican tax reform policy—its effect of enlarging the wealth gap in the United States should at least cause political conservatives to pause. Another compelling reason to pause is the relation of wealth disparity to civil unrest. This association is noted by such eminent thinkers as Plato, Aristotle, Thomas More, and Guillaume Budé. In fact, Plato and Aristotle go so far as to suggest that wealth disparity is the most significant factor leading to civil unrest. If the ultimate objective of conservatives is to "conserve" the status quo, then they also have a vested interest in acting to reduce the causes of civil unrest. While the repeal of the estate tax may appear to be beneficial in the short run—especially in financial terms—in the long run it could be disastrous. Fortunately, some wealthy Americans have a more long-term perspective on this issue.

On Sunday, February 18, 2001 the *New York Times* published on its editorial page a petition from an organization called "Responsible Wealth" opposing ongoing political initiatives, including proposed legislation to repeal the United States' estate tax (this petition is reproduced on the following page). Remarkably, the signatories to the petition included some of the nation's wealthiest individuals—persons whose families could certainly be expected to benefit financially from the repeal of the estate tax. The key point in the petition is that the repeal of the estate tax "would leave an unfortunate legacy for America's future generations" because it would "enrich America's millionaires and billionaires while hurting families who struggle to make ends meet."

The petition signatories resemble closely the "equitable" persons referred to in Plato's *Laws* and Aristotle's *Ethics* and *Politics* who work over the course of generations to reduce the likelihood of civil unrest by reducing the extent of disparities in wealth. They are willing to "be satisfied with less than [their share] even though [they have] the law on [their] side" (*Ethics* 1138a). The signatories are willing to forego the apparent benefit of reduced estate taxes even though they would be legally entitled to it. Also like the equitable, as defined by Aristotle, the modern signatories are taking into account consequences for their regime that span many generations.

One noteworthy difference is that the modern signatories, unlike Aristotle's equitable persons, are *publicly* advocating for their position. Aristotle's equitable persons needed to work discreetly to accomplish their goal—their efforts either had to be hidden from public view, or explained away in altruistic terms. Exposure involved personal risk. The fact that the petition

If the estate tax is eliminated, someone else will pay.

YOU.

LET'S FIX THE ESTATE TAX, NOT REPEAL IT.

We believe that repeal of the estate tax would be bad for our democracy, our economy, and our society. Repealing the estate tax, a constructive part of our tax structure for 85 years, would leave an unfortunate legacy for America's future generations.

Only the richest 2 percent of our nation's families currently pay any estate tax at all. Repealing the estate tax would enrich the heirs of America's millionaires and billionaires while hurting families who struggle to make ends meet.

The billions of dollars in lost state and federal revenues will inevitably be made up either by increasing taxes on those less able to pay or by cutting Social Security, Medicare, environmental protection, and other government programs so important to our nation's continued well-being.

The estate tax exerts a powerful and positive effect on charitable giving. Repeal would have a devastating impact on public charities ranging from institutions of higher education and land conservancies to organizations that assist the poor and disadvantaged.

We recognize the importance of protecting America's family farms and small businesses, and the estate tax has many special provisions that do so. This concern—the rationale usually advanced for eliminating the estate tax—can be addressed by amending the existing estate tax system.

William H. Gates, Sr. • Steven C. Rockefeller • David Rockefeller, Jr. • George Soros • Agnes Gund • Henry and Edith Everett • Peter Barnes • Richard and Jing Lyman • Robert E. Cook • George and Jane Russell • Eileen Rockefeller Growald • Frank and Jinx Roosevelt • Paul Newman • and more than 200 other signers

Call or visit our website and sign the statement showing your support for the estate tax.

RESPONSIBLE WEALTH
A Project of United for a Fair Economy

37 Temple Place, 2nd floor, Boston, MA 02111 (617) 423-2148 **www.responsiblewealth.org**

Op Ed section only
Sunday 02/18

Responsible Wealth "Estate Tax" Job Number: **6301**
Colors: **B&W** Ad Size: **quarter page 6.25" x 10.25"**
Pub: **The New York Times** Material Specs: **0**
Insertion Date: **02/18/01** Local Contact: **Jon Jackson**
Shipping Address: **The New York Times, COF/Team D - 6th Floor, 229 West 43rd St, New York, NY 10036**
telephone: **212.556.1167**

Prepared by Underground Advertising • Pier 9, #116, San Francisco, CA 94111
415.433.9334 • www.undergroundads.com

signatories are publicly stating their position and seeking support for it is, in my view, a very hopeful sign for modern liberal democracy.[2] Another hopeful sign is that the petition signatories unwittingly are applying a critical lesson of equity from classical political thought, one which Thomas More unsuccessfully attempted to transfer into the early modern era.

In any event, the contemporary debate over whether the estate tax should be repealed highlights the practical contemporary value of my reexamination of the classical and Renaissance roots of equity. My study provides a solid theoretical foundation for the efforts of the petition signatories; it also provides a touchstone for nominal conservatives to assess what is really in their long-term self-interest.

A significant hurdle remains, I think, before this lesson from classical political thought will be taken seriously. This hurdle involves the continuing pervasive appeal of cold-war anti-communist rhetoric, even in a post cold-war era. We must learn to reappreciate the value of the texts of the great political thinkers of the past—even the ones that seem to sympathize with or promote communism as an ideal—to reap the benefits of the practical applications of their thoughts. In light of liberal democracy's apparent victory in the cold-war against communism, we can afford to be magnanimous and reassess even ideas that continue to seem obnoxious to many. For both profound Christian thinkers like Thomas More as well as for persons who continue to take seriously the arguments of classical political thought, like the American founders, "communism" meant something more than is encompassed by its recent history and stereotypes. Communism represented a social ideal we might usefully reconsider, not as a practical objective, but as a kind of touchstone to consult—in an appropriately delicate manner—when addressing political matters.

Appendix A

Equity in Hobbes' *Leviathan*

EQUITY AND THE ORIGINS OF INEQUALITY IN CHAPTER 15 OF HOBBES' *LEVIATHAN*

Political philosophers and theorists have struggled continuously with how to justify property ownership in civil society, particularly gross disparities in quantity and/or quality of ownership. Particularly problematic is determining how to persuade purportedly equal persons, at the stage of the initial contract which initiates civil society, that they should agree to enter a civil society with the foreknowledge that it will contain such disparities. After all, why should anyone willingly agree at the outset that someone else may be justified in having more than oneself? Hobbes deals with this issue in chapter 15 of his *Leviathan* in the context of rather perplexing discussions of "equity" and "equality" amongst persons. In these discussions Hobbes sets forth the principles of property distribution amongst the "equal" persons forming civil society. But in doing so, he purposefully presents conflicting accounts of both "equity" and "equality." Hobbes then fails to resolve the conflicts, at least upon the surface of the text. Instead, he invites those of his readers who recognize and wish to resolve these conflicts to meditate deeply on the contrasting passages and upon the relationship of equity and equality in his system.[1]

This appendix will show that Hobbes' discrepant presentations of both "equity" and "equality" in chapter 15 of *Leviathan* are in fact connected. The discrepancies are designed to persuade persons of extraordinary ability to enter into a civil society commencement pact containing principles of nearly absolute equality amongst the compacting parties. Hobbes "quietly" assures these extraordinary persons that the civil society so founded will in fact recognize their extraordinary status; this civil society will not only allow inequalities to exist, but will also require of its arbitrators and judges that they recognize the extraordinary status of some society members and take such inequalities into account when interpreting law and determining disputes.

Why Hobbes chooses the term "equity" to play such an important role in *Leviathan* appears to be related to the evolution of the concept of equity in the English Renaissance, which I discussed in Chapter One, an evolution which culminates in the political sphere in Francis Bacon's fashioning of the concept as a tool or reflection of raw sovereign power.[2] For present purposes let it suffice that Hobbes transforms the term from its accepted meaning and use in sixteenth and early seventeenth century England to an extent equal or greater than the transformation to his own purpose of the term "natural law."

The natural law in which Hobbes deals with "equity," the eleventh, is central among the fifteen secondary laws of nature set forth in Chapter 15 of *Leviathan*. [3] This is the second time Hobbes defines the term. The first definition of equity occurs earlier in chapter 15, in the extensive discussion of the third natural law, which deals with justice. Here Hobbes discusses equity as he attempts to distinguish the sort of justice called for in *Leviathan* from the Aristotelian conceptions of "commutative" and "distributive" justice. It is in apparent opposition to this latter notion that Hobbes constructs his first definition of equity. Aristotle, he notes, means by distributive justice, the distribution of "equall benefit, to men of equall merit" (15:14). Hobbes objects, insisting that "merit" in an inherent sense is beside the point, having previously shown (13:1–3) that men, in all essential respects, are equal, and are indistinguishable on the basis of inherent merit. Hobbes instead asserts that merit results from grace; what is commonly perceived as the giving of benefits based on "merit," in fact should be conceived as the rendering of something as a "free gift and not [an] obligation" (Raphael 1988, 166). In this context then, Hobbes defines equity as the act of the arbitrator or judge in distributing "to every man his own" (15:15). Presumably, if all persons are equal in all relevant respects, the distribution to which he alludes will also partake of this equality.

Before turning to the contrasting definition of equity in the eleventh natural law, and comparing it with the original version in the third natural law, we must observe what happens to Hobbes' seemingly rigid principle of equality in the intervening discussions of his ninth and tenth natural laws.[4] The shift that occurs here respecting equality purposefully sheds light on the immediately following shift to the meaning of equity. The ninth natural law is framed as an injunction against pride,[5] and provides *"[t]hat every man acknowledge other for his Equall by Nature"* (15:21)(emphasis in original); the tenth natural law is integrally related and enjoins arrogance, which consists of a man's insistence in reserving "*to himselfe[at the entrance into conditions of peace,] any Right, which he is not content should be reserved to every one of the rest*" (15:22)(emphasis in original). The problem with such a reservation, of course, is that it would violate the ninth natural law "that commandeth the acknowledgment of naturall equalitie" (Ibid.). Thus the "sin" of arrogance necessarily involves and encompasses the *lesser* "sin" of pride, and at root both relate to the problem of someone of extraordinary ability objecting to the equality principle in the terms of the peace, without which principle peace and civil society will not be achieved.[6]

The sensitive point Hobbes avoids here is set forth with remarkable clarity in the discussion of the ninth natural law, and consists of an express acknowledgment, in the form of an alternative argument, that some men may not be equal.[7] Addressing such persons, he states: "if Nature have made men unequall; yet because men that think themselves equall, will not enter into conditions of Peace, but upon Equall termes, such equalitie must be admitted" (15:21). It is imperative that persons of extraordinary ability assent to the fiction of their inequality, since only in civil society can they be adequately compensated.[8] And the only way to get others to agree to enter into civil society is to persuade them that all parties to the compact acknowledge equality, and that distribution of benefits, including personal property will be based upon the equality principle.[9] But the assent of persons of extraordinary ability will not occur unless they can be assured they will be unequally compensated, and such assurance cannot be explicitly contained in the terms of the original peace; in fact, its terms must on the surface oppose unequal compensation. The dilemma becomes, there can be no peace without an assent to equality by all, but those of extraordinary ability won't assent to this fiction unless they can be persuaded that the equality principle of the civil society to which they are agreeing to enter will in practice allow them to be unequally compensated for their abilities.

Hobbes' solution to this dilemma involves redefining—or at least clarifying—what he means by equity. After raising the equality problem in the ninth and tenth natural laws, Hobbes immediately turns to equity in the eleventh natural law and, without explanation, presents a different formulation of equity than in the third natural law. Instead of having the arbitrator or judge distribute "to every man his own," Hobbes now asserts that it is the arbitrator or judge's job to "*deale Equally between them*" (15:23)(emphasis added). This formulation, at first glance, appears simply to clarify the earlier definition and to ensure that a radical equality applies to the equitable distribution of benefits. But Hobbes adds a transformative qualification when he notices that "[*dealing*] *Equally between them*" requires, "the equall distribution to each man, of that which in reason belongeth to him" (15:24) (emphasis in original). Hobbes' revised definition of equity provides to the persons of extraordinary ability the assurances they need that Hobbesian civil society, in practice, will recognize and compensate their unequal abilities in unequal fashion.[10]

Hobbes does not explicitly explain the distinction he is making. Such an explanation would prevent people from assenting to the peace pact at the outset. Any assurances of inequality must be obscure, and are intended to be noticed only by the persons of extraordinary ability themselves and, once the pact is in place, by the arbitrators and judges. Later in *Leviathan*, in the chapter dealing with "Civill Lawes," Hobbes makes clear that the arbitrator or judge must "meditate" most carefully on "that principall law of nature called *Equity*" in order to obtain a "*right understanding*" thereof. (26:27)(emphasis in original). And the first thing they must notice is the remarkable rise in the stature of equity—by chapter 26 it has become the "principall law of nature." To determine why, the arbitrator or judge would naturally turn to the discussion of equity in chapter 15. These arbitrators or judges would find the two discrepant version of equity there. This in turn would cause them to determine how equity interacts with the equality principle, and eventually would compel them to consult the qualifications about equality set forth in the discussion of the ninth natural law. Then, presumably, they would appreciate how equity and equality interact, and realize the origin, place and role of inequality in Hobbesian civil society.

Appendix B[1]

Hugonis Grotii de Aequitate, Indulgentia et Facilitate

LIBER SINGULARIS
CAPUT I. DE AEQUITATE

Cum Justitia (universalis dicta) in legum observatione consistat, cum qua aequitas maxime pugnare videtur, ut & indulgentia atque facilitas: haec quomodo inter se convenient & distinguantur, viro bono & inprimis[2] jurisconsulto intelligere necessarium est.

Hugo Grotius
On Equity, *Indulgentia* and *Facilitas*

CHAPTER I: ON EQUITY

Since justice, taken as a whole, consists in following the law[3], and since equity, *indulgentia* and *facilitas* appear to be at war with law, it is therefore necessary, first of all, to understand in what ways good men consider these terms to be similar and in what ways different, especially by those good men who are learned in law.

Et ut de aequitate primum loquamur, ejusque *homonymias* evitemus, scire oportet, aequitatem aut aequum de omni interdum jure dici, ut cum jurisprudentia ars boni & aequi dicitur: interdum de jure naturali absolute, ut cum Cicero ait, jus legibus, moribus & aequitate constare; alias vero de hisce rebus, quas lex non exacte definit, sed arbitrio viri boni permittit: saepe etiam de jure aliquo civili propius ad jus naturale accedente, idque respectu alterius juris, quod paulo longius recedere videtur, ut jus Praetorium, & quaedam jurisprudentiae interpretationes.

In order to speak first about equity,[4] and avoid its homonyms,[5] we ought to know that it is said of all right,[6] from time to time: it is said to be equitable and fair,[7] just as jurisprudence is said to be the art of what is both good and fair. Sometimes this is also said absolutely about natural law,[8] as when Cicero says right consists in law, custom and equity. But at other times, with respect to those things which the law does not define exactly, it is said that a good man can determine these at his discretion. Often too, something of the civil law[9] itself appears to move closer to natural law, and other legal systems have [for a little while] been seen to move a little further away from it, as is the case with the praetorian law,[10] and certain interpretations of jurisprudence.

Proprie vero & singulariter aequitas est virtus voluntatis, correctrix ejus in quo lex propter universalitatem deficit.

Aequum autem est id ipsum, quo lex corrigitur. Nominis sui originem a Graecis traxit, qui [eikos], Dorice vero [aikos] dixere, id est, quod aliqui congruit, ac respondet. Cum enim inaequalibus idem non possit esse aequale, res autem saepe sunt inaequales, lex vero una semper atque eadem; necessario consequitur, alia virtute opus esse, quae inaequalibus rebus suam cuique aequalitatem praestet, unde haec virtus [aequitas] latinis, graecis vero [epieikeia] dicitur.

Equity, rightly and specifically understood, is a virtue of will, which corrects that which law lacks on account of its universality.

Equalness is the means by which law is corrected. The Greeks originally called this means *eikos*, but in Doric it is called *aikos*; because it suits and answers to some certain situation. Although things often are unequal, since the same thing cannot be equal to unequal things, the law is always one and the same. Consequently, it is necessary that there is some virtue which provides its own equality to unequal things, which virtue is called by the Latins *aequitas*, and by the Greeks *επιείκεια*.

Est porro voluntatis habitus, non intellectus: graecis enim intelligendi virtus, id quod aequum est, *εὐγνωμοσύνη* dicitur, latinis autem aequi prudentia vertitur, quae sese ita ad aequitatem habet, ut jurisprudentia ad justitiam.

Equity is a disposition of will, not of intellect: for the Greeks the virtue of the intellect, that which is called equalness, is called *eugnomosyne*.[11] The Latins mean by it knowledge of equalness. Equalness has the same relation to equity, as jurisprudence has to justice.

Esse autem hanc virtutem necessariam, ita colligitur: quoniam vaga & lubrica hominum ingenia ad eum finem, quo vera natura ducit, dirigi non possent, nisi artis quibusdam regulit, quae ex naturae ipsius principiis desumerentur: eae autem regulae ad coercendos homines cum finitae esse deberent, ipsa autem rerum atque actionum materia infinita sit, sequebatur multa saepe occurrere, quibus illae regulae non satis congruerent. In quibus oportuit non regulam, sed ejus qui regulam dedisset mentem atque propositium sequi, id quod erat omnia dirigere ex principiis naturae; unde ad ipsa naturae principia recurrendum fuit, ut ita ex infinito suppleretur, quod finito deerat: perfecta enim norma rei infinitae finita esse non potest. Quo pertinet, quod philosophi & jurisconsulti dixere, leges, non his, quae nunquam accidere possunt, sed illis, quae plerumque accidunt, aptari.

The reason that the virtue of equalness is necessary is because the aimless and slippery characters of men cannot be directed to that end to which true nature leads, except by certain artificial rules, derived from the beginnings of nature itself. Although these rules for coercing men must have limits, the actual circumstances and actions to which they must be applied are infinite. It followed that many things often occur, to which those limited rules could not be fitted. In these circumstances it was necessary not to follow the rule, but to determine the mind and purpose of the lawgiver, which we know was to derive all rules from the beginnings of nature. It was necessary to return to the beginnings of nature itself so that that which the [necessarily] finite [rules] lacked could be supplied by the infinite. For the finished standard for infinite things cannot be finite. Because of this the following pertains, as the philosophers and experts in law have said: laws are fitted to things which usually happen, not to those things which can never happen.

Legem ergo cum dicimus (quae aequitatis objectum est) late ejus vocem sumimus, & non tantum constitutiones civiles, sed & ipsas juris gentium atque ipsius naturae notitias comprehendimus, quae etsi nec scripto, nec jure proprie constant, universaliter tamen concipiuntur, ut: reddendum depositum: neque enim locum habet in furioso ensem reposcente.

Therefore, when we speak of law which is the object of equity, we apply the term broadly, not only about civil constitutions, but we also include the concepts of the gentile law[12] and the law of nature themselves, although they do not consist of written [law], nor do they consist exclusively of right; nevertheless these concepts are conceived of universally, so that, a sword being left in trust, it should not be surrendered, though its rightful owner demands it back, if he is mad.

Quin illa etiam, quae Deus extra ordinem vetat aut praecipet, comprehendere non dubitamus: quia is defectus, quem aequitas corrigit, non semper est ex defectu auctoris, quanquam is in humanis legibus plerumque concurit; sed ex defectu materiae, quae certae & definitae regulae non est capax. Unde etiam Dei leges ex notitiis naturae impressis ab ipso Deo supplere minime absurdum est, ut cum dicitur: non occides, supplebimus, nisi tuendae vitae, aut publicae animadversionis causa.

Rather, we readily [employ this all encompassing broad interpretation of a law subject to equity], except in cases where God specifically forbids or requires something. Law and equity mostly exist in a state of conflict in human law, and as law is the defective part, equity corrects it. But, this defect in law is not the result of fault on the part of the lawgiver, but rather a defect in the nature of law, which is not capable of certain and fixed rules. However, since God's laws are imprinted in nature by God himself, it is foolish to try to add anything to them, as when it is said we will make complete the prohibition against killing by excepting cases of self defense and public execution.

Sed prima naturae principia, & quae leges virtutem ponunt, nihil nisi vitium tollunt, aequitatem non recipiunt: illa, quia id quod suppletur necesse est legibus praestantioribus suppleri; principia autem prima naturae leges sunt praestantissimae, ut: Deum esse colendum, atque amandum. Hae vero leges, quia virtutes ipsae, vitia infinita, propter universalitatem non deficiunt, ut: non moechaberis, non furaberis, vivendum pie, honeste, sobrie.

The first principles of nature which will never allow adjustment by equity [are those which require us to] worship and love God. [The laws associated with this] are absolute, such as "thou shall not commit adultery or steal," and "you must live a pious, honest, moral life."

Caeterum & ad leges inferiorum potestatum, & ad patrum, maritorum, dominorum imperia, ad vota etiam, pacta, & testamenta aequitas pertinet: idque dupliciter, aut enim verba atque conceptus jubentium, voventium, paciscentium, testantium corrigit, prout casus ex ipsorum praesumta mente poscit: aut etiam cum mens expressa est, legem ipsam, qua jussa, vota, pacta, testamenta servari jubentur, restringit ex superioribus. Prioris exemplum est: promisit quidam constituto die, certo loco adesse: si tempestas obest, aequitas supplet id, quod pacto deest. Si pactum est, ne quis de dolo teneatur, lex ipsa, quae pactum servare jubet, exceptionem patitur.

But, equity relates to laws of lesser authority, as well as to the rule of fathers, husbands and lords, and to agreements, wills and vows. In addition, on two accounts, it reforms both words and conceptions of ordering, contracting, and bequeathing, just as it requires of events something which the intention takes for granted. And even when the intention is clear, equity (from its superiority) restrains the law itself, whereby orders, vows, agreements and wills are ordered to observe it. An example of this is if someone undertakes to be present for a special purpose, on a certain agreed upon day, and at agreed upon place, and weather prevents him from coming there, equity makes complete that by which he falls short of the agreement. So even in the case where an agreement is recognized as [legal and binding] by all persons free from guile, even then, the law, which itself orders the observation of the agreement, allows an exception.

Cum autem aequitas frequentissime circa leges poenales versetur, falluntur qui putant leges semper ita aequitate corrigi, ut poena minuatur, cum etiam aequitate intendi illae possint. Ut si lex sit de homicidii praescriptione post vicennium, excipiemus parricidium, & augebuntur legum supplicia ob circumstantias delictum gravantes, aut quia delictis grassantibus severiori exemplo opus est.

Equity is most frequently used [in relation to] the penalties associated with law. They are deceived who think that the law's shortcomings are always corrected by equity diminishing the penalty; it is also possible that equity will increase the penalty. So if after 20 years an objection arises to a homicide law, we will set it aside in the case of parricide, and the punishment for this crime will be increased [either] because of its aggravating circumstances, or because it is necessary to set [a harsher] example of such a crime.

Correctionem cum dicimus ejus, in quo ob universalitatem lex deficit, primum excludimus eas leges, quae inhonestum quid praecipiunt simpliciter, aut id, quod ex officio necessario faciendum est, vetant. Si dubitatio oriatur, quum tota lex, sumta secundum mentem claram legislatoris, pugnat cum lege naturae, an non hic quoque aequitas locum habeat? Nullus defectus ex universalitate est, sed sequenda lex hoc casu: quamquam enim de legis justitia dubitatur, non tamen & hoc dubitatur, an in dubio valere debeat legis autoritas, quod quidem perquam durum est, sed, ita lex scripta est, inquit Jurisconsultus; & plerumque habet aliquid ex iniquo omne magnum exemplum, quod adversus singulos utilitate publica pensatur. Contra has enim, cum vim obligandi non habeant, aequitatis remedio opus non est. Ostendimus praeterea eorum, quae in lege obscure dicta sunt, interpretationem aut productionem lege ad casus similes.

When we say that it is a correction of what the law lacks on account of its universal statement, we first set aside those laws which plainly deter dishonest acts, as well as those things which these laws are duty bound to forbid. Moreover, if doubt should arise when a law is taken according to the distinct understanding of the legislators, shouldn't equity have a role [even here], when a law fights with the law of nature? In the following case, [however], the law must be followed whether or not it is defective on account of its universal statement: in the case where the justice of a law is doubted, but its authority is not; while this result is quite harsh, such is the nature of written law according to the lawyer. Typically, every great example [of law] has something unfair [about it], which opposition [to fairness] is weighed separately, case by case—the unfairness counterbalanced by [a law's] public usefulness. These examples have no need of an equity remedy, since they are [applied case by case, and are] not binding [as precedent]. We explain obscure laws, [in terms of] how to interpret and apply such laws, by referring to [the way other laws are interpreted and applied to] similar cases.

Sit autem haec correctio, non tollendo legis obligationem, sed declarando legem in certo casu non obligare: quod si apparet, nemo ad contraria obligari potest. Unde leges, quae ipsa intentione pugnant, altera per alteram necessario abrogatur. Sit autem interdum, ut non intentione, sed casu pugnent, quam *ek peristaseos nomon machen* graeci vocant: quod ubi sit, necessario in illo casu lex una per alteram exceptionem patitur. Ut, augur collegam coram populo nominet: damnatus publico judicio, cum populo ne agat: si augur damnatus sit, addetur priori legi exceptio ex posteriori. Unde sequitur, omnes leges, quae aliquo casu inter se committi possunt, ita subordinatas esse, ut altera alteri cedat: quae autem cedere debeat, facile definiri non potest, sed hoc ipsum e naturalibus principiis pendet, quae docent, fortiorem esse legem jubentem permittente: vetantem jubente: poenalem non poenali: generali particularem; statim implendam, ea quae moram patitur: imprimis vero pertinentem ad majora, pertinenti ad minora: ita in legibus, etiam divinis, cedunt spectantes ad proximum, spectantibus ad Deum: ceremoniales moralibus: & in humanis legibus eae quae ad privatam utilitatem pertinent, iis quae ad publicam; unde lex ad reddendum depositum, exceptionem patitur in depositore, cujus bona publicata sunt; & lex, capitalia crimina morte punienda esse, intelligenda est, nisi magna pars populi, aut unus populo admodum & summopere necessarius peccaverit.

However, there is this [type of] amendment, which does not address the law's power to bind, but which instead declares law to be non-binding in certain cases. If this amendment is supplied, no one can be bound to the contrary. Whence it is necessary for one or another of these laws to be repealed, when they [begin to] fight with their intentions. Sometimes, however, there are laws that don't fight with their intentions, but with the event itself, from the particular circumstances, a conflict,[13] as the Greeks say: which, when this happens, it is necessary that the law exempts one or another. Thus, if a seer appoints a colleague in the presence of the people, and if this seer acts against the people's wishes and is condemned in a public trial, then, if he is convicted, his earlier appointment will be reversed. Whence it follows, all laws which can be linked together by some event, so [that these laws are] subordinate to the event, [face the difficulty that] some laws must yield to others, but which must yield to which is unclear. This difficulty is resolved [when] the beginnings of nature are considered, since all laws teach yielding to the stronger commanding law. Consequently,

a. a command yields to a prohibition;
b. that which is not concerned with punishment yields to that which is;
c. the general yields to the particular;
d. that which permits delay yields to that which must be done at once;
e. that which pertains to the smaller yields to that which pertains to the greater;
f. those looking at nearby human things yield to those looking at god;
g. ceremony yields to morality; and
h. in human law, that which pertains to the private utility yields to that which pertains to the public utility.

Whence an exception is allowed in the case of a deposit, which the law requires to be returned [upon demand of its owner]; this exception is the public good. Moreover, the law which provides the punishment of death for a capital crime [cannot apply when] the majority of people either [commit this crime], or when only one person [commits it] when that person's actions are completely and exceedingly unavoidable.

Idem sic quoque probatur: vis obligandi, ut in pactis ita in lege neque ex scriptura, neque ex verbis proficiscitur, sed ex ipsa mente & voluntate. Vult autem nemo contraria, & legislatoris voluntas fuit, ut omnes observarentur, quatenus fieri potest; noluit ergo legislator suam valere, ubi exceptionem lex altera suppeditat, & consequenter eo casu non obligabit. Unde recte a nonnullis dictum est: aequi esse hominis non legem, sed legislatorem respicere. Hac de causa jus strictum quatenus opponitur aequitati, jus esse negamus, sed ita dici aequivoce, ut hominem pictum, hominem dicimus. Opponitur ergo aequitas stricto huic juri, ut bonum malo. Eo autem juri, quod lex ipsa dictat, in casibus non excipiendis opponitur, ut bonum diversum bono, & bonum bono melius.

Thus, this is also proven to be good: the binding force of contracts and law proceeds not from the writing or the words [themselves], but from the intention and sense. But, all is observed, in so far as it can be, in accordance with the intent of the legislator, and no one wishes otherwise. Therefore, the legislator will not act if the law provides for an exception; he is not obligated to. Whence many rightly say that a law is not the work of a just man unless it provides for an exception. From this cause, to the extent strict right is set against equity, we deny [it] to be right [in a larger sense], but with equal voice it is said that it is just [in a narrow sense], in the same way we call a man's portrait, a man. Therefore, equity is opposed to this strict right in the same way good is by evil. But, in cases where no exception opposes [the application of the law], there law states what is [truly] right, as where a lesser good is not opposed by a [greater], and where a greater good is not opposed by a [lesser] good.

Restat videre, quibus personis aequitate uti conveniat. Nos eam, cum justitiae pars sit, omnibus & cuivis convenire posse non dubitamus adhibita tantum distinctione.

It remains to be seen what people should be allowed to resort to equity. We do not doubt, that when law is a part of justice [in a larger sense], everyone can unite by applying such a distinction [between law and equity].

Aut enim evidens est exceptio, qua lex suppletur, ut in lege hac: cives omnes ad comitatum veniant: exceptio, nisi morbus impediat: & haec exceptio tum fieri potest a privato, tum a judice, si judicanda veniat.

The exception is clear by which law is made complete in this case: when all citizens are required to attend an assembly, an exception will be made in the case where someone cannot attend because disease prevents him: in such a case a judge can make such an exception, if he is so empowered.

Aut dubia est exceptio, quia ambiguum est, utrum aequius, utrumve publico utilius sit, legis verba sequi, aut non sequi. Sed iterum distinguendum: aut enim res moram patitur aut non: si non patitur moram, faciet privatus id, quod in re dubia recte ratiocinando aequius & melius inveniet; ita tamen, ut si dubius maneat, nec se recte explicare posit, legis verba sequatur: quod & in judice, si res subito dijudicanda sit, locum habebit. Sin moram res patitur, consulendus est legislator, sive summus, sive inferior, qui legem posuit, ut ipse sit mentis suae verique juris interpres. Et hactenus de aequitate.

When the exception is doubtful because it is ambiguous, either the letter of the law is followed or it is not, depending on whether it is more just, or whether it is more publicly useful. But, a distinction has to be made whether the matter permits delay or not. If it permits no delay, it will be handled privately—and what is more just and better in such a case will be uncovered by thinking rightly. However, [if no delay is permitted and] if doubt remains, [and] right thinking cannot determine the matter, then the letter of the law should be followed; [thus, the strict letter of the law] continues to have a role in judging in matters that must be decided immediately. If, however, the matter permits delay, the legislator who enacted the law [must decide the matter], whether such person is of the highest order, or a lesser, so that he himself is the interpreter of his own intentions and the way the law [should apply in this case]. So much for equity.

Appendix C

Equity in Cicero's *Verrine Oration*

FACTS AND LAW NOTWITHSTANDING: CICERO'S VERRINE STRATEGY

One all too overlooked aspect of Cicero's legal cases is that they are in fact *legal* cases. They are designed to address a specific set of facts, and to defend or attack specific individuals. Cicero's overriding objective is to win. He has pre-determined rhetorical and legal strategies to achieve his objective. Much ink has been devoted over the ages to analyzing his rhetorical strategies. Much less attention has been paid to the legal context and strategies of his cases. This essay constitutes a preliminary exploration of a portion of the legal context of Verres' trial (or at least Cicero's report of the speeches he intended to deliver at the trial) and a reconstruction of what appears to have been Cicero's legal strategy.

In this appendix I explore Cicero's Verrine legal strategy, and its problematic implications. The passages I focus on in *Verrines* II.4 deal with Verres' "theft" from Gaius Heius ("Heius") of the Praxiteles Cupid statue (the "Cupid"), and his "theft" from Prince Antiochus of the jewel encrusted lamp stand ("jeweled lamp stand").

During his term as *Quaestor* of Sicily in 75 (a position roughly equivalent to a treasurer), Cicero earned a reputation there for fairness and integrity. Verres, on the other hand, during his term as Governor of Sicily in 73–71, was known for his "unusual cruelty and rapacity." Following Verres' term, all of the Sicilian states but Syracuse and Messana (current day Messina) sent delegations to Rome to retain Cicero as their *patronus* to prosecute their extortion case against Verres. Cicero accepted the case, one of the few instances in which he acted as prosecutor. His motivations were not entirely disinterested. He stood to gain both politically and professionally if he could defeat Quintus Hortensius, the greatest orator of the time, whom Verres had retained to defend him. (Mitchell 1986, 5–6)

Roman provincials, with an extortion claim against their governor for property unjustly seized, could complain to the *Praetor Peregrinus*, a position created to handle complaints of non-Roman citizens against Roman citizens. While non-Roman citizens could represent themselves, they typically hired a Roman Citizen with oratory skill as their *patronus* to argue their case for them. Provincials could not utilize the law that applied to Roman citizens, the *ius civile*. Instead they had to rely upon the *ius gentium*, the basic law that was considered to apply to Roman citizens and others alike—or at least the law that governed all civilized peoples. The *ius gentium* is far less rigorous and strict than the *ius civile*. The *ius gentium* was "free from the trammels of [the *ius civile*] and [had] the indefinite possibilities of equity" (Greenidge 1901, 48–49).

Having the "indefinite possibilities of equity" overstates the case—the flexibility of the *ius gentium* certainly had limits. For instance, the remedies available to the Sicilians in the extortion court under the *ius gentium* did not include the return of the objects stolen by Verres. If successful, they could only recover money. In an extortion case, by the time of the *lex sulla* (c. 81) (an expansion of the *lex calpurnia* (c.149) and the *lex acilia* (c.123–22), the original extortion laws), a successful party in an extortion trial would recover *twice* the estimated value of the object(s) extorted (Mitchell 1986, 3; Greenidge 1901, 422). Remarkably, the prosecuting party's *own* estimate was the value adopted by the court (Stein 1961, 85). Critical to the logic of this system is the opportunity afforded the defendant after judgment and before execution to return the stolen property in lieu of the monetary fine (*Ibid.*). Presumably, the defendant would rather return the property than pay what inevitably must have been an exorbitant amount of money. An added incentive to the principal provincials who pursued successful extortion claims was that they were rewarded with Roman Citizenship together with an exemption from military service (Mitchell 1961, 2).

Cicero faced several large problems in dealing with the two thefts focused on in this essay. Some of these problems were inherent in the sort of property that was stolen, others relate to Cicero's strategy. My analysis suggests that if Cicero actually had had to present the rest of his case, it would have looked considerably different than what we see in the set speeches he claims he would have presented. If a skilled orator were on hand to respond to Cicero's allegations, he would have taken full advantage of these problems—something Cicero would surely have wanted to avoid.

The first major difficulty Cicero faced was that the type of property Verres was accused of unjustly taking was not *res mancipi*, which consisted primarily of land, slaves and agricultural animals. Rather it was *res nec mancipi*, which consisted of everything else. The difficulty is that *res mancipi* requires certain formal methods of transfer (e.g. laying hands on the object in front of an official, who recorded the event), *res nec mancipi* did not. In the case of Heius, Cicero had to overcome the glaring fact that Verres had documents reflecting Heius sold him the Cupid. Reading between the lines, we can appreciate by the extraordinary rhetorical lengths to which Cicero went, how great a problem he considered this to be. Cicero, as I will show, would have been able to overcome this problem largely due to the fact that he had at his disposal the equitable principles contained in the *ius gentium*. He did not need to satisfy the strict requirements of the *ius civile*.

The other big problem with the Heius portion of the case was the fact that Heius was from Messana—one of the two Sicilian states sending delegations *in support* of Verres! Moreover, if we are to believe Cicero, Heius was likely the most important personage in the Messana delegation. As a practical matter, Cicero resolved this problem by calling Heius as a witness. In the American legal system, Heius would be what is called a "hostile" witness; that is, his testimony would be presumed to be in favor of Verres. Consequently, any favorable testimony that Cicero could elicit from Heius would be more credible than otherwise. This principle seems to be the case in Roman courts as well. Calling Heius as a witness was probably no great risk to Cicero's case—though in the abstract it might seem like a daring and dangerous move. Cicero knew what answers Heius would give to his questions. After all, prudent lawyers do not ask questions to which they do not already know the answers.

In the case of Prince Antiochus, Cicero faced three major hurdles. The most glaring one, and the ultimately insurmountable one from a legal perspective, is relevance. Cicero was retained by Sicilians to recover property or its value from other Sicilians. While Prince Antiochus happened to be in Sicily when Verres stole the jeweled lamp stand from him, he was not Sicilian, and there is no indication Cicero represented him. The other two big problems Cicero faced were the fact that the jeweled lamp stand had not yet been dedicated to the Roman People, and that it had not been pulicly displayed.

Addressing first the theft by Verres of Prince Antiochus' jeweled lamp stand, it should be noticed that objects dedicated to the Roman People, *res publicae*, are also characterized as *res quorum commercium non est.* (Watson 1968, 13–14) That is, such objects cannot be sold or transferred—or even privately owned. Cicero, in effect, accuses Verres of stealing a *res publicae*—a far more serious charge than provincial pilfering. [1] Presumably, the gravity of this charge alone, taken together with the fact that Verres does appear to have taken the object, would influence the jury against Verres even if the charge were irrelevant to the case. Moreover, Cicero paints a remarkable picture of the object in the minds of the jury—he would probably claim he was compelled to do this, since no one had seen the lamp stand, including Cicero, in all liklihood. This picture would plant in the jury members a longing to see the object. They would realize that they would have been able to see it had it been dedicated to the Roman People as planned. Instead, this "artificially" created desire is frustrated by Verres' theft, further influencing the jury against him.

Turning to the case of Heius' Cupid, Cicero had to address the problem of Heius' contract with Verres. But the existence of a contract aggravates his problem since no contract is even required for the transfer of *res nec mancipi*. The presence of a contract where one is not necessary would appear to make the transfer legally unassailable. Fortunately for Cicero, the *ius gentium* rather than the *ius civile* was the law of the case. Under the *ius civile*, ~~an unambiguous contract foreclosed looking further into the intentions of~~ the parties or the circumstances of the transaction. Moreover, the fact that one party appears to have struck a remarkably good deal was irrelevant, even in a situation of unequal bargaining power or knowledge (Stein 1961, 91). Under the *ius gentium*, on the other hand, various equitable principles were applicable to the transaction, even if the contract was seemingly unambiguous. The most important of these equitable principles relating to the Heius contract is the one that imposed a good faith requirement (*ex fide bona/bonae fidei*) on the parties to the contract.[2] Cicero clearly sets forth evidence proving Verres' bad faith. Consequently, he could easily succeed on this point under the *ius gentium*.

Along related lines, the equitable principles of the *ius gentium* allowed the plaintiffs to prove their case by establishing that the transaction involved duress (*exceptio doli*) and/or fraud (*exceptio metus*) (Stein 1961, 81). Heius certainly was under duress from Verres to "sell" the Cupid and the contract clearly was fraudulent. Again, Cicero could establish this, at least circumstantially, with ease. Finally, as a last line of defense, Cicero might try to argue that the equitable principle of unjust enrichment applied. This equitable principle, though, appears to have been conceived of narrowly. It might only apply in situations in which the object of the contract has been frustrated by an event outside the parties' control (Stein 1961, 87). Cicero probably could not meet such strict requirements of proof on this point.

Finally, we come to Cicero's fixation on the Cupid to the exclusion of all of the other statues Verres stole from Heius. What about this particular statue, apart from its artistic merit—a characteristic that was probably lost on his Roman audience—prompts him to narrow his focus to this one? An obvious answer, of course, is the contrast Cicero is able to create between Verres and Gaius Claudius, the *Praetor* who had borrowed this very Cupid statue for a special holiday display in the forum, then returned it. This contrast also highlights the fact that the statue was displayed in Rome and is likely to have been seen by many of the jury members, unlike most or all of the rest of the objects Verres stole, including, of course, the jeweled lamp stand. But an even more important reason for choosing to fixate on the Cupid statue is *quod erat consecratus* (2:4). As with an item which was *res publicae*, an item which was *res sacra*, something dedicated under authority of the Roman People to the gods above—that is, consecrated—is *res quarum commercium non est* (Watson 1968, 2–3). That is, once consecrated, the object was not Heius' to sell—it could not be usucapted by a human being. Cicero appears to be walking a fine line here—he is at least implying the more serious crime of *sacrilegium*—a crime for which Verres is not being prosecuted, and a crime that appears to be beyond the jurisdiction of the extortion court. He is surely setting Verres up for the *sacrilegium* type charges he hammers in the "Henna Ceres statue" episode (48ff). A crowning problem with Cicero's line of attack here is that Heius, since he does not *own* the Cupid, is not the proper party to complain of its taking—this responsibility and right probably belongs to the Bacchic priests.

Notes

NOTES TO THE INTRODUCTION

1. Factors weighing in on the side of literary as opposed to other treatments include one identified by Aristotle; he observed that literature (poetry), in contrast to history, is "more philosophic and of graver import that history, since its statements are of the nature rather of universals, whereas those of history are singulars" (*Poetics* 1451b). It may also be that authors of literary works are more sensitive than others to meaning shifts in language. Perhaps they possess a special ability or talent for achieving or creating a sense of perspective which may not be possible for persons caught up in the sweep of events; put differently, such authors may well be able to perceive and process contemporary changes more quickly than others. They may also be more willing to explore controversial "cutting edge" changes in concepts, since they can disguise what they are dealing with in the structure of the fictionional narrative—creating ambiguities behind which they can protect themselves from accusations of expressing unorthodox or even dangerous opinions. A prime example of this is the way Thomas More handles communism in *Utopia.* See Chapter Three, below.
2. Chapter Two consists of an analysis of key passages from Plato's *Laws* and Aristotle's *Rhetoric*, *Ethics*, and *Politics* addressing *επιείκεια*; the chapter includes original translations of select passages.
3. See Chapter Three.
4. However, whether the people have ever fully accepted the new conception is an open question. Certainly the English people did not immediately accept the new conception of what should be considered fair. This is reflected in the elevated importance of the concept of mercy in the late sixteenth and early seventeenth century in England. Unfortunately, mercy was not specifically designed to address the problems that the *επιείκεια* derived meaning of equity had done. Mercy is much less flexible than equity—in jurisprudence its function is largely limited to the pardoning of an offender in one fashion or another, following a final determination at law. It is a

gross tool for fashioning a "fitting" result, and it certainly cannot disguise the laws' inability to fashion one. The problems that resulted from the loss of those meanings of equity derived from *επιείκεια*, and the employment of mercy to address the problems formerly dealt with by equity, are evident in, for instance, Shakespeare's *Measure for Measure* and *Merchant of Venice.*

5. This tension is evident, for instance, in Francis Bacon's attempts on the one hand to systematize English law, by among other things reducing equity to a series of maxims, and, on the other hand, his actions as James I's attorney general promoting the primacy of the Chancery court's equity jurisdiction in the English legal system.
6. The use of equity as a political tool appears in large part to rely upon an *επιείκεια* based understanding of equity because such equity could adjust outcomes regardless of what the letter of the laws might otherwise provide. In this sense equity based on *επιείκεια* could be seen as overruling the laws, and could be used as support for the Chancery's overruling of Common Law court decisions. This perspective of course ignores the fact that equity based on *επιείκεια* is designed to work quietly with the laws, not opposing them for all to see. The political abuse of equity based on *επιείκεια* certainly violated its *spirit.*
7. Understanding the full complexity of More's and Spenser's uses of equity requires more than a survey of the history of the idea of equity, it also requires delving into equity's ambiguous role in sixteenth century England's legal and political arenas, and the larger forces that were at work in the era effectively eliminating some meanings of equity, and transforming others. The multiple perspectives from which equity must be approached has resulted, naturally enough, in considerable confusion as to its meaning. John Austin, a prominent 19th century legal historian seeking to provide a general characterization of equity—one encompassing its sixteenth century meanings, succinctly expresses this confusion:

   > The applications of the term 'equity' are extremely numerous. . . . Of all the various objects denoted by this most slippery expression . . . I will briefly advert to a few of the numerous meanings which are not infrequently attached to that most ambiguous term. (Austin, 61)

8. At its most profound level (as opposed to its practical jurisprudential application), equity is not associated with the ideal *per se*. Rather it is concerned with how to influence practice from the standpoint of an ideal starting point. Consequently, what equity deals with is necessarily less than ideal and very practical. But it aims to raise the practical as close as possible to the ideal—or, at least, equity is employed by persons who seek to accomplish this end.
9. Aristotle, in his *Ethics*, compares the flexibility of *επιείκεια* with the Lesbian rule, a flexible leaden measuring device used to align unevenly shaped paving stones.

10. It is clear that Plato also considered justice in economic terms as is clear in the *Laws* where he describes the inevitable "money loving that goes with justice" (737a).

NOTES TO CHAPTER ONE

1. The contemporary elevation of the principles of liberty and individual freedom are in considerable tension with the notion of unlimited judicial discretion, especially in Anglo-American jurisprudence. We do not trust others—perhaps especially those in office of public trust—to make decisions affecting our lives or increasingly the society in which we live. We prefer the application of the "rule of law," and tend to accept even problematic applications of this principle so long as they can be justified on the basis of the equality principle.
2. This example as well as the ones that follow are enumerated in Jesse Katz, "A big zero—how intolerant we've become" *Sacramento Bee*, 22 March 1998, Forum 1.
3. The zero tolerance problem has drawn considerable attention. The American Bar Association, at its February 2001 meeting, publicly criticized the use of zero tolerance policies in schools "without regard to the circumstances or nature of the offense or the student's history." "Lawyer's group targets rules on "zero tolerance" in schools." *Sacramento Bee*, 15 February 2001, A3.
4. Zero tolerance is by no means the only area in which this problem arises. Other examples of this tension between equality and justice arise in areas such as affirmative action, "three strikes" laws, and drug sentencing guidelines prohibiting judicial discretion.
5. There are two sorts of disguise that must be distinguished here. The first is the intentional sort contemplated by Aristotle. In his view, the defective nature of laws must be concealed so that the rule of law could be established and maintained. Equity was the cloaking device that made the laws appear flexible enough to achieve proportional results in individual cases, even though the laws were too rigid by nature to accomplish such precise results, as a consequence of their general statement. Since the early modern period the defective nature of laws has been unintentionally disguised by the view that laws are in fact sufficient to achieve sufficiently proportional results in individual cases. Ironically, this shift seems to make their defective nature all the more obvious.
6. Consider for example Lincoln's comments on the rule of law in his 1838 "Lyceum" address:

   > Let reverence for the laws be breathed by every American mother, to the lisping babe, that prattles on her lap—let it be taught in the schools, in seminaries, and in colleges;—let it be written in Primmers, spelling books and Almanacs;—let it be preached from the pulpit, proclaimed in legislative halls, and enforced in courts of justice. And, in short, let it become the *political religion* of the nation; and let the

old and young, the rich and the poor, the grave and the gay, of all sexes and tongues, and colors and conditions, sacrifice unceasingly upon its altars. (emphasis in original)

7. For the Holmes quote see his dissenting opinion in *Black & White Taxicab Co. v. Brown and Yellow Taxicab and Transfer Co.*, 276 U.S. 518, 533 (1928).
8. The principal objection to natural law based views is our egalitarian distrust of anyone who might possess virtues we do not and our bias in favor of defending individual liberty rather than promoting the common good. We are, of course, tremendously suspicious of "aristocratic" notions generally, in spite of the pronounced element in this direction in both the theory and practice of the founding fathers. However uncomfortable the notion, we need to remind ourselves occasionally that the roots of our regime are intimately connected with notions of aristocracy.
9. For a more detailed discussion of concepts relating to equity in Roman law, see Appendix C.
10. Cicero thus clearly anticipates the sixteenth century ce trend already discussed.
11. As if this isn't already confusing enough, there are additional ancillary pre-Christian Roman meanings of *aequitas*. As you might expect, these meanings all come from one or another of Cicero's works, and they all appear to derive to a greater or lesser extent from Aristotelian *επιείκεια*. For instance, in his *De Finibus* and *Pro Murena*, Cicero states that it is "inequitable" to punish all transgressions in the same fashion. While this sort of *aequitas* does not address the unique circumstances of individual cases, it does recognize that there is a problem punishing in similar ways crimes of varying degrees; that is, equality cannot simply be identified with justice. Some aspects of equality tend to undermine the authority of law, since decisions pursuant to these will be viewed as unfair, as unjust. Cicero provides yet another meaning for *aequitas* in his *Topica*. There he describes the civil law as "a system of equity established between members of the same state for the purpose of securing to each his property rights." This meaning of *aequitas* does not obviously relate to Aristotelian *επιείκεια*, at least not Aristotle's explicit treatments of it. But it does relate to Aristotle's implicit treatment in the *Politics*, which in part deals with the problems of distributive justice, as discussed more fully in Chapter Two.

    In addition, there were various equitable precepts in praetorian law and the gentile law, which in contractual situations, for instance, required that the parties to a contract act in good faith, and excused non-performance of contractual obligations when fraud or duress were involved. These also seem to relate to Aristotelian *επιείκεια*, in that they examine the unique circumstances of individual cases; they intervene between the law and its application to a case.
12. I utilize here Clinton Walker Keyes' Loeb Classical Library translation. Obviously, the reference to God here is generic. We should note, however, that Cicero himself does not appear to fully adopt the Stoic position on

natural law. See Strauss and Cropsey 1973, 170–172. Nor does Cicero associate *aequitas* with the natural law.

13. As Landau notes, the typical Christian Latin formulation was "*Nihil enim aliud est equitas quam deus*" (130).
14. In the formulation of *επιείκεια* in Aristotle's *Rhetoric, επιείκεια* requires that the judge take into account the weakness of human nature—in this context, *επιείκεια* requires elements of what we identify today as mercy.
15. Consider in this regard Cephalus' description of what old age is like in Book I of Plato's *Republic* (359a). Also relevant is the Athenian Stranger's praise of the Cretan law that allows old men, when no young people are present, to discuss the merits and defects of the regime's laws with magistrates and others of like age (Laws 634d-e).
16. Terrence has an interesting alternative formulation "*ius summum saepe summa est malitia.* See Hamburger 1950, 452.
17. A consequence of this shift from the theoretical to the practical is the radical narrowing of natural law evident by the beginning of the seventeenth century—there was very little that everyone could agree was equal and fair. We should distinguish here between what everyone considers fair generally—if such agreement can even be posited, and what people in a particular regime might consider fair in a particular legal case, given all of the facts and circumstances.
18. Prudence may be indirectly associated in some sense with transcendent notions or standards of a sort.
19. Shakespeare explores this problem in depth in his *Merchant of Venice.*
20. A useful formulation provides "*rerum convenientia quae in paribus casis paria iura desiderat et bona omnia aequiparat.*" (an equivelance which promotes the application of the same laws to the same cases and ensures justice and equality) (Mclean 1992, 175).
21. One of the issues raised in Shakespeare's *Measure for Measure.*
22. One of the issues explored by Spenser in *The Faerie Queene* Book V. This was also an issue in the second trial of Mary Queen of Scots.
23. Of course Plato also attempted to show how his theory applied in practice, for instance in his *Laws.* Also, his *Seventh Letter* suggests he attempted to apply his theories in real life situations—with nearly disastrous results, it should be noted.
24. Machiavelli continues: "For a man who wants to make a profession of good in all regards must come to ruin among so many who are not good. Hence it is necessary to a prince, if he wants to maintain himself, to learn to be able not to be good, and to use this and not use it according to necessity."
25. See the discussion of Aristotle, *Politics,* 3.10 and Plato, *Laws,* Book V, 735a & ff in Chapter Two.
26. "Natural law theories before the seventeenth century were dominated by a principle of theistic origins—that God was the source of all laws perceived

as natural by human reason" (Hochstrasser 2000, 4). These laws were very wide-ranging—for the most part they correspond to the Stoic conception of natural law.

27. Chapter one of Grotius' "*De Aequitate, Facilitate, et Indulgentia*" is translated into English for the first time (to my knowledge) in Appendix B to this book.
28. For Grotius, the natural law which could exist independently of divine law, flowed from the principle that people were social by nature—but the society to which they were naturally drawn was minimal—the key factor being to keep others off what is one's own (an ancestor of private property theory). The focus on one's own, on the individual, carries over to a nascent theory of some individual rights—rights as something an individual possesses (as long as they are consistent with the basic notion of keeping others off what is one's own). While Grotius agrees that people are impelled by a natural desire to preserve their own being, he, unlike Hobbes, sees this as subject to a person's rational faculty. See Strauss and Cropsey 1987, 386–395; Haakonssen 1999, 239–265.
29. In his early work, *On Secular Authority*, Luther depicted the "true religion . . . as being more divorced from the life of the civil community . . . as being more private and more personal . . ." Luther sought to "subject all hierarchies and earthly superiors to [the fundamental liberty and equality of all Christians.]" (Hopfl 1991, x).
30. It is beyond the scope of this study to consider the obvious tension between Bacon's choosing to create a utopia and Machiavelli's rejection of all utopias. For some elements to consider with respect to this tension see Strauss and Cropsey 1987, 368.
31. Not surprisingly, Bacon appears to be one of the first who began formulating this series of maxims—probably taking his cue from Fortescue and St. German. As Lord Chancellor, Bacon attempted as much as possible to codify Chancery's practices—that is, to restrict discretion and flexibility. See Coquillette 1992, 45, 206.
32. This is in fact how I interpret Thomas More's final and most significant use of *aequitas* in his *Utopia*. There, More attempts to combine Aristotelian equity (which he apparently encountered in its original form during his humanistic studies—after he began to study Greek) with "biblical equity" in an attempt to formulate a new equity that might respond to some of the real world problems being faced at the outset of the early modern period.
33. In 1975 the University of Cambridge Faculty of Law awarded Baker the Yorke Prize for this essay.
34. According to Baker, "English humanists were characteristically men of affairs rather than speculative scholars" (29). As one might expect, Baker has difficulty in accounting for Thomas More, a remarkable combination of a speculative scholar and a man of affairs. Baker's solution appears to be

to selectively disregard More's speculative side, and draw upon his practical side.

35. For present purposes Chancery court equity can be considered similar to the less esoteric sort of Aristotelian equity
36. Baker's observation is really quite insightful. As will be described at length in Chapter Two the theory advocated by both Plato and Aristotle views extreme communism as the ideal. They are clear, however, that it is an unachievalble one in practice. But they are guided by this ideal as they describe the best achievable situation. They both seek to improve regimes until they approach extreme communism as closely as possible—they suggest that a ratio of four or five to one, between the wealthiest and poorest segments of society is achievable. When I spoke with Professor Baker in the summer of 2001 at Cambridge, he indicated that he was not familiar with Plato and Aristotle's treatments of *επιείκεια*.
37. The quotation is from Pollard, J. Baker also cites with favor Thomas Elyot's admonition that "where all things are common there lacketh order: and where order lacketh, there all things are odious and uncomely" (36). Baker's description of "common wealth" as 'the most universal ethical and political concept of English Renaissance" was not laudatory (34). According to Baker, "universal political concepts" "failed utterly to give any help in the solution of actual problems," and, consequently, were worthless (36). Baker's test of whether "common wealth" was of any value was whether it was "a source of [new] law;" he discounts any significance "common wealth" might have "merely to explain existing principles of law" (35). This is a very inadequate and limiting measure of the extent of the influence of the idea of "common wealth" in English jurisprudence. At any given time, new laws are a very small fraction of all laws pertaining to any given society. Baker's text ensures the outcome he is seeking by excluding all the laws that the idea of "common wealth" did pertain to.

NOTES TO CHAPTER TWO

1. The first use of *επιείκεια* is the only one in which it is mentioned by someone other than the Athenian Stranger (*Laws* 635a). Kleinias, the Cretan, employs the term to describe the Athenian Stranger's proposal that it is fitting for the three of them, Megilius, the Spartan, is the third, to discuss what is praiseworthy and blameworthy in the laws of the Cretan and Spartan regimes. The word used by Kleinias is *επιεικως*. The Athenian Stranger had previously alluded to a "presumed" law common to both Crete and Sparta, which prohibits the young from inquiring which laws are finely made and which not, but which allows the old to discuss such things among themselves, in the presence of a magistrate, provided no young person is present (Strauss 1988, 30). Thus, in a certain sense, the entire text of Plato's *Laws*,

in some fundamental way, is equitable—equity (in the form of *επιείκεια*) is somehow the necessary context for any serious conversation that addresses the merits and defects of laws, especially laws of the specific regime governing the society of which the debaters are members.

The third use of *επιείκεια* describes the old men who are in charge of selecting laws for a regime. In this case the context is the education of the children. Specifically, the Athenian Stranger indicates that "education is the drawing and pulling of children toward the argument that is said to be correct by the law and is also believed, on account of experience, to be correct by those who are most [equitable] and oldest" (*Laws* 659d). The Greek word is *επιεικεστάτοις*.

The sixth use also describes the character of particular old men. In this case, the context is identifying who will recognize the merits of the regime being established in the new colony. The particular elements of the new regime focused on here are the way the new regime deals with allocation of wealth and property and the limits placed upon the acquisition of wealth. Regarding this, the Athenian Stranger says:

> [t]he amount of good that the system now being laid down will do for all the cities that follow it . . . is forever unknown to the evil man and knowable only by him who has become experienced and [equitable] through habituation. For under such a system great money-making is impossible. (741d-e)(The Greek word is *επιεικεστάτοις*.)

The tenth and final use of *επιείκεια* occurs in the final book of the *Laws*, and is like the first use of *επιείκεια* in that it occurs in the context of a critique of laws. In this case it involves the selection by the "Guardians of the Laws" (those initially in charge of the colony to be established) of "pieces of legislation [composed] by [equitable] men which are not unseemly" (957a-b) (The Greek word used is *επιεικων*). These laws will be reviewed by the Guardians, modified as necessary, tested by experience, and then set in place as "final [and] . . . unchangeable." The equitable men who composed these laws are equitable presumably for the same reasons the old men referred to in the first, third, and sixth uses of *επιείκεια* were equitable: namely, they have become experienced and decent through habituation.

2. The Greek word is *επιεικέστατα*.
3. In the second usage, *επιείκεια* is used to characterize the infamous drinking party described by the Athenian Stranger (649a-650b). The Greek word is *επιεικη*. The drinking party the Athenian Stranger proposes, unlike the notoriously unstructured drinking parties of the Athenians, is actually designed as a careful test of the characters of the participants, since the more they drink, the less they will be able to disguise from the sober test-leader their character flaws. The virtues of the test are that it is cheap, safe and quick. He does not however say that the test is the most accurate or best way to accomplish this goal! The Athenian Stranger appears to praise the pleasure

loving quality of the Athenians (who were notorious for their less structured drinking parties), and the Athenian regime's willingness to allow their people to indulge in such pleasures. However, what the Athenian Stranger really appears to be doing is critiquing the Cretan and especially the Spartan regimes, and their discouragement of the enjoyment of pleasure. See Strauss 1989, 232–33. He certainly is not defending the licentious practices of the Athenians, or the Athenian regime that allows them.

The ninth use of *επιείκεια* refers to laws and customs of the Spartans and Cretans that are equitable and therefore worth considering for the new colony (836b). The Greek word is *επιεικως*. But the context for this comment is to juxtapose these equitable laws with the Spartan and Cretan laws and customs concerning the regulation of sexual desire—these, according to the Athenian Stranger, are exactly the opposite of what the new colony will want to adopt. Just before this passage, the Athenian Stranger mentions "the fact that it's impossible to get terrifically rich [in the new colony] is no small benefit to moderation" (836a). So, as with the second usage, the ninth involves a critique of the pleasurable.

4. *Laws* 735a & 736d.
5. The translation here is my own.
6. The translation here is my own. The Greek word is *επιεικεία*.
7. There appears to be considerable uncertainty whether there can be any assurance as to the quality of the people selected for the colony. After all they have not been raised under the laws of the regime being established. Consequently, a purge will probably be necessary eventually. Hence the digression at this point. It is interesting to note that the "drinking party" method of testing character will not be employed. Instead they will employ "thorough testing—with every sort of persuasion over a sufficient period of time—[to] discover those who are bad among the people trying to become citizens in the present city and prevent them from entering." 735b-c.
8. *Laws* 736d. The translation here is my own.
9. The translation is my own. The Greek word is *επιείκειαν*.
10. Perhaps such persons are self-identified—insightful readers of texts such as the *Laws* who project themselves into the roles of reformers.
11. The Athenian Stranger again appears to be suggesting that the new colony is not really avoiding the problem. "This danger, as we assert, we're avoiding; nevertheless, it is more correct to discuss it, at any rate, and show how we might find a way out if we were not escaping it." 737a
12. This appears to be one explanation for this extended digression. Equity must be part of the new colony if the good laws initially established are to persevere.
13. And finally, equity appears, in the natures of these reformers, to point back towards the word's root definition: reasonableness and moderation in the exercise of one's rights, and the disposition to avoid insisting on them too

rigorously. Or should we describe a reformer as an "equitable man [who], in a spirit of justice, demands less than legal justice allows him[?]" Or perhaps as one who takes both less and more: less of "say wealth and honors and power, while taking, or even in order to be able to take, something else, perhaps leisure, and what it brings to the best men, without measure?" *Laws* 737b.

14. The translation is my own. The Greek word is *επιεικης*.
15. Following a long tradition, I will translate *επιείκεια* as "equity." See Arnhardt 106.
16. Speech and argument "have the power to encourage and stimulate young men of generous mind . . . [they also] can cause a character well-born and truly enamored of what is noble to be possessed by virtue. . . . *Ethics*, at 1179b.
17. It is intriguing to notice the close proximity of the remarkable passage on universal law/the law of nature (earlier in chapter 13 at 1373b) to the passage on equity.
18. See Hamburger 1965, 89–90 and Arhnardt 106 on the touchstone quality of this passage in Aristotle.
19. What Aristotle means by "equitable" persons is not clear here.
20. The jurors were the judges in Athens. Compare the passage at *Politics* 1281b where Aristotle indicates the types of office suitable to the multitude—"deliberating and judging."
21. On arbitrators, see Aristotle's *The Athenian Constitution* 53.2–7. Arbitrators were appointed from among men 59 years of age.
22. See *Ethics* 6.8.1141b23–33. The statesman's "practical wisdom" deals "with particular facts."
23. See *Ethics* 6.8.1141b23–33. The legislator's "practical wisdom" is "supreme and comprehensive."
24. The audience to whom the *Ethics* is aimed is men "well brought up in [their] habits and not dominated by passion." They are "more concerned with the honor to be won by political life than for the virtue that merits it." Strauss and Cropsey at 123; *Ethics* 1.3.1095a2–11.
25. See Cropsey, at 252. "[I]t appears that Aristotle dealt with all of the moral virtues but one in a mere one and a half books[.]"
26. This of course raises the issue of distributive justice, discussed immediately below.
27. Stewart here explains that chapter 11 of Book V is, together with chapter 9, a kind of appendix to Book V.
28. See *Ethics* 5.9.1136b31–1138a3.
29. See also Strauss and Cropsey 129. Aristotle's discussion "certainly raises a question about the simple justice of law and law-abidingness."
30. "For there are some beings—including, no doubt, the gods—who cannot have too much of these goods" (*Ethics* 5.9.1137a27–29).

31. I differ with Cropsey regarding whether this group "does not point in direction of philosopher king" (Cropsey 265). It seems to me that the argument, once equity and the equitable are adequately accounted for, points in the direction of the philosopher king—or at least in the direction of the best aristocracy.
32. What Aristotle does not explicitly say in this passage on equity is that the precision of law is inherently incompatible with the subject matter to which it is applied—human actions. Human action is infinitely variable–for "the endless possible cases [that could arise] . . . a lifetime would be too short" to address these by law (*Rhetoric* 1.13.1374a30–35). Aristotle highlights the problem with the subject of human action at the outset of the *Ethics*:

    > Our discussion will be adequate if it achieves clarity within the limits of the subject matter. For precision cannot be expected in the treatment of all subjects alike, any more than it can be expected in all manufactured articles . . . Therefore, in a discussion of such subjects, which has to start from a basis of this kind, we must be satisfied to indicate the truth with a rough and general sketch: when the subject and the basis of a discussion consist of matters that hold good only as a general rule, but not always, the conclusions reached must be of the same order (1.3.1994b.13–22).

    Though on the surface Aristotle is careful to make it seem like equity follows the law, it is clear that law always "falls short by reason of its universality." *Ethics*, at 5.10.1137b27; see also *Rhetoric*, 6.8.1142a.23–27:

    > That practical wisdom is not scientific knowledge is (therefore) evident. As we stated, it is concerned with ultimate particulars, since the actions to be performed are ultimate particulars. This means that it is at the opposite pole from intelligence. For the intelligence grasps limiting terms and definitions that cannot be attained by reasoning, while practical wisdom has as its object the ultimate particular fact, of which there is perception but no scientific knowledge.
33. (quoting *Ethics* 6.8.1141b23–33). Prudence is primarily concerned with adapting "universals reflected in the moral virtues to the particular circumstances in which moral action must take place. Hence prudence is highly dependant on experience" (131). "The exercise of equity is, it would seem, analogous to an aspect of the prudence of political men or citizens acting in a particular case"(129).
34. See Strauss 1988, 30–32.
35. See also *Politics*, at 5.7.1307b1–5.8.1307b37. Changing a regime for the better, of course, involves destroying the existing regime.
36. The bracketed translation is my own. Carnes Lord's translation which I replaced reads as follows: "Thus it is clear what the equitable is, that it is just, and better than just is one sense of the term. We see from this, too, what an equitable man is. A man is equitable who chooses and performs

acts of this sort, who is no stickler for justice in a bad sense, but is satisfied with less than his share even though he has the law on his side. Such a characteristic is equity; it is a kind of justice and not a characteristic different from justice."

37. In the next passage, Aristotle effectively subordinates law, and necessarily that which *follows* upon it, when he observes that laws "are necessarily poor or excellent and just or unjust in a manner similar to the regimes" to which they belong. He anticipates here his subsequent discussion in chapters 15–16 where the rule of the best laws is compared qualitatively with the rule of the best person(s), and the rule of the best laws is found wanting. *Politics* 3.11.21. Aristotle continues "if nothing else, it is evident that laws should be enacted with a view to the regime. But if this is the case, it is clear that those [enacted] in accordance with the correct regimes are necessarily just, and those [enacted] in accordance with the deviant ones, not just." (3.11.21) The problem is of course with polity, which consists of a mixture of two deviant types of regime. In order for his logic to work, the sum must be more than its parts, and two wrongs must equal a right. Aristotle appears to be trying to create a mixed regime, leaning towards oligarchy, which is ripe for reformation in the direction of aristocracy. The equitable appear to be the critical element if this transformation is to take place.
38. It has been suggested that we must approach *Politics* 3.10–3.15 employing the assumption that Aristotle's presentation here is "radically ironic" in nature, much like Plato's political writings. Strauss 1989, 4; Strauss and Cropsey 1973, 121.
39. As Strauss observes: "The few wise men cannot sit beside each of the many unwise men and tell [them] exactly what it is becoming for [them] to do. The few wise men are almost always absent from the innumerable unwise men. All laws, written or unwritten, are poor substitutes but indispensable substitutes for the individual rulings by wise men. They are crude rules of thumb which are sufficient for the large majority of cases. . . ." (Strauss and Cropsey 1973, 75).
40. Carnes Lord chooses to translate *epieikes* as "respectable." To preserve the consistency of the translation I substitute "equitable" for his "respectable."
41. In other words, when they rule, the equitable look to virtue, whereas the oligarch looks to wealth, and the democrat to freedom. See 4.7.4–5; 4.8.7
42. Polity is defined in 2.6.16 as a mixture of democracy and oligarchy—a mixture that is halfway between the two.
43. We must approach *Politics* 3.10–3.15 employing the assumption that Aristotle's presentation here is "radically ironic" in nature, much like Plato's political writings (Strauss 1989, 4; Strauss and Cropsey 1973, 121).
44. Since they are outside the regime and its laws, what standard will the equitable look to when changing the laws? Aristotle answer appears to be that

the standard is "what is right." 3.15.6. The determination of "what is right," requires the intellectual virtue of prudence—the practical intellectual virtue.

45. The lower ratio allows the *polis* to avoid the "civil war" which "harsh poverty" and extreme "wealth" lead to. *Laws* 744e.
46. It is unclear whether Aristotle's "mistake" is in fact intentional here.

NOTES TO CHAPTER THREE

1. The principal early modern English treatments of equity can be found in the works of Sir John Fortescue, Christopher St. German, Edmund Plowden, William Lambarde, Richard Hooker, Thomas West, Sir Thomas Elyot, and Sir Edward Coke. Two other more extensive treatments of equity should be mentioned: Edward Hake's *Επιείκεια: A Dialogue on Equity in Three Parts*; and William Perkins' *ΕΠΙΕΙΚΕΙΑ: or a Treatise of Christian Equity and Moderation.*
2. Except where specifically noted otherwise I employ in this chapter the Surtz translation from the Yale edtion of the Complete Works of St. Thomas More. The pagination of translated passages is from the paperback edition of *Utopia* published in conjunction with the complete works project.
3. As I argue in the Introduction and Chapter One, the concept of equity, the recorded history of which begins in classical Greece, was by More's time being radically changed through the influence of such diverse phenomena as the Reformation, the political innovations attributed to Machiavelli, the rise of a more scientific conception of law, and the narrowing of the scope and authority of natural law.
4. The reason mercy is incapable of performing equity's function is essentially because equity is employed prospectively in order to fashion an appropriate outcome to a case. Mercy, however, typically is employed retrospectively via the pardon power, and remits an inappropriate outcome already rendered.
5. In Chapter One I sketch the development of the Court of Chancery's equity jurisdiction, and address the controversy between it and the Common Law Courts that resulted in James I's 1616 decision in favor of the Court of Chancery's equity jurisdiction.
6. See Chapter One's discussion on equity's origin in the Greek *επιείκεια*, and how equity's essential role involves disguising the insufficiency of laws by making them *appear* to be able to achieve appropriate outcomes in individual cases.
7. Numerous scholars have noted the Crown's abuse of the Court of Chancery's equity jurisdiction by the early seventeenth century, and have suggested that this abuse was a contributing cause to the events of 1642. See e.g. Levack 1973, 1–2, 144–45. As discussed below, I interpret More's offer to return the equity jurisdiction to the Common Law courts as an attempt to avoid such a crisis.

8. According to Machiavelli, political counselors who advise rulers based on a theoretical model, such as an "utopian" ideal, will be ruined, whereas those who render political advice employing as their touchstone the way political matters operate in the "real" world, will thrive. In *Utopia*, Raphael Hythlodaeus' *words* agree with the Machiavellian position—he asserts he will be ruined if he attempts to become a royal councilor. But his *actions* belie his words, and by means of equity Raphael succeeds admirably in conveying effective advise based on the model of an "utopian" society without ruining himself. As discussed below, focusing on equity also helps to account for the late addition to the text of Book I of *Utopia* of the passage in which Raphael's actions prove him to be a successful counselor. This scene relates Raphael's circa 1498 visit to England and his conversation that took place there with Lord Chancellor Morton.
9. By absolute or extreme communism, I mean a political system in which the ratio between the wealthiest and poorest segments of society are one to one, for all practical purposes—there is no problem of wealth disparity in such a regime.
10. Guillaume Budé's introductory letter to *Utopia*, discussed below, clearly identifies this limitation. See also Raphael Hythlodaeus' discussion of the problems associated with private property at pages 50–52, and 148–49.
11. *Aequitas* is most extensively dealt with in what is commonly termed the "Treatise on Law," which consists of Aquinas' *Summa Theologiae*, I-II, QQ. 90–97.
12. More himself was to push some of these reforms in his famous and biting 1518 letter to Oxford defending the new education, particularly the study of Greek.
13. Linacre was in Italy until 1499. While Grocyn was teaching at Oxford when More was in attendance, it is not believed that More began his study of Greek then, or even that Greek played any part of the formal curriculum prior to Linacre's return from Italy.
14. More, in his letter to Dorpius, indicates he studied the Greek works of Aristotle with Linacre. By 1500 copies of Plato's *Republic* and *Laws* were certainly available in England in Latin in Ficino's *Opera Platonis* (1st ed. 1484). Copies of Decembrio's Latin translation of the *Republic* were apparently in England as early as 1450. While Greek texts, including Platonic dialogues, were beginning to appear in England before 1500, there is little historical record of these. In 1537 the historical record of these texts really begins when John Claymond, President of Corpus Christi College, Cambridge, gave his collection of Greek manuscripts to the College, including the *Republic* and *Laws*. See generally, Jayne 1995, Ch. 2.
15. Both were trained lawyers who entered Royal service. Budé's service included being an ambassador, the royal secretary, and royal librarian. Budé is perhaps most famous today for founding the library that forms the nucleus of the Biblioteque Nationale. In addition he was largely responsible for persuading

Francis I to create the trilingual *collège royal* (Latin, Greek & Hebrew). His major works include the *Annotations in xxiv Pandectarum libros* (1508), *De Asse* (1515), *Commentaria linguae Graecae* (1529), and *De Transitu Hellenismi ad Christianismum* (1534).

16. Erasmus certainly knew More better personally, but it seems to me that Budé, because of his legal background and his professional experience, may have been more in tune with certain aspects of the way More thought.
17. Here we see that More's reverence for the ancients is not unqualified. This is the only instance I am aware of in which an early humanist elevates a contemporary above the ancients in this way.
18. The matters addressed in the letter are roughly as follows (for convenience I refer to the Logan, Adams & Miller's *Utopia* edition's Latin paragraph structure):
    1. Acknowledges Budé's debt to Lupset for providing him copies of More's *Utopia* and especially Linacre's translation of Galen.
    2. Describes Budé's country house activities as he peruses the *Utopia.*
    3. Relates the ingrained characteristic of greed in human nature—and how this gets reflected in the civil order.
    4. Describes how the problem of greed is amplified in countries which must deal with both civil and canon law. One possible contrast Budé is making here is between the nations of Continental Europe and England.
    5. Suggests that there is a lack of justice in contemporary nations when measured by the rule of Christ. The then current conception of justice is also distant from its older sense of giving to each his due. ("*simplicitas*"is highlighted here—see note 22 below)
    6. Sets forth the current argument that the law of nature (as an ancient and authentic code) supports the rule of the strongest (i.e., if strong, one is entitled to more goods and authority).
    7. Describes Christ and his disciples as teachers and practitioners of communism.The Ananias episode from *Acts* V.1–11 is cited, but *no reference is made to Ananias' dishonesty*—instead Budé suggests he is sentenced to death for violating the rule of communion!
    8. Suggests that the place called Utopia is also known as Udepotia. Asserts that the Udepotians' good fortune (in holding to the true customs and authentic wisdom of Christianity) is attributable to three divine institutions: equality of all good and evil things among the citizens; a dedication to peace and tranquility; and utter contempt for gold and silver.
    9. Raises the question of how Utopia is preserved from the chief vice of the rest of the world, avarice.
    10. Asserts that it is preserved because it is located outside bounds of known world (both spatially and temporally).

11. Relates how we really owe our knowledge of Utopia to Thomas More, not Raphael Hythlodaeus. "He it is who has shaped the city . . to the standard of a model and a general rule, and added all those touches which give beauty, order and authority to a magnificent work." (13)
12. Reveals that Budé considers More so highly both because of *Utopia*, and because of Peter Giles' and Erasmus' praise of him.
13. Continues with farewell to Lupset, and greeting to Linacre.
14. Concludes with greeting sent to More. Includes passage identifying *Utopia* as seedbed of elegant and useful concepts.

19. Some scholars have begun to address Budé's letter as complex, but hesitate to view it as a critique. See e.g. Schoeck 1977, 285ff; Sylvester 1977, 293–94; and Wooten 1999, 7–9. As is evident in much of the extensive Budé-Erasmus correspondence, Budé was quite proud and jealous of his scholarly achievements. Consequently, his praise of other scholars never seems to be unqualified.
20. In this passage, a man named Ananias desires to join the disciples communal community. To do so he must sell all his possessions and donate the proceeds to the community. But he secretly holds some money back. When confronted by Peter, Ananias simply drops dead. Later, Peter confronts Ananias' wife Sapphira, who does not know her husband has died, but who knows he held money in reserve. She too drops dead. The passage in no way supports Budé's assertion that Ananias is condemned to death for violating the law of communion. Instead, the main factor appears to be their dishonesty. Budé, presumably, expects that his readers would realize the significance of his mischaracterization of the passage.
21. The Latin text for this passage is as follows:

    "A uero CHRISTVS possessionum conditor & moderator, Pythagoricam communionem & charitem inter asseclas suos relictam, luculento sanxit exemplo, damnato capitis Anania ob temeratam communionis legem. Quo certe instituto CHRISTVS omne iuris istius ciuilis pontificijque adeo recentioris argmentosa uolumina, inter suos quidem ab rogasse mihi uidetur. Quod ipsum ius hodie arcem tenere prudentiae uidemeus, ac fata nostra regere. (*Complete Works,* Vol. 4, 8–10)

    The bracketed words in the text corresponding to this note ("shining" and "sanctified") is my emendation of the Surtz translation use of "significant" and "ratified" respectively, as translations for *luculento* and *sanxit*. It seems to me that Budé is drawing his readers attention to the Ananias passage by his idiosyncratic treatment of it as well as his use of provocative language. In my view, the Surtz translation of these words is much too subdued.
22. My preliminary conclusions about the overriding message of Budé's letter is that he is differing from Raphael, and also Erasmus, on the core teaching of Christianity. Raphael, of course, contends that communism is the core

teaching. He further suggests, in problematic fashion, that the teaching is rather explicit and that we would know this if we heeded the also problematic admonition of Christ that we be forthright rather than indirect. Erasmus claims that *caritas* (charity/love) is the central tenet of Christianity, and that this implies communism. (Prolog. *Adages*. Vol. 31, p. 15, *Collected Works*). Budé responds by highlighting a different tenet of Christianity—the "prescription of evangelical" *simplicitas*—of forthrightness, truthfulness. His reason for doing so, perhaps, is because he identifies "avarice" as the key human fault preventing the achievement of anything resembling pure communism—Plato appears to agree with him on this point (*Laws* 736e-737a). Raphael, in contrast, identified pride as the key human fault. The reason Budé identifies *simplicitas* as a key Christian teaching can be found in the central passage of his letter—specifically in his allusion to the Ananias passage from *Acts*. It is generally acknowledged that the message of the Ananias passage is not that Christ, by the example set by his disciples, advocated communism—at least this isn't the main message—it is rather that faced with the prospect of absolute communism, Ananias' avariciousness, his human nature, asserted itself and prevented him from telling the truth. Ananias' dishonesty is his crime, and it is for this he is punished. Intriguingly, Christ is described here by Budé as the "founder and controller of all property" (Logan, Adams & Miller 1995, 13). He is also described in the letter as the "founder of our human condition" (Ibid., 11). In some way, Budé's letter suggests that Christ appears to be responsible for the problem of the human fault of avariciousness—or at least it associates avariciousness more with Christian than classical times. Consequently, in the Christian era, *simplicitas* becomes elevated to counteract the "new" or newly emphasized problem of avariciousness. But the problem is wonderfully complex. How we should interpret *simplicitas* is itself wrought with difficulties. How can we know that "what Christ whispered in the ears of his disciples" has been interpreted by them correctly in the formation of their communist community? How can we know that they are "shouting from the rooftops" the same message they were whispered by Christ? And finally, is living by example the same thing as "shouting from the rooftops?"

23. Thus Budé initially raises what Aristotle identified as the critical political problem caused by disparity in wealth. Then, immediately afterwards, in the central paragraph of the letter, Budé cryptically refers to the ideal answer to this political problem—a regime that adopts communism. Finally, in the next paragraph, Budé raises the key fault in human nature (avariciousness) that in practical terms prevents communism being a solution. Thus, the structure of Bude's letter is consistent with the interpretation I will present of equity in More's *Utopia* (Book II), an interpretation suggesting that the practical message of the text is consistent with the classical solution to this problem—the ancients agreed that communism was not a practical solution.

24. *Amicorum communia omnia* (between friends all is common), or in Greek, *Τα των φίλων κολνά*. Erasmus, *Adagia*, 29.
25. In Chapter Two I discuss how Plato, in the *Laws*, points out that the highest form of equity involves acting outside the laws of the regime in order to improve the form of the regime in the direction of absolute communism. I return to this issue at the end of this chapter when I deal with More's final usage of equity in Book II, where he links equity and communism.
26. The "original" version of Book I revolved around two hypothetical situations—Surtz labels these two hypotheticals the first and second "royal councils." The first involved Raphael positing himself as a counselor at the court of the French King addressing the "most perplexing question" of "what is to be done with England?" (41). The second of the "royal councils" involved an unspecified king's court at which Raphael is to provide counsel respecting a king's desire to amass wealth, presumably largely for the purpose of financing wars of imperial expansion. Neither of these hypotheticals deals with the sort of pressing "domestic" problem dealt with in the Lord Chancellor Morton passage. As will be addressed below, this suggests that equity might primarily be concerned with domestic issues.
27. We should keep in mind, however, that this later Roman formulation of equity, while acknowledging a problem with laws, minimizes the nature of laws' defectiveness and fails to address and even conceals equity's paramount role according to Aristotle: its role in producing a result in legal cases that satisfies the sense of justice/fairness of the members of the society. This satisfaction in turn helps to preserve the rule of law, thereby preserving civil order.
28. Consider for examples of political mercy the pardons of Aumerle and Carlisle at the end of Shakespeare's *Richard II*, or the debate over whether Mercilla should be merciful towards Duessa and pardon her in Book V of Spenser's *The Faerie Queene*.
29. We should note that only in the Lord Chancellor Morton example, and not in the two hypotheticals, does Raphael do all three things proposed by Peter Giles: entertain with his learning, furnish examples, and assist with counsel.
30. The Latin word used is *servus*—which can mean servant *or* slave.
31. Later, the More persona sets much reduced goals, after he feels compelled to disclose his method for rendering "wise" counsel.
32. Literally, the people of much nonsense.
33. Notice that the nation of the Polylerites, althought fictional, is located within the bounds of the known world—a significant difference, I would suggest, between Books I and II.
34. Notice the isolation of this land—it is as much an "island" as Utopia—but it has more control over contacts with the outside. Consider the comments made by Plato's Athenian Stranger in Book IV of the *Laws* respecting the location of the new Cretan colony—and his assertion of how fortuitous it was that it would be located inland, not on the sea (704a-707b).

35. One explanation for Raphael's seeming contradiction of his words by his actions, is that, since he doesn't appreciate the different understanding of equity in England, he doesn't realize that Lord Chancellor Morton will take his suggestion seriously and even accept it. If the understanding of equity in England had been the same as that on the continent, Raphael's argument would be more familiar to Morton and therefore not as persuasive.
36. Suarez, while writing in the early seventeenth century, accurately reflects the status of equity a century earlier.
37. Morton also does not attempt to act pursuant to a divine law-based understanding of equity, though Raphael fishes for this as well.
38. Raphael particularly likes the works of Plato.
39. It is not at all clear Aristotle says this in the *Rhetoric*. Whether it can be inferred is even questionable. Really, this is an outgrowth of the development of the later concept of a higher law controlling equity, which occurs after Aristotle's time.
40. See note 63, below, and accompanying text.
41. Aristotle's careful treatment of this sort of equity occurs in the *Ethics*. See generally Chapter Two.
42. Morton's selection of the pardon power is understandable. What other options were there that Morton could draw upon that could circumvent the ordinary legal processes? We should observe that a mere century after More identifies mercy as equity's replacement, Shakespeare could be seen treating matters exclusively in terms of mercy which in More's time would have required the application of equity. Shakespeare scholars continue to struggle with this shift, continually reading equity into some of the plays since the dramatic situations appear to them to demand it.
43. Consider Maxim 750 of Publius Syrus (c. 42 BCE) "Pardon one offence, and you encourage the commission of many."
44. Roper reports that More had prepared in advance a defense for all of the decisions he had made to date, in the event they refused. Roper also reports that More liked Chief Justice Fyneux's statement that "whoso taketh from a justice the order of his discretion taketh surely from him more than half his office." On this same matter, Roper reports that More told him "I perceive son, why [the Common Law judges] like not [to make equitable decisions], for they see that they may by this verdict of the jury cast off all quarrels from themselves upon them, which they account their chief defense."
45. Only "those few with the insight of Sir Thomas More, could see that English jurisprudence would ultimately derive more benefit from the equitable development of the common law [than from the separate development of equity in Chancery]" (Baker 1978, 43).
46. Numerous scholars have made this connection. See for example Levack 1973, 1–2, 144–45.

47. Here is another example of Raphael's "continental" perspective: the royal prerogative there tended to be more extensive than in England, where it did not outweigh all law.
48. The easiest place to access a copy of Henry VIII's markup of the coronation oath is as an inset piece at the beginning of Henry Ellis' 1827 book *Original letters, illustrative of English History*, Series 2. The text of the original oath and the oath as marked up is reproduced at 176–77. The original of this document is at the British Library BM Cotton, Tiberius, E8, Folio 89. American scholar Thea Cervone has been working on trying, as part of a forthcoming publication in connection with an ongoing study, to affix a date on Henry's markup based on handwriting analysis. I thank her for drawing my attention to it.
49. There are a number of logical problems with this passage that should be noticed. If Christ advocates forthrightness, why is he whispering? How do we know what the disciples shout is what Christ whispered? Certainly the stage is set in this example that some things cannot and should not be expressed openly. Forthrightness is not an absolute.
50. See Chapter One.
51. Notice that Raphael relies on Christ here, not his "favorite" author Plato! Plato certainly has a different position with respect to indirect counsel—consider the "noble lie." Budé's elevation of the evangelical prescription of *simplicitas* probably is in part a reaction to this *Utopia* passage.
52. I suspect that the limited goals proposed by the More persona involve counsel on issues of foreign affairs, and that portion of the king's revenues devoted to foreign affairs.
53. One thing that More as author seems to be addressing here is the distinction between the situations in the two hypotheticals in which the foreign affairs of a kingdom, and the ways a king finances his foreign affairs, are respectively addressed. Domestic affairs—supposedly what kings should be mainly focusing on—and what should be the main subject of wise counselors is not addressed in the original structure of Book I. One message More appears to be conveying is that the effectiveness of wise counsel in foreign affairs, and a kings finances with respect thereto, is severely limited. Certainly in such areas counsel by indirection is absolutely necessary, and the objectives of such counsel are quite modest—little positive good can be accomplished.
54. The passage in *Acts* that reveals the disciples were living in communal fashion is presented as merely a detail of a teaching about being honest—being forthright.
55. Certainly, based on the two hypotheticals in the "original" structure of Book I, equity does not appear to play a role in matters related to foreign relations, or the way in which revenue is raised for them. Aristotle's treatment of equity in the *Rhetoric* and *Ethics* also seems to be limited to matters of domestic concern. A related difficulty can be seen in the reliance of early

modern scholars for what equity means on the way Hugo Grotius treats it in his *De Jure*. Since the *De Jure* involves above all else matters of foreign relations, these scholars should instead consult Grotius *De Aequitate*, his specific short work devoted to equity. I completed what I believe to be the first published English translation of this work as part of my dissertation. I have included this translation as Appendix B to the book.

56. This is the nub of the difference between More and Machiavelli—between Machiavelli and a more classically oriented approach. The traditional classical view is that theory governs practice. Machiavelli asserts that practice should determine theory. Under both approaches, at least in this context, the ends justify the means to a large degree. Only in the classically oriented approach, the ends are more worthwhile in that they are directed towards preserving or improving the "commonwealth."
57. I think my translation of *aequitatis* as equity is absolutely necessary, for the reasons set forth in the text. The Latin for this sentence is: *Hic aliquis velim cum hac aequitate audeat aliarum iustitiam gentium comparare, apud quas dispeaream si ullum prorsus comperio iustitiae aequitatisque vestigium*. (Logan, Adams & Miller 1995, 242). Raphael's switch from *aequalibus* to *aequitas*, I think, prevents an accurate translation of *aequitas* as "fair" here, at least to the extent that fair implies a sort of equality rather than equity. See *Yale Edition*, p.104 at l. 16ff. The way translators have dealt with this passage vary. None appear to be adequate. While Adams' translation is better than most, correctly setting up the first part of the comparison—the "equity" of Utopia—he fails to translate literally the second part of the comparison, the "justice and equity" of existing European nations. Instead he translates the second part of the comparison "justice and fairness" (243). Wooten uses "fair dealing" for the first part, and simply "justice" for the second (157). Ogden completely reverses the terms in the first part. He compares the "justice" of the Utopians with the "justice and equity" of other nations (80). Surtz is consistent, if not accurate, rendering *aequitas* as "fairness" in both parts of the comparison (147).
58. I mean to distinguish between the ideal sort of communism practiced by the Utopians from the achievable *practical* alternative closest to their sort of regime.
59. Plato, in a critical passage from the *Laws* that will be addressed below, speaks in terms of the "money-loving that goes with justice" (737a). Consider also Raphael's second hypothetical in Book I, as well as the paragraph that occurs just before the center in Budé's letter.
60. Raphael soon utters another oath, "so help me God," which merely amplifies the point emphasized by his first oath. (148).
61. The Surtz translation says that Raphael has finished his "story." The Latin text does not suggest that what Raphael has recounted is a "story"—a fiction.
62. The five contenders are, in order, the multitude, the wealthy, the equitable, the one who is best of all, and the tyrant.

63. At the risk of unnecessary repetition, I will summarize here the relevant information from Chapter Two. The role these "equitable" persons play, their "practice," is addressed in Aristotle's *Politics*. There we learn there that they are the group best deserving to rule in the *Polis*, at least in the best achievable regime. Frustratingly, however, this astounding piece of information proves to be of little help since we immediately learn that, though deserving, they apparently will never succeed in ruling, since they will be prevented by the inevitable power struggle between the poor multitude and the wealthy few; the best achievable regime will not emerge while the struggle continues. Put differently, the prime factor that prevents the emergence of the best possible regime and the rule by those best deserving, is the extent of the disparity in wealth between the poor multitude and the wealthy few. The *Politics* makes clear what the group of "equitable" persons are best capable of doing—rule in the best *achievable* regime, the one closest to the *impossible* ideal. The *Politics* does not, however, answer the even more tantalizing question of what their "practical" role is in typical existing regimes where the struggle between the poor multitude and wealthy few dominates. The answer to this is contained in Plato's "political work par excellence," the *Laws* (Strauss 1988, 29).

In Book V of Plato's *Laws*, the Athenian Stranger teaches that absolute communism is an admirable, but practically unattainable goal, and that "harsh poverty" and/or extreme wealth in a regime inevitably "breed civil war and faction" (744d-e). Aristotle, in Book II of the *Politics*, explains why absolute communism is impractical: "For the refined may well become disaffected, on the grounds that they do not merit [mere] equality" (1267a1-b1, 2.7.18). For an early modern treament of this problem see Appendix A. Consequently, a practical compromise short of the ideal must be sought where there can be established a "limit of poverty." This limit, according to Plato, should be a ratio of four to one between the wealthiest and poorest segments of a society (744e); Aristotle appears to be slightly less strict on this point, allowing the ratio to be as high as five to one. (*Politics*, 1266b1, 2.7.4). The critical difficulty according to Plato is how to achieve such a ratio in an existing regime and avoid "the terrible, dangerous strife occasioned by redivision of land, canceling of debts, and redistribution." The only safe way to do this is for there to be in the regime:

> a continual supply of reformers from among those who possess an abundance of land and many debtors . . . who must be willing, out of a sense of [equity], to share in some way what they have with any of their debtors who are in distress, forgiving some of the debts and parceling out some of the land. (736d-e)

The Athenian Stranger emphatically calls our attention to this "device," for he stipulates that it is the "most important source of a city's preservation;" it "provides a sort of sturdy foundation upon which someone can later build whatever political order befits such an arrangement;" and it is the only "escape, broad or narrow," from "the money-loving that goes with justice," and its consequences (736e-737a).

This passage from Plato's *Laws* addresses both the practical role of the mysterious "equitable" persons *and* the relation of the concept of equity to communism; it reveals that these two things are inextricably intertwined. The group of equitable persons act out of a sense of equity; their practical actions are guided, in other words, by political theory. Their main goal is to improve an existing regime by *surreptitiously* reducing the wealth to poverty ratio. Their motivation is not simply philanthropic; rather they are acting to construct "a sturdy foundation . . ." for a subsequent, improved regime. The "political order [that] befits such an [improved regime]," in Aristotelian terms, is the rule by those best deserving to rule, those who excel all others not on the basis of wealth, numbers or power, but in terms of virtue.

64. Pangle's translation is quite accurate here. See Benardete 2000, text following n.10.
65. As I have shown, the position taken by the More persona in Book I on "indirect" counsel, is itself dangerous—it raises the distinct possibility that his counsel should not be trusted. How much more dangerous would it be for More the author, if he were to be associated with the advocacy of communism, or something approaching it.
66. Of course such persons would be viewed as a threat by the rulers of the regime. After all, they are laying the foundations for their own group to rule—or at least enhance this possibility.
67. More writes in dialogue form which means that nothing is spoken in his own voice. Moreover, the More persona he creates in the text expressly rejects the notion of absolute communism as impractical. More further shields himself by writing the work in Latin rather than the vernacular, and he has it published on the continent rather than in England. Another way of looking at this is that More did not intend for all readers of *Utopia* to understand the relation of equity and communism, and all that it implied. That would be far too dangerous—political suicide at the very least. In all probability he only wanted like-minded persons—such as his humanist friends—to understand.

NOTES TO CHAPTER FOUR

1. In Book V, Artegall, the knight of justice and protagonist of Book V, gets sidetracked from his quest to free Irena from Grantorto—a task assigned to him by *The Faerie Queene*. Artegall enters the land of the Amazons and agrees to fight their queen, Radigund. He defeats her in trial by combat, a mode of settling disputes Artegall has previously repudiated. When he removes the helmet from her fallen figure he is overcome with pity upon seeing her beauty, and voluntarily submits to her rule—her beauty effectively captivates him.

Radigund takes Artegall prisoner and constrains him to dress as a woman and perform women's work such as sewing. Britomart, betrothed to Artegall, and whose offspring by him are destined to rule Britain (as earlier prophesied by Merlin), is a warrior in her own right, though she remains disguised as a man during her exploits until her battle with Radigund. When Britomart learns of Artegall's submission to Radigund, she stifles her anger and jealousy, and sets off to rescue him. On her way she stops at Isis Church, where she is initiated into the mysteries of Isis, who is said to represent equity. She then hurries on to the land of the Amazons and fights and defeats Radigund, beheading her. Britomart then assumes rule of the Amazon nation with the sole objective of reforming the regime to prepare it for return to male rule. Her final act in *The Faerie Queene* is voluntarily to tender control of this nation to the freed and recovered Artegall.

2. Many scholars have identified two centers to Book V, the first being the Isis Church passage in Canto vii, the second being the events occurring at Mercilla's court in Canto ix (Stump 1982, 87–89). Scholars have differed over which of these passages is "the conceptual heart" of Book V (87). I align with those scholars who identify the Isis Church passage as the conceptual heart for the following reasons. First, the Isis Church passage occurs at the numeric center (the exact bisection) of Book V (Fowler 45). Second, justice, as an Aristotelian rather than a Christian virtue, is more closely identified with equity than mercy—in fact, as previously noted, equity was still considered to be the very essence of justice at the beginning of the Renaissance in England. Classically, mercy was not associated with justice, except for those elements of equity which we now identify as relating to mercy (see Chapter One). This distinction appears to be made in Book V—equity is explicitly identified by the narrator as part of justice, but the narrator introduces mercy by pointing out that "Clarkes doe doubt . . /Whether this heauenly thing . . . /To weeten Mercie, be of Iustice part" (V.x.1.1–3). Consequently, equity, and its treatment at Isis Church, appears to be thematically much more central to justice than mercy. Third, as discussed in Chapter Two, Aristotle not only distinguished between unjust persons (people who take more than their shares) and just persons (persons who take just their shares), he adds a third category—the most just persons. These he describes as equitable. Equitable persons are satisfied with fewer than the shares to which the laws entitle them. The discussion of equity at the center of Book V appears to reflect an appreciation for equity's relationship to the core of justice in the Aristotelian scheme.
3. The extent of Spenser's knowledge of Greek is uncertain. However, Greek was part of the standard curriculum in his grammar school and at Cambridge during the years he attended (Judson 1945, 14; Hamilton 1990, 131). Aristotle's *Ethics* and *Politics* were also required reading at Cambridge at the time. It is also clear that Spenser was interested in Plato, as he himself

translated into English the dialogue *Axiochus* (since determined to be spurious). Perhaps the most persuasive evidence of the extent of Spenser's knowledge of Greek and of Aristotle and Plato comes from Spenser's friend Lodowick Bryskett, who in his *A Discourse of Civill Life*, describes Spenser's erudition. In the dialogue Bryskett complains that he is not capable of the "exacting study demanded by Plato and Aristotle" (Judson 106). Bryskett then entreats Spenser to help him on this score

> knowing him to be not only perfect in the Greek tongue, but also very well read in philosophy, both moral and natural. . . . For, of his love and kindness to me, he encouraged me long sithens to follow the reading of the Greek tongue, and offered me his help to make me understand it. (quoted in Judson 106).

4. The sort of equity associated with Artegall's justice, equity based on equality, was gradually becoming predominant in late sixteenth century English jurisprudence. Artegall's name associates him with equality (*égalité*), not equity (*équité*).
5. As Eggert notes, Artegall follows in the footsteps of Guyon. Guyon destroyed the Bower of Bliss with "rigour pitilesse" (II.xii.83.2) Eggert associates this destruction with an initial unsuccessful attempt at defeminization of *The Faerie Queene's* poetry (26). Artegall is also associated with Hercules in that Hercules is reported to be the father of Osyris, who according the Isis priest's interpretation of Britomart's dream, is an analogue for Artegall in all relevant respects. Guyon and Talus also bear a certain resemblance in their rigidity.
6. See Chapter One.
7. Richard Eaden, in a sermon delivered around 1600, also discusses the problems inherent in equity's use of a flexible measure:

   > It were beyond all credit, if it did not offer itself to all eyes, how many sleights this witlesse wittie, and learnedly unlearned age hath devised to make the rules of good and evill like that leaden rule of Lesbia, pliable to purposes, and to serve turnes: how many pleas iniustice hath found out to justifie it selfe out of iust lawes; how many shadowes ungodlinesse to shroud it selfe under the law of God. (quoted in Gallagher, 148–49)

   As discussed in Chapter One, the leaden rule of lesbia is associated with equity based on *επιείκεια*. As previously noted, the rule of Lesbos was a malleable measuring device, probably made of lead, used by road builders to fit together uneven paving stones. Aristotle first associates it with *επιείκεια* in the *Ethics* (5.10; 1137b). See Chapter Two.
8. Implicitly it would seem that Artegall's equity based on equality is associated solely with a rigorous justice based purely on the positive laws, whereas Isis' equity based on *επιείκεια* looks beyond the laws to at least a general sensibility of what is fair, if not to a transcendent standard.

9. For discussions of the transformation of equity's meaning in sixteenth century England as it was developing in politics and jurisprudence see the Introduction, and Chapter One.
10. As Eggert notes, Radigund's beauty and its power over Artegall is itself a metaphor for the superior power of "feminine" poetic modes, of which digression is one, over "masculine" ones (23–29).
11. I discuss below the reasons why Spenser takes such care to conceal what he is doing.
12. Isis is the wife of the god Osyris. Isis and Osyris are purported to represent an Egyptian king and queen who were subsequently deified (Hamilton 1977, 573, note to V,vii,2–4).
13. While Britomart is in disguise as a knight, it later becomes apparent that the temple priests had seen through her disguise and know she is a woman.
14. The priest's full description is:

    Magnificke Virgin, that in quaint disguise
    Of British armes doest maske thy royall blood,
    So to pursue a perilous emprize,
    How couldst thou weene, through that disguised hood,
    To hide thy state from being vnderstood?
    Can fro th'immortall Gods ought hidden bee?

    If we assume the omniscience of the gods of Isis Church is suspect, then there are other ways to explain the priest's piercing of Britomart's disguise. Most likely, the priest identified Britomart the previous night when she fell asleep without her helmet at the foot of the altar. There is some suggestion that the priests knew she was a woman before admitting her to Isis Church, since they barred entry to Talus. .
15. It should be noted that clemency is really only a part of classical equity, not all. Classical equity's objective is to produce a fitting result—it is entirely possible that what is fitting is more severe than what the laws dictate if there are aggravating circumstances that the law does not take into account. See Appendix B.
16. Moreover, as noted in Chapter One, describing equity as having a controlling power over laws would be highly controversial in England in the early 1590's, when the general trend in English jurisprudence was to consider equity as "following" the law rather than leading it. The beginning of the tremendous struggle between the equity and common law courts, that would temporarily give the equity jurisdictions the ascendance, was still a decade away.
17. Aristotle's formulation for *επιείκεια* intends its operation to be hidden so as to preserve the impression that the laws themselves are capable of producing fitting results in particular cases. See Chapter Two.
18. Of course Spenser's probable audience for the "ensample" of these passages will know that there really is no controlling power of equity of the sort described at Isis Church—women are merely meant to think there is.

19. The succession controversy will be discussed later in the chapter in more detail
20. An interesting analogue to Eggert's distinctions between feminine flexibility and masculine rigidity, is Plato's description of the rigid "woof" and flexible "warp" of all regimes. It is particularly interesting to note that Plato's Book V digression in his *Laws* opens with the discussion of the woof and warp, then moves on to the topic of regime change, and equity's role in this process. See Chapter Two.
21. I discuss Spenser's audience in more detail later in the chapter. As Lowell Gallageher observes, Spenser captivates his audience by causing a "rupture of the narrative scheme" of Book V—the digression of the central episodes (152). Focusing on how men have resorted to a feminine mode in devising the bait of the secret controlling power of equity reveals how Britomart is unwittingly recruited to the masculine cause.
22. Upon entering Castle Joyous, Britomart "greatly wondred" at the "superfluous riotize,"—its fantastic and beautiful artistic adornment (III,i,33.6,8). Even so, she was not captivated in the same way or to the same extent as her companion the Redcrosse knight, who almost immediately disarms (42.6). Britomart, however, lifts her vizor, revealing her eyes and gender to Malecasta's knights. This action, together with her later complete disarmament when she goes to bed, appear to be the causes of her later wounding by Gardante.
23. "Idol worship is the enemy of spiritual vision in Book III, the Legend of Chastity, not just in the 'fowle Idolotree' before Cupid's statue in the house of Busirane (III,vi,49), but also in the cult that surrounds the false Florimell, twice identified as as 'Idole'" (Hamilton 1990, 388). This should be relevant to Britomart, of course, since she was Book III's knight of Chastity. It is also useful to keep in mind that "[i]dolotry is Redrcosse's fate when he accepts Duessa as his companion. In her ornaments, in the mists she stirs up to becloud reason, and in her playing on the victim's fears (of which she is in part composed), she represents the idolatry that follows upon 'errours' (the monstor Error) and 'superstition' . . ." (Hamilton 1990, 387). Not all idols in *The Faerie Queene* are suspect, however, nor are all pagan practices necessarily evil. In each case the circumstances must be examined to determine the proper interpretation. The combination of factors I have pointed out should "encourage further investigation [by the reader]," and certainly should have placed Britomart on her guard (Hardin, 102).
24. The customary interpretation of the Isis Church episode does not view it critically (Kermode 50; Stump 93; Knight 293–94). *The Spenser Encyclopedia* suggests that idol worship is acceptable at Isis Church (388). I believe I have provided good reason to depart from the customary interpretation.
25. As Lowell Gallagher notes, the priest has the "authoritative" "last word on the subject" of the dream, and "the reader is left . . . to contend with certain disjunctions between the dream and its translation" (156).

26. Possibly Britomart's own tendency towards fiction—towards artifice and guile make her particularly susceptible to it. We learned earlier that Britomart is accustomed to framing "diuerse plots" and masking them in "strange disguise" (III,iii,51.9). Moreover, when she is on her guard she readily employs guile to defeat guile (III,xii,28.1–2).
27. The chief priest, as his title implies, is clearly male (V,vii,20.5,9). And based on his attire and the other symbols reminiscent of the "old church," he could well be a catholic priest—perhaps even a Jesuit.
28. Apparently, a play like *Gorboduc*, famously critiqued by Sir Phillip Sidney in his *Defence of Poesy*, and written by the queen's cousin Thomas Sackville (later her Lord High Steward) and Thomas Norton, both law students, was not subject to this edict, in spite of its thinly veiled allusion to the succession issue. It was written by nobles and performed only twice—at court for Twelfth Night, 1562, and a command performance two weeks later for Elizabeth.
29. Moreover, fresh in Spenser's mind would be the fate of the Parliamentarian Peter Wentworth, imprisoned initially from August to November 1591 and again from February 1593 until his death in prison in 1597 (Spenser published Books 1 through 3 of *The Faerie Queene* in 1590. Books 4 through 6 were first published in 1596). Wentworth wrote a short treatise entitled *A Pithie Exhortation to her Majestie for Establishing her Successor to the Crowne.* He prudently did not publish it, instead presenting a copy to Elizabeth through an intermediary. However, copies were distributed, resulting in his first arrest. After his release, he attempted to lobby support for his position on the succession in the Parliament of 1593, which led to his second arrest. The example made of him probably foreclosed any public discussion of the succession during the balance of that Parliament (Williams, 384). Adding bitter irony to Wentworth's plight was that his judge was Thomas Sackville, Lord Buckhurst, the co-author of *Gorboduc.* Spenser could certainly not expect his even less transparent historical allegory to escape the notice of a person with Sackville's literary credentials. Sackville is likely part of Spenser's select audience. The issue is not that Sackville must fail to appreciate what Spenser is saying, rather it is that Spenser must say it in a way that only his select audience will understand. Wentworth's problem was his indiscretion.
30. Eggert explores the significance of the feminine centers of various of *The Faerie Queene*'s books (32–33).
31. While neither Mary nor Elizabeth were formally "legitimized" by Henry VIII, the 1543 Succession effectively did so Act, by placing them in the line of succession (Cauthen xxiv; Somerset 14).
32. There was of course a jurisdictional problem in Mary's case. Should a foreign monarch be subject to the laws of England? It makes much more sense that only subjects could commit treason. Another obvious problem was whether Mary's Catholocism should bar James.

33. A less likely claimant, also a woman, Lady Margaret Strange, was also colored by possible illegitimacy. Lady Strange would succeed to Katherine's claim (and that of Katherine's younger sister Mary) if they Grey girls were excluded by virtue of illegitimacy (Somerset 105). Henry VII's line is noteworthy for the number of its female heirs and the recurring problem of illegitimacy.
34. Doleman's theory is criticized in Shakespeare's *Richard II* (Axton 93).
35. Perhaps another way to think about the "moderate" Puritans is that they possessed a higher degree of prudence than the more extreme Puritans.
36. Britomart's actions, as described earlier, were as follows:

    During which space she there as Princess rained,
    And changing all that forme of common weale,
    The liberty of women did repeale,
    Which they had long userpt; and them restoring
    To mens subiection, did true Iustice deale: (V.vii.42.3–7)
37. Others in this select audience might be identified by looking among the men to whom Spenser wrote dedicatory sonnets (Hamilton 1977, 739–43).
38. Recall here how Plato deals with the issue of regime change in his work devoted to "government such as might best be," the *Laws*. In his Book V digression, Plato suggests there that for regime change to occur without civil unrest, it must occur behind the scenes, veiled from the existing government. A select group of men, acting out of a sense of equity, must take action gradually to effect the change. Spenser is using equity in a similar fashion to try to achieve regime change in England. Something about equity's flexible, shifting nature (at least equity based on *επιείκεια*)—its behind the scenes application—lends itself to the task of regime change. Spenser's objective as regards regime change, the shift to a masculine monarch, is more modest than Plato's, who sought to reduce the disparity between the wealthiest and poorest segments of society. Consequently, he is not constrained by Plato's timeframe for such change, which is measured in generations. But Spenser is bound by equity's secrecy element—the head of the existing regime cannot perceive that such a change is being attempted.
39. See e. .g. Chaucer's *Wife of Bath's Prologue and Tale*. There the reader learns that what women secretly desire above all else is "maistrie" over men—according to the *Prologue* and *Tale* men do not know this, and most women are ignorant as well that this is their deepest desire. Those who are aware and who achieve dominance, exercise it discreetly—they do not act tyrannously like Radigund. Jankin, the Wife of Bath's fifth husband, grants Alison (the Wife of Bath's name) "maistrie" in a situation analogous to Artegall's submission to Radigund. Jankin has "beaten" Alison in a domestic quarrel; Artegal has "beaten" Radigund in battle. Both men are overcome by emotion afterwards and, as a result, voluntarily submit to be ruled

by these women. But unlike Radigund, Alison does not act tyrannously. She readily grants Jankin's one requested condition, and agrees to maintain the outward appearance of subservience to Jankin in public. Similarly, the unnamed old witch in the *Tale,* whom the unnamed knight has agreed to marry in exchange for being told the secret of what women desire most—mastery over men—acts most graciously to the knight after he has granted her mastery over him. The knight makes the grant after being offered the choice of accepting the witch (who he has agreed to marry in exchange for learning the secret) as old, ugly, and chaste, or young, fair and unchaste. After his submission the witch grants his implicit wish that she be young, fair and *chaste*. Moreover, thereafter she even "obeyed him in every thing/ That mighte doon him plesance or lyking" in spite of her mastery over him (399–400).

NOTES TO THE AFTERWORD

1. "A cut in the capital gains tax rates in 1997 to 20 percent from 28 percent encouraged long-term holders of assets, like privately owned businesses, to sell them, and big increases in executive compensation thrust corporate chiefs into the ranks of the nation's aristocracy. [2003's] tax cut reduced that rate [further] to 15 percent" (p. A1).
2. Thomas Pangle, in the context of discussing a recurring debate over the influence of the political thinker Leo Strauss, suggests the "liberal democracy" is "the best regime in our epoch" (Pangle 10).

NOTES TO APPENDIX A

1. John Locke, I suggest, found this way of dealing with the inequality of property ownership issue problematic, and in his *Second Treatise* forefronted and explicitly justified inequalities of property ownership.
2. In 1615, after engineering the resolution of the dispute between the common law and Chancery courts in favor of Chancery's equity jurisdiction, Bacon could assure James I that Chancery was "the [Court] of the king's absolute power" (Cropsey 12).
3. Chapter 15, it should be noticed, is the central chapter of the first two books of *Leviathan.*
4. Hobbes provides:

   > Nature hath made men so equall, in the faculties of body, and mind; as that though there bee found one man sometimes manifestly stronger in body, or of quicker mind then another, yet when all is reckoned together, the difference between man, and man, is not so considerable, as that one man can thereupon claim to himselfe any *benefit,* to which another may not pretend, as well as he. . . .

> And as to the faculties of the mind . . . I find yet a greater equality amongst men, than that of strength. For prudence, is but experience; which equall time, equally bestowes on all men, in those things they equally apply themselves unto. That which may perhaps make such equality incredible, is but a vain conceit of ones owne wisdome . . . (13:1–2)(emphasis added).

Noticeably excluded from this equality principle (at least as to faculties of mind) are men of science.

5. It is curious that the injunction against pride, the greatest of the seven deadly sins, is not the centermost of the nineteen total natural laws. This honor is reserved for the immediately following and related, but distinct injunction against the offense of arrogance, dealt with in the tenth natural law.
6. Consequently, Hobbesian civil society is founded upon a fiction of equality—a noble lie of sorts.
7. We are not told whether these "unequal" men are exclusively the men of science of 13:2.
8. The possibility of property possession in excess of what could be accumulated in the state of nature is, of course, a great motivating factor for assenting.
9. Notice, however, that the distribution to "every man of his own," Hobbes original equity formulation, is sufficiently ambiguous as to allow the possibility that some men might receive more benefits than others.
10. At least one critic has observed the problem Hobbes presents of equity and equality in chapter 15, but he does not pursue what Hobbes intends by his the conflicting presentation—he simply posits it as a puzzle:

    > But it is not at all clear why the distribution of "that which in reason belongeth" to a man should be an equal distribution. Hobbes has told us in chapter 13 that all men are roughly equal in natural powers, and here in chapter 15 he says that the ninth law of nature requires men to acknowledge their natural equality. But he cannot think that the possession of property should always "in reason" be equal. He simply does not explain what he thinks. (Raphael 168)

    Consider also Hugo Grotius' comment on equity and equality in Appendix B at page 129.

NOTES TO APPENDIX B

1. I have designed Appendix B as a facing page Latin-English translation. The English translation is the first of which I am aware. I also believe this is the first modern English or American reproduction of the Latin text. I utilize the text of the 1670 Amsterdam edition of the *De Jure*, to which the "*De Aequitate*" is attached as an appendix. As indicated in the Introduction, scholars like Kahn and Hutson have recently made much of Grotius' treatment of

equity. However, such scholars appear to rely upon Grotius' periodic comments about equity in Grotius' *De Jure*. They do not cite his work devoted to equity translated here, the *De Aequitate*.

2. While the text spells this *inprimis*, I have translated it as *imprimis*.
3. When "law" is used herein, it is used in its collective sense of "all laws," except when context makes clear a specific law is being referred to.
4. Typically, *aequitas* is defined as "fairness, impartiality and justice." (*Oxford Latin Dictionary*). It is also defined as "the recourse to general principles of justice to correct or supplement the provisions of law." (*Oxford English Dictionary*—"equity" entry). However, it also has various nuances, most of which are no longer recognized. We must remember that *aequitas* is the word used to translate the Greek *επιείκεια*, which is defined as "reasonableness and moderation in the exercise of one's rights, and the disposition to avoid insisting on them too rigorously." (*Oxford English Dictionary*—"equity" entry). All of these differing definitions must be kept in mind—Grotius is clearly aware of them and is using or playing off of all of them.
5. *Homonymias*.
6. *Ius* has a tremendous range of meanings (see the quote from Bracton, below). Here, in distinction to *lex*, I take *ius* to mean "that which is good and just, the principles of law, equity, the right." (*Oxford Latin Dictionary*). When so used, I will consistently translate *ius* as "right." *Aequitas* would look to the principles of *ius*, so understood, to determine how to amend/complete *lex*. Bracton says of *ius*:

    > *Jus* is derived from justice and is used in a number of different senses. For it is sometimes used for the *ars boni et aequi* itself, or for the written body of *jus*. It is called the art of what is fair and just, of which we are deservedly called the priests, for we worship justice and administer sacred rights. *Jus* is sometimes used for natural law which is always fair and right; sometimes for the civil law only; sometimes for praetorian law only; sometimes for that which results from a judgment, for the praetor is said to *jus* even when he does it unjustly, the word referring not to what he in fact did but what he ought to do. . . . Sometimes it stands for the law in all its rigor, as when we distinguish between law and equity. Bracton, *De Legibus* (Introduction—*What Jus Is*).

7. *Aequum* is sometimes considered to be a synonym of *aequitas*, especially in translation. But the distinction being made here suggests *aequum* is to be considered to mean that sort of fairness associated with equality. This distinction is particularly difficult today, as we tend to identify equality as the essential component of fairness—to be virtually a synonym of equity. Following a long tradition, I will consistently translate *aequum* as "fair."
8. *Ius naturale* is defined as the "ideal law implanted in man by nature." I will translate it here as "natural law." Paragraph 11 of the "Prolegomena" to Grotius' *De Jure Belli ac Pacis* contains Grotius' famous statement that

natural law would still have force and exist "even if we should concede that which cannot be conceded without the utmost wickedness, that there is no God, or that the affairs of men are of no concern to Him." (Kelsey translation). Also consider the following from paragraph 16: "For the very nature of man, which even if we had no lack of anything would lead us into the mutual relations of society, is the mother of the law of nature."

9. *Ius civile* originally meant the law of and for Roman Citizens. Bracton's description is useful:

   > Civil law, which may be called customary law, has several meanings. It may be taken to mean the statute law of a particular city. Or for that kind of law which is not praetorian; it sometimes detracts from or supplements natural law or the *jus gentium*, for law different from that outside sometimes prevails in cities by force of custom approved by those who use it, since such custom ought to be observed as law. Civil law may also be called all the law used in a state [or the like], whether it is natural law, civil law or the *jus gentium*.

10. *Ius praetorian* is the law introduced by the edicts of the praetors and other magistrates, sometimes having an equitable quality about it.
11. Literally, "good at figuring things out."
12. *Ius gentium*, originally was the law available to non-Roman citizens. Its meaning expanded to mean the law available to citizens and aliens alike. Often, it equates with *ius naturale*.
13. *Ek peristaseos nomon machen*

NOTES TO APPENDIX C

1. I was unable to determine what the penalty was for stealing a *res publicae*, or who was entitled to commence an action for such a theft. Such issues are probably irrelevant in any event, since they would not be part of the "real" case.
2. Amazingly, until recently the majority of American state jurisdictions did not impose a good faith requirement on contracting parties, except to the extent that they were required to do so pursuant to the Uniform Commercial Code.

Bibliography

Alford, John A. “Literature and Law in Medieval England.” *PMLA* 92:4 (Sept. 1977) 941–951.

Allen, Carleton Kemp. *Law in the Making*. Oxford: Clarendon 1964.

Allen, Ward. “The Tone of More’s Farewell to Utopia.” *New Literary History*. 6 (1975) 108–18.

Ames, Russell. *Citizen Thomas More and His Utopia*. Princeton: Princeton UP 1949.

Anastaplo, George. *The American Moralist: Essays on Law, Ethics, and Government.* Athens: Ohio UP 1992.

———. *The Constitution of 1787: A Commentary*. Baltimore: The John Hopkins UP (1989).

———. *Human Being and Citizen*. Chicago: Swallow 1975.

———. “On Trial: Explorations.” *Loyola University of Chicago Law Journal* 22:4 (1991) pp 765–1118 (section entitled “Thomas More, The King, and The Pope”).

Anderson, Judith H. ““Nor Man It Is”: The Knight of Justice in Book V of Spenser’s *Faerie Queene*.” *PMLA* 85 (1970) 65–77.

Anderson, Perry. *Lineages of the Absolutist State*. Norfolk: Thetford 1974.

Aptekar, Jane. *Icons of Justice: Iconography & Thematic Imagery in Book V of The Faerie Queene*. New York: Columbia UP 1969.

Aquinas, St. Thomas. *Summa Theologiae*. New York: Blackfriars/McGraw-Hill 1964.

———. *The Treatise on Law: [Being Summa Theologiae, I-II, QQ. 90 thorugh 97]* Trans. and Ed. R.J. Henle, S.J. Notre Dame: U of Notre Dame P 1993.

———. *Basic Writings of Saint Thomas Aquinas*. Anton C. Pegis ed. New York: Random House 1944 (2 vol).

Aristotle. *Nichomachean Ethics*. Martin Oswald trans. Indiana*polis*: Bobbs-Merrill (The Library of Liberal Arts) (1962).

———. *The Politics*. Carnes Lord trans. Chicago: University of Chicago P (1984).

———. *The Rhetoric and The Poetics of Aristotle*. W. Rys Roberts and Ingram Bywater trans. New York: The Modern Library (1954).

Arnhardt, Larry. *Aristotle on Political Reasoning*. DeKalb: Northern Illinois UP 1981.

Austin, John. *Lectures on Jurisprudence or the Philosophy of Positive Law.* Robert Campbell ed. New York: John Cockroft 1875.

Axton, Mary. *The Queen's Two Bodies: Drama and the Elizabethan Succession*. Royal Historical Society Studies in History. London: Royal Historical Society (1977).

Bacon, Sir Francis. *Collection of some principal rules and maxims of the common lawes of England.* London: John More 1639.

———. *The New Atlantis.* In The Harvard Classics 3. New York: Collier 1909.

Baker, J.H. *An Introduction to English Legal History.* London: Butterworths, 3rd ed., 1990.

———. "English Law and the Renaissance." Constituting the Introduction to *The Reports of Sir John Spellman Volume II.* London: Seldon Society 1978 (volume 94 of The Publications of the Seldon Society).

Baldwin, Anna P. *The Theme of Governement in Piers Plowman.* Cambridge: D. S. Brewer 1981.

Barnes, Harry Elmer and Teeters, Negley K. *New Horizons in Criminlogy.* 3rd Ed. Englewood Cliffs, N.J.: Prentice Hall 1959. (especially chapter 19 entitled "The Transportation of Criminals")

Barratt, Alexandra. "The Characters 'Civil' and 'Theology' in 'Piers Plowman.' *Traditio*. v. 38 (1982) 352–364.

Barton, J. L. "Equity in the Medieval Common Law." *Equity in the World's Legal Systems.* Ralph Newman ed. Brussels: Établissements Émile Bruylant (1973).

Baumer, Franklin Le Van. *The Early Tudor Theory of Kingship.* New Haven: Yale UP 1940.

Benardete, Seth. *Plato's Laws: The Discovery of Being.* Chicago: Uof CP 2000.

Benson, Pamela Joseph. "Praise and defense of the Queen in *The Faerie Queene,* Book V." *Edmund Spenser.* Andrew Hatfield ed. London: Longman (1996) 161–76.

Berman, Harold J. *Law and Revolution: The Formation of the Western Legal Tradition.* Cambridge: Harvard UP 1983.

Bertman, Martin A. "Justice and Contra-Natural Dissolution." *Hobbes Studies,* vol. X (1997) 23–37.

Bevington, David M. "The Dialogue in *Utopia*: Two Sides to the Question." *Studies in Philology* 58 (July 1961) 496–509.

———. "Introduction." *The Complete Works of William Shakespeare Volume IV.* David M. Bevington ed. New York: Bantam 1988. (The book has no pagination. The page numbers I provide begin with the first page of the Intrduction)

Bieman, Elizabeth. "Britomart in Book V of *The Faerie Queene.*" *University of Toronto Quarterly* Vol. 37 (1967–68) 156–174.

Bierman, Judah. "Science and Society in the *New Atlantis* and other Renaissance Utopias." PMLA 78 (1963) 492–500.

Birnes, William Jack. "Patterns of Legality in *Piers Plowman.*" Diss. NYU. 1974.

Biscardi, Arnaldo. "On *Aequitas* and *Epieikeia.*" *Aequitas and Equity: Equity in Civil Law and Mixed Jurisdictions.* ed. Alfredo Mordechai Rabello. Hebrew U.: Jerusalem 1997.

Bloom, Harold. *Shakespeare: The Invention of the Human*. New York: Riverhead Books 1998.

Bogdanos, Theodore. *Pearl: Image of the Ineffable*. University Park: Pennsylvania State UP., 1983.

Borroff, Marie. *Pearl: A New Verse Translation*. New York: Norton 1977.

Bowen, Catherine Drinker. *The Lion and the Throne: The Life and Times of Sir Edward Coke*. Boston: Little, Brown and Co. 1956.

Brann, Eva. "An Exquisite Platform. *Utopia*." *Interpretation* 3 (1972) 1–26.

Campbell, W. E. "The *Utopia* of Sir Thomas More." *The King's Good Servant*. Papers Read to the Thomas More Society of London. Ed. Richard O'Sullivan. Oxford: Basil Blackwell (1948) 26–39.

———. *More's Utopia and His Social Teaching*. 1930. New York: Russell and Russell 1973.

Cauthen, Irby B. Jr. "Introduction." *Gorboduc or Ferrex and Porrex*. Regents Renaissance Drama Series. Lincoln: U of Nebraska P (1970).

Cicero. *De Finibus*. The Loeb Classical Library. Trans. H. Rackham. Cambridge: Harvard UP 1914.

———. De Re Publica. The Loeb Classical Library. Trans. Clinton Walker Keyes. Harvard UP 1914.

———. *Pro Murena*. The Loeb Classical Library. Trans. Louis E. Lord. Cambridge: Harvard UP 1937.

———. *Topica*. The Loeb Classical Library. Trans. H. M. Hubbell. Cambridge: Harvard UP 1949.

Cohen, Stephen. "From Mistress to Master: Political Transition and Formal Conflict in *Measure for Measure*." Criticism. 41:4 (1999) 431–464.

———. "The Quality of Mercy": Law, Equity and Ideology in *The Merchant of Venice*. *Mosaic*. 27:4 (1994) 35–54.

Coles, Paul. "The Interpretation of More's *Utopia*." The Hibbert Journal 55 (1957) 365–370.

Condon-Clarke, Mrs. *The Complete Concordance to Shakespeare*. London: Bickers 1881.

Coquillette, Daniel R. *Francis Bacon*. Series: Jurists: Profiles in Legal Theory. Stanford UP: Stanford. 1992.

Crimes, S. B. "Sir John Fortescue and His Theory of Dominion." Transactions of the Royal Historical Society. 4th Series, Vol. XVII (1934) 117–147.

Cropsey, Joseph. *Political Philosophy and the Issues of Politics*. Chicago: UofCP 1977.

———. "Introduction" to Thomas Hobbes *A Dialogue Between A Philosopher and a Student of the Common Laws of England*. Chicago: UCP (1971) pp 1–48.

Davis, J. C. *Utopia and the Ideal Society: A Study of English Utopian Writing 1516–1700*. Cambridge: CambridgeUP 1981.

———. "More, Morton, and the Politics of Accommodation." *The Journal of British Studies* 9:2 (1970) 27–49.

Davitt, Thomas E. S.J. "St. Thomas and the Natural Law." In *Origins of the Natural Law Tradition*. Arthur L. Harding ed. (SMU Studies in Jurisprudence I) Dallas: SMUUP 1954. 26–47.

Dickenson, John W. "Renaissance Equity and *Measure for Measure*." *Shakespeare Quarterly* 13 (1962) 287–297.

Doe, Norman. *Fundamental Authority in Late Medieval English Law*. Cambridge: Cambridge UP 1990.

Eccles, Mark. *A New Variorum Edition of Shakespeare: Measure for Measure*. New York: MLA 1980.

Eggert, Katherine. *Showing Like a Queen: Female Authority and Literary Experiment in Spenser, Shakespeare, and Milton*. Philadelphia: University of Pennsylvania UP, 2000.

El-Gabalawy, Saas. "Christian Communism in *Utopia*, *King Lear*, and *Comus*." *University of Toronto Quarterly* 47 (1978) 228–237.

Ellis, Henry. *Original letters, illustrative of English history*. Volume 2. London: Harding, Triphook, & Lepard, 1824.

Fehrenbacher, Don. *Abraham Lincoln: A Documentary Portrait Through His Speeches and Writings*. Stanford: Stanford UP (1964).

Fletcher, Angus. *The Prophetic Moment: An Essay on Spenser*. Chicago: UC Press (1971).

Fortescue, Sir John. *De Natura Legis Naturae*. London: Privately Printed 1869 (No. 1 in Garland's series "Classics of English Legal History in the Modern Era") (Trans. Hon. Chichester Fortescue, M.P.)

Fortier, Mark. "Equity and Ideas: Coke, Ellesmere, and James I." *Renaissance Quarterly* 51.4 (1998) 1255–1279.

Fowler, Alistair D.S. *Spenser and the Numbers of Time*. London: Routledge 1964.

Gallagher, Lowell. *Medusa's Gaze: Casuistry and Conscience in the Renaissance*. Stanford: Stanford UP 1991.

Geoghegan, Vincent. *Utopianism and Marxism*. New York: Methuen 1987.

Gilbert, Felix. "Sir John Forescue's 'Dominum Regale et Politicum.'" *Medievalia et Humanistica*, II (1944), 88–97.

Goldsmith, M.M. "Hobbes on Law." In *Cambridge Companion to Hobbes*. Cambridge: CambridgeUP (1996) 274–304.

Grace, Damian. "*Utopia*: A Dialectical Interpretation." *Miscellanea Moreana: Essays for Germain Marc'hadour.* Eds. Clare M. Murphy, Henri Gibaud, Mario A. Di Cesare. *Medieval & Renaissance Texts & Studies*, v. 61. Binghampton: Medieval and Renaissance Texts & Studies 1989. 273–302.

Graziani, René. "Elizabeth at Isis Church." *PMLA* Vol. 79 (1964) 376–89.

Greenblatt, Stephen. *Renaissance Self-Fashioning: From More to Shakespeare*. Chicago: UChicagoUP 1980.

Greenidge, A. H. J. *The Legal Procedure of Cicero's Time*. Oxford: Clarendon Press, 1901.

Grotius, Hugo. *De Jure Belli et Pacis*. (includes "De Aequitate, Facilitate et Indulgentia" as an appendix) Amstelaedami, spud Joonnem Blaev, 1670.

Guy, J.A. *The Public Career of Sir Thomas More*. London: Harvester 1980.

———. *Tudor England*. Oxford: Oxford UP 1988.

———. "The King's council and Political Participation." *Reassessing the Henrician Age: Humanism, Politics and Reform 1500–1550*. Essays by Alistair Fox and John Guy. Oxford: Basil Blackwell 1986 121–47.

Haakonssen, Knud. " Hugo Grotius and the History of Political Thought." *Grotius, Pufendorf and Modern Natural Law*. Knud Haakonssen ed. Ashgate: Aldershot. 1999

Halpern, Richard. *The Poetics of Primitive Accumulation*. Ithaca: CornellUP 1991.

Hamburger, Max. "Equitable Law: New Reflections on Old Conceptions." *Social Research*. 17:4 (1950) 441–460.

———. *Morals and Law*. New York: Biblo and Tannen 1965.

Hamilton, A.C. *The Faerie Queene*. ed. A. C. Hamilton. London: Longman (1977).

———. *The Spenser Encyclopedia*. Toronto: University of Toronto P. 1990.

Hamilton, Robert. "More's *Utopia*." *Hibbert Journal* 44 (1946) 242–47.

Harbison, E. Harris. "Machiavelli's *Prince* and More's *Utopia*." *Facets of the Renaissance*. Ed. William Werkmeister. Harper & Row: New York (1959) 41–57.

Hardin, Richard F. *Civil Idolotry: Desacralizing and Monarchy in Spenser, Shakespeare, and Milton*. Newark: U. of Delaware P. 1992.

Harding, Arthur L ed. *Origins of the Natural Law Tradition*. SMU Studies in Jurisprudence I Dallas: SMUUP 1954.

Hargrave, Francis. *A Collection of Tracts Relative To The Law of England From Manuscripts*. Vol. 1. Oxfordshire: Professional Books Ltd. 1982 (originally published 1808).

Haskett, Timothy S. "The Medieval English Court of Chancery." *Law and History Review* 14:2 (1996) 245–313.

Hastings, Margaret. "More and Fortescue." *Moreana* 36 (1972) 61–63.

Havelock, Eric A. *The Greek Concept of Justice: From its Shadow in Homer to its Substance in Plato*. Cambridge: HarvardUP 1978.

Hexter, J. H. "Intention, Words, and Meaning: The Case for More's *Utopia*." *New Literary History* 6 (1975) 529–41.

———. *More's Utopia: The Biography of an Idea*. The History of Ideas Ser. 5. 1952. Westport, CT.: Greenwood, 1976.

———. "Thomas More and the Problem of Counsel." *In Quincentennial Essays on St. Thomas More*. Ed. Michael J. Moore. (1978) 55–66.

———. "Thomas More: On the Margins of Modernity." *Journal of British Studies* 1 (1961) 20–37.

———. *The Vision of Politics on the Eve of the Reformation: More, Machiavelli, and Seyssel*. New York: Basic Books 1973.

Hobbes, Thomas. *Leviathan*. Ed. Richard Tuck. "Cambridge Texts in the History of Political Thought." Cambridge: CambridgeUP (1996).

———. *A Dialogue Between A Philosopher and a Student of the Common Laws of England*. Chicago: UCP (1971).

Hochstrasser, Tim J. *Natural law theories in the early Enlightenment*. Cambridge: Cambridge University Press (2000).

Hogrefe, Pearl. *The Sir Thomas More Circle*. Urbana: U of Illinois UP 1959.

Holdsworth, Sir William. *A History of English Law*. Vol. 4. London: Methuen, 1925.

———. *Sources and Literature of English Law*. Oxford: Clarendon, 1925.

———. *Some Makers of English Law*. Cambridge: Cambridge UP, 1938.

Hooker, Richard. *Of The Laws of Ecclesiastical Polity: The Fifth Book*. Ed. Ronald Bayne. London: Macmillan 1902.

Hostettler, John. *Sir Edward Coke: A Force for Freedom*. Chichester UK: Barry Rose Law Publishers 1997.

Hough, Graham. *A Preface to The Faerie Queene*. New York. Norton. (1962).

Hughes, Paul L., and Larkin, James F. Eds. *Tudor Royal Proclamations: Volume I, The Early Tudors (1485–1553)*. New Haven: Yale UP 1964.

Hurstfield, Joel. "The Succession Struggle in Late Elizabethan England." *Elizabethan Government and Society: Essays Presented to Sir John Neale*. S. T. Bindoff, J. Hurstfield, and C. H. Williams eds. London: Athlone (1961) 369–396.

Jaffa, Harry V. "Chastity as a Political Principle: Measure for Measure." *Shakespeare as a Political Thinker*. John Alvis & Thomas G. West eds. Durham: Carolina Academic Press 1981.

———. *Original Intent and the Framers of the Constitution*. Washington: Regnery Gateway (1994).

———. The *Conditions of Freedom: Essays in Political Philosophy*. Baltimore: John Hopkins University Press 1975.

Jameson, Frederic. "Of Islands and Trenches: Naturalization and the Production of Utopian Discourse." *Diacritics* (June 1977) 2–27.

Jay, Martin. "Must Justice Be Blind?: The Challenge of Images To The Law." *Law and the Image*. Eds Costas Douzinas and Lynda Nead. Chicago: University of Chicago Press 1999.

Jayne, Sears Reynolds. *Plato in Renaissance England*. Dordrecht: Kluwer Academic 1995 (International Archives of the History of Ideas #141).

Jones, Emrys. "Commoners and Kings: Book One of More's *Utopia*." Medieval Studies for J.A.W. Bennet. Aetatis LXX. Eds. P.L. Heyworth, and Dan Davin. Oxford: Clarendon 1981 255–72.

Judson, Alexander C. *The Life of Edmund Spenser*. (Volume 11 of *The Works of Edmund Spenser: A Variorum Edition*. Edwin Greenlaw et. al. eds) Baltimore: John Hopkins UP 1945.

Kahn, Victoria and Hutson, Lorna. *Rhetoric and Law in Early Modern Europe*. New Haven: YaleUP 2001.

Kantorowicz, Ernst H. *The King's Two Bodies: A Study in Medieval Political Theology*. Princeton: Princeton UP 1957.

Kaske, R.E. "Two Cruxes in 'Pearl': 596 and 609–10." *Traditio*. v.15 (1959) 418–428

Kautsky, Karl. *Thomas More and His Utopia*. New York: Russell & Russell 1959 (first published in English in 1890).

Kavka, Gregory S. *Hobbesian Moral Theory and Political Theory.* Princeton: PrincetonUP 1986.

Kean, P.M. *The Pearl: An Interpretation.* New York: Barnes & Noble, 1967.

Keaton, George W. and L. A. Sheridan. *Equity.* 2nd ed. Oxfordshire: Professional Books Ltd., 1976.

———. *A Case-book on Equity and Trusts.* 2nd

Kenyon, Timothy. *Utopian Communism and Political Thought in Early Modern England.* London: Printer Publishers 1989.

Kermode, Frank. *Shakespeare, Spenser, Donne.* London: Routledge & Kegan Paul, 1971.

Kinney, Arthur. *Humanist Poetics: Thought, Rhetoric, and Fiction in Sixteenth-Century England.* Amherst: UmassUP 1986.

———, and Dan S. Collins, eds. *Renaissance Historicism: Selections from English Literary Renaissance.* Amherst: UMass UP 1987.

Kisch, Guido. "Humanistic Jurisprudence." *Studies in the Renaissance.* 8 (1961) 71–87.

Knight, Nicholas, W. "The Narrative Unity of Book V of *The Faeire Queene*: 'That Part of Justice Which is Equity.'" *RES* Vol. 21 (1970) 267–294.

———. "Equity in Shakespeare and His Contemporaries." *Iowa State Journal of Research* 56:1 (1981) 67–77.

———. "Equity, *The Merchant of Venice* and William Lambarde." *Shakespeare Survey* 27 (1974) 93–104.

———. "Equity and Mercy in English Law and Drama (1405–1641)." *Comparative Drama* 6:1 (1972) 51–67.

Kojève, Alexandre. "Tyranny and Wisdom." In Strauss, Leo. *On Tyranny.* New York: The Free Press (1991) pp. 135–176.

Lamont, W. D. "Justice: Distributive and Corrective." *Philosophy* 61 (1941) 3–18.

Landau, Peter. "Aequitas in the 'Corpus Iuris Canonici.'" *Aequitas and equity: equity in civil law and mixed jurisdictions : papers presented at the Second International Conference on Aequitas and Equity.* Alfredo Mordechai Rabello ed. (The Hebrew University of Jerusalem, May, 1993). Jerusalem: Hebrew U (1997).

Landman, James Henry. "Langland, Chaucer, Fortescue: Force of Law and Popular Voice, 1377–1471." Diss. U. of Minnesota. 1996.

Lander, J. R. *The Limitations of English Monarchy In the Later Middle Ages.* Toronto: U. of Toronto P 1989.

Lane, Robert. "'The sequence of posterity': Shakepeare's *King John* and the Succession Controversy." *Studies in Philology.* 92 (1995) 460–81.

Lefebvre, Charles. "Natural Equity and Canonical Equity." *Natural Law Forum.* vol. 8 (1963) 122–136 (trans. Jeanne Rodes).

Leslie, Marina. *Renaissance Utopias and the Problem of History.* Ithaca: Cornel UP 1998.

Levack, Brian P. *The Civil Lawyers in England 1603–1641.* Oxford: Claredon Press 1973.

Lever, J. W. "Introduction." *Measure for Measure.* New Arden ed. London: Methuen 1965.

Levin, Joel. "The Measure of Law and Equity: Tolerance in Shakespeare's Vienna." *Law and Literature Perspectives*. Bruce Rockwood ed. New York: Peter Lang 1996.

Lewis, C. S. *English Literature in the Sixteenth Century Excluding Drama*. Oxford: Clarendon Press 1954.

Lewis, Jayne Elizabeth. *The Trial of Mary Queen of Scots: A Brief History with Documents*. In *The Bedford Series in History and Culture*. Boston: Bedford 1999.

Leyden, W. von. *Arisotle on Equality and Justice: His Political Argument*. New York: St. Martin's Press. 1985.

Lindley, David. "The Stubborness of Barnardine: Justice and Mercy in *Measure for Measure*." *Shakespeare Yearbook*. 7 (1996) 333–351.

Loades, David. *The Tudor Court*. Dorchester: The Dorset Press 1992.

———. *Power in Tudor England*. (British Studies Series) London: MacMillan 1997.

Logan, George M. *The Meaning of More's Utopia*. Princeton: Princeton UP 1983.

Ludwig, Hans-Werner. "Thomas More's *Utopia*: Historical Setting and Literary Effectiveness." *Intellectuals and Writers in Fourteenth-Century Europe*. Eds. Piero Boitani, and Anna Torti. Cambridge: Brewer 1986 244–64.

Luther, Martin, and Calvin, Jean. *Luther and Calvin on Secular Authority*. Ed and trans. Harro Hopfl. Cambridge Texts in Political Thought. Cambridge UP: Cambridge. 1991

Lyon, Bruce. *A Constitutional and Legal History of Medieval England*. New York: Norton 1980.

Machiavelli, Niccolò. *The Prince*. Trans. Harvey C. Mansfield, Jr., Chicago: U of CP 1985.

Maclean, Ian. *Interpretation and Meaning in the Renaissance: The Case of Law*. Cambridge: Cambridge UP 1992.

Maine, Henry Summer. *Ancient Law: Its Connection with the Early History of Society, and its Relation to Modern Ideas*. London: John Murray 1861.

Maitland, F.W., and Francis C. Montague. *A Sketch of English Legal History*. New York: Putnam, 1925.

———. *Equity: A Course of Lectures*. Cambridge: Cambridge UP, 1936.

———. *Selected Historical Essays of F. W. Maitland*. Helen M. Cam, ed. Cambridge: Cambridge UP 1957.

Manuel., Frank E., and Fritzie P. Manuel. *Utopian Thought in the Western World*. Cambridge: Harvard UP 1979 ("The Passion of Thomas More." 116–49)

Marin, Louis. *Utopics: Spatial Play*. (tran. Robert A. Vollrath) (Contemporary Studies in Philosophy and the Human Sciences) New Jersey: Humanities Press Inc. 1984.

———. "Toward a Semiotic of Utopia: Political and Fictional Discourse in Thomas More's *Utopia*." *Structure, Consciousness, and History*. Eds. Richard Harvey Brown, and Stanford M. Lyman. Cambridge: Cambridge UP, 1978 262–82.

Marshall, John S. "Richard Hooker and the Origins of American Constitutionalism." In *Origins of the Natural Law Tradition*. Arthur L. Harding ed. (SMU Studies in Jurisprudence I) Dallas: SMUUP 1954. 48–68.

Maxey, Chester C. "Strange Interlude." *Political Philosophies*. Rev. Ed. New York: McMillan, 1948 (ch. 9, pp. 125–53)

Mcneil. David O. *Guillaume Budé and Humanism in the Reign of Francis I*. Geneva: Librairie Droz 1975 (Travaux D'Humanisme et Renaissance no. CXLII)

Mermel, Jerry. "Preparations for a politic life: Sir Thomas More's entry into the king's service." *The Journal of Medieval and Renaissance Studies* 7:1 (1977) 53–66.

Mitchell, T. N. *Cicero's Verrines II.1*. London: Macmillan, (translation and commentary) 1986.

Moore, Kathleen Dean. *Pardons: Justice, Mercy, and the Public Interest*. New York: Oxford UP 1989.

Moore, Michael J. *Quincentennial Essays on St. Thomas More*. Boone N.C.: Albion 1978.

Moorman, Charles. *The Works of the Gawain-Poet*. Hattiesburg: Mississippi UP 1977.

More, Thomas. *Utopia*. Edward Surtz, S.J. ed. (based on G.C. Richards translation). New Haven: YaleUP 1964 (paperback English only edition based on the Yale Edition of the Works of St. Thomas More).

———. *Utopia*. Edward Surtz S.J. and J. H. Hexter eds. Vol. 4 of *The Yale Edition of the Complete Works of St. Thomas More*. New Haven: Yale UP 1965. (Latin text and English translation).

———. *Utopia*. George Logan, Robert M. Adams and Clarence H. Miller eds. (Robert M. Adams trans.—based on his translation first appearing in the 1975 Norton Critical Edition of *Utopia*) Cambridge: Cambridge UP 1995. (Latin text and English translation).

———. *Utopia*. David Wooten ed. & trans. Indianapolis: Hackett 1999 (includes *The Sileni of Alcibiades* by Erasmus).

———. *Utopia*. H. V. S. Ogden ed. & trans. Wheeling: Harlan Davidson 1949. (Crofts Classics ed.).

Mowat, Barbara. "Historical Background." *Measure for Measure*. William Shakespeare. New York: WSP (The New Folger Shakespeare Library) 1997 225–238.

Neill, Kirby. "Spenser on the Regiment of Women: A Note on *The Faerie Queene*." *Studies in Philology*. 34 (1937) 134–37.

Nelson, William, ed. *Twentieth Century Interpretations of Utopia*. Englewood Cliffs, N.J.: Prentice Hall 1968.

———. The Poetry of Edmund Spenser: A Study. New York: Columbia UP (1963).

Newman, Ralph A. *Equity and Law: A Comparative Study*. New York: Oceana 1961.

———. Ed. *Equity in the World's Legal Systems: A Comparative Study*. (California Western School of Law Studies in Jurisprudence I) Brussels: Établissements Émile Bruylant 1973.

Ogilvie, Sir Charles. *The Kings Government and the Common Law 1471–1641*. Oxford: Oxford UP 1958.

Palmer, Robert C. *English Law in the Age of the Black Death: 1348–1381*. Chapel Hill: UNCUP 1993.

Pangle, Thomas. "Leo Strauss's Perspective on Modern Politics." (Forthcoming in Dutch translation in *Nexus*, Journal of the Nexus Institute, Tilbug University)

Pater, Walter. *Appreciations: With an Essay on Style*. London: Macmillan 1924.

Phelps, Charles E. *Falstaff and Equity*. Cambridge: Riverside 1901.

Phillips, James E. "Renaissance Concepts of Justice and the Structure of *The Faerie Queene*, Book V." *Huntington Library Quarterly.* 33 (1970) 103–120.

———. "The Woman Ruler in Spenser's Faerie Queene." *Huntington Library Quarterly*. 5 (1941) 211–34.

———. "The Background of Spenser's Attitude Toward Women Rulers." *Huntington Library Quarterly*. 5 (1941) 5–32.

Plato. *The Laws*. Thomas L. Pangle trans. New York: Basic Books (1980).

———. *The Republic*. Allan Bloom trans. New York: Basic Books (1968).

Plowden, Edmund. *The Commentaries, or Reports of Edmund Plowden*. London: S Brooke 1816.

Plucknett, Theodore F. T. *A Concise History of the Common Law*. 5th ed. Boston: Little, Brown, 1956.

———. "Introduction to St. German's *Doctor and Student,"* appearing in the Seldon Society's 1974 edition, T. F. T. Plucknett and J. L. Barton, eds. (xi-lxvii*)*, London: Seldon Society.

Pollock, Frederick. *A First Book of Jurisprudence: For Students of the Common Law*. London: MacMillan 1923.

Pound, John. *Poverty and Vagrancy in Tudor England.* Seminar Studies in History. New York: Longman 1986.

Quattrocki, Ed. "Injustice, Not Counsilorship: The Theme of Book One of *Utopia*." *Moreana* 31–32 (1971) 19–28.

Rabello, Alfredo Mordechai. *Aequitas and Equity: Equity in Civil Law and Mixed Juriscictions*. Jerusalem: Hebrew UP 1997.

Radin, Max. "A Juster Justice, A More Lawful Law." *Legal Essays in Tribute to Orrin Kim McMurray*. Max Radin and A. M. Kidd eds. Bereley: UC Press 1935.

Raphael, D. D. "Hobbes on Justice." In *Perspectives on Thomas Hobbes*. Ed. G. A. J. Rogers & Alan Ryan. Oxford: Oxford UP (1988) pp. 153–70.

Reuger, Zofia. "Gerson's Concept of Equity and Christopher St. German." *History of Political Thought* 3:1 (Spring 1982) 1–30.

Riley, Rev. Lawrence Joseph. *The History, Nature and Use of EPIKEIA in Moral Theology*. Series: The Catholic University Of America Studies in Sacred Theology (2nd Series) No. 17. Washington DC: Catholic UP (1948)

Schaeffer, John D. "Socratic Method in More's *Utopia*." *Moreana* 69 (1981) 5–20.

Schanzer, Ernest. *The Problem Plays of Shakespeare: A Study of Julius Caesar, Measure for Measure, Antony and Cleopatra*. New York: Schocken Books 1963

Schless, Howard H. "*Pearl*'s 'Princess Paye' and the Law." *The Chaucer Review*. 24:2 (1989) 183–85.

Schoeck, R.J. "'A Nursery of Correct and Useful Institutions': On Reading More's *Utopia* as Dialogue." In *Essential Articles for the Study of Thomas More*. R. S.

Sylvester and G. P. Marc'hadour. eds. (The Essential Articles Series). Hamden: Archon Books 1977 281–289.

———. "Common Law and Canon Law in Their Relation to Thomas More." *St. Thomas More: Action and Contemplation: Proceedings of the Symposium Held at St. John's University, October 9–10, 1970*. Ed. Richard S. Sylvester. New Haven: Yale UP 1972. 15–56.

———. "Strategies of Rhetoric in St. German's *Doctor and Student*." *The Political Context of Law: Proceedings of the Seventh British Legal History Conference Cantebury 1985*. Eds. Richard Eales and David Sullivan. London: Hambledon 1987 77–86.

———. "Lawyers and Rhetoric in Sixteenth-Century England." *Renaissance Eloquence: Studies in the Theory and Practice of Renaissance Rhetoric*. Ed. James J. Murphy. Berkeley: U Cal P 1983. 274–291.

———. "More's *Utopia* and Intertextuality." *Intertextuality and Renaissance Texts*. Gratia: Bamberger Schriften zur Renaissanceforschung. 12. Renaissanceforschung: H. Kaiser-Verlag, 1984 83–110.

———. "The Ironic and the Prophetic: Towards Reading More's *Utopia* as a Multidisciplinary Work." *In Quincentennial Essays on St. Thomas More*. Ed. Michael J. Moore. (1978) 124–34.

Schotter, Anne Howland. "The Paradox of Equality and Hierarchy of Reward in *Pearl*." Renascence. 33:1 (Autumn 1980) 172–79.

Sebba, Leslie. "Clemency in Perspective." *Criminology in Perspective: Essays in Honor of Israel Drapkin*. Lexington Ma: Lexington Books. 1977.

Seldon, John. *Table Talk*. London: Wm. Pickering, 1847.

Sharpe, Kevin. *Politics and Ideas in Early Stuart England: Essays and Studies*. New York: Pinter, 1989.

———, and Lake, Peter eds. *Culture and Politics in Early Stuart England*. Palo Alto: Stanford UP, 1994.

Shugar, Debora Kuller. *Political Theologies in Shakespeare's England*. London: Palgrave 2001.

Simpson, A. W. B. *Legal Theory and Legal History: Essays on the Common Law*. London: Hambledon (1987). (chapter 12 is entitled "The Rise and Fall of the Legal Treatise: Legal Principles and the Forms of Legal Literature").

Simpson, A. W. B., ed. *Biographical Dictionary of the Common Law*. London: Butterworths, 1984.

Slavin, Arthur J. "Tis far off, And rather like a dream": Common Weal, Common Woe and Commonwealth." *Explorations in Renaissance Culture* 14 (1988) 1–27.

Sokol, B. J., and Sokol, Mary. "Shakespeare and English Equity Jurisdiction: *The Merchant of Venice* and the Two Texts of *King Lear*." *The Review of English Studies*. 50:200 (1999) 417–439.

Somerset, Anne. *Elizabeth I*. New York: Random House (Anchor) (1991).

Southall, Raymond. "More's *Utopia*: The Case for a Palace Revolution." *Literature and the Rise of Capitalism: Critical Essays Mainly on the Sixteenth and Seventeenth Centuries*. London: Lawrence & Wishart, 1973 11–20.

Spenser, Edmund. *The Faerie Queene*. A. C. Hamilton ed. London: Longman 1977.

St. German, Christopher. *Doctor and Student*. T. F. T. Plucknett and J. L. Barton, eds. London: Seldon Society, 1974.

Steinrager, James. "Plato and More's *Utopia*." *Social Research*, 36 (1969) 357–72.

Stevens, Richard G. "On the Practicality of More's *Utopia*." *Social Research*, 33 (1966) 30–46.

Stewart, J. A. *Notes on the Nichomachean Ethics of Aristotle*. Oxford: Clarendon Press 1892.

Still, Judith. "Dreams of the Ends of Markets: The Model of Women's Work in Plato, More, and Rousseau." *Paragraph*, 15 (1992) 248–60.

Stein, Peter. "Equitable Principles in Roman Law." *Equity in the World Legal Systems: A Comparative Study*. ed. Ralph A. Newman. Etablissements Emile Bruylant: Brussels (1973) pp. 75–92.

Strauss, Leo. *On Tyranny*. New York: The Free Press (1991).

———, and Joseph Cropsey, eds. *History of Political Philosophy*, 3rd Ed. Chicago: UofCP 1987.

———. *The City and Man*. Chicago: U of CP 1964.

———. *Persecution and the Art of Writing*. 1952. Chicago: U of CP 1988.

———. *The Rebirth of Classical Political Rationalism*. Chicago: U of CP 1989.

———. *An Introduction to Political Philosophy*. Wayne State UP 1989.

———. *What is Political Philosophy*. The University of Chicago Press: Chicago 1988 (reprint of 1959 edition by The Free Press)

———. And Cropsey, Joseph. *History of Political Philosophy 3rd Ed*. The University of Chicago Press: Chicago 1987.). (2nd ed. 1973).

Stump, Donald V. "Isis Versus Mercilla: The Allegorical Shrines in Spenser's Legend of Justice." *Spenser Studies: A Renaissance Poetry Annual III* (1982) 87–98.

Surtz, Edward. *The Praise of Pleasure: Philosophy, Education, and Communism in More's Utopia*. Cambridge: Harvard UP 1957.

Sylvester, R. S. and Marc'hadour, G. P. eds. *Essential Articles for the Study of Thomas More*. (The Essential Articles Series). Hamden: Archon Books 1977.

———. ""Si Hythlodaeo Credimus": Vision and Revision in Thomas More's Utopia." In *Essential Articles for the Study of Thomas More*. R. S. Sylvester and G. P. Marc'hadour. eds. (The Essential Articles Series). Hamden: Archon Books 1977. 290–301.

Tarkov, Nathan and Pangle, Thomas. "Epilogue: Leo Strauss and the History of Political Philosophy." Leo Strauss and Joseph Cropsey. *History of Political Philophy* 3rd ed. Chicago: U of Chicago P. (1987).

Thirsk, Joan. Ed. *The Agrarian History of England and Wales: Volume IV 1500–1640*. Cambridge: CambridgeUP 1967.

Tinkler, John F. "Praise and Advice: Rhetorical Approaches in More's *Utopia* and Machiavelli's *The Prince*." *The Sixteenth-Century Journal*, 19 (1988) 187–207.

Trapp, J.B. "Introduction to Volume 9." *The Complete Works of St. Thomas More*." J. B. Trapp ed. (xvii -xciii), New Haven: Yale UP, 1979.

Ullman, Walter. *The Medieval Idea of Law as Represented by Lucas de Penna: A Study in 14th Century Legal Scholarship*. London: Methuen 1946.

Van Zyl, D. H. *Cicero's Legal Philosophy*. Digma Publications: Roodepoort 1986.

Villeponteaux, Mary. "*Not as women wonted be*:" Spenser's Amazon Queen." *Dissing Elizabeth: Negative Representations of Gloriana*. Durham: Duke UP (1998).

Walker, David. M. *The Oxford Companion to Law*. Oxford: Clarendon Press 1980.

Watson, Alan. *The Law of Property in the Later Roman Republic*. Oxford: Clarendon Press, 1968.

Wegemer, Gerard B. *Thomas More on Statesmanship*. Washington, D.C.: CatholicUP 1996.

Weir, Alison. *The Life of Elizabeth I*. New York: Balentine 1998.

White, R. S. *Natural Law in English Renaissance Literature*. Cambridge: Cambridge UP 1996.

White, Thomas I. "Festivitas, Utilitas, et Opes: The Concluding Irony and Philosophic Purpose of Thomas More's *Utopia*." In *Twentieth Century Interpretations of Utopia*. William Nelson, ed. Englewood Cliffs, N.J.: Prentice Hall 1968. 135–150.

———. "Pride and the Public Good: Thomas More's Use of Plato in *Utopia*." *Journal of the History of Philosophy*. 20 (1982) 329–54.

———. "The Key to Nowhere: Pride and *Utopia*." In *Interpreting Thomas More's Utopia*. Ed. John C. Olin. New York: FordhamUP 1989.

White, Helen C. "The *Utopia* and Commonwealth Tradition." In *Social Criticism in the Popular Religious Literature of the Sixteenth Century*. 1944. New York: Octagon, 1973. 41–81.

Wilkin, Robert N. "Cicero and the Law of Nature." In *Origins of the Natural Law Tradition*. Arthur L. Harding ed. (SMU Studies in Jurisprudence I) Dallas: SMUUP 1954. 1–25.

Wilkinson, B. *Constitutional History of England in the Fifteenth Century (1399–1485)*.

Williams, Penry. *The Later Tudors: England 1547–1603*. Oxford: Clarendon (1995).

Wilson, Richard. "The Quality of Mercy: Discipline and Punishment in Shakespearean Comedy." *The Seventeenth Century*. 5 (1990) 1–41.

Wood, Ann Douglas. The *Pearl*-Dreamer and the 'Hyne' in the Vineyard Parable. *Philological Quarterly*. 52:1 (January 1973) 9–19.

Woods, Susanne. "Spenser and the Problem of Women's Rule." *Huntington Library Quarterly*. 48 (1985) 140–58.

Wooten, David. "Introduction" to Thomas More's *Utopia*, David Wooten, ed. & trans. Indiana*polis*: Hacket 1999.

Index

T

U

V

W

X

Z